J. Redhouse

The Diary of H.M. the Shah of Persia,

During his Tour through Europe in A.D. 1873

J. Redhouse

The Diary of H.M. the Shah of Persia,
During his Tour through Europe in A.D. 1873

ISBN/EAN: 9783744746113

Printed in Europe, USA, Canada, Australia, Japan

Cover: Foto ©ninafisch / pixelio.de

More available books at **www.hansebooks.com**

THE
OF
H.M. THE SHAH OF

H.M. THE SHAH OF PERSIA.

DIARY OF H.M. THE  OF PERSIA

THE DIARY

OF

H.M. THE SHAH OF PERSIA

DURING

HIS TOUR THROUGH EUROPE IN A.D. 1873.

BY J. W. REDHOUSE,
MEMBER OF THE ROYAL ASIATIC SOCIETY,
CORRESPONDING MEMBER OF THE ORIENTAL SOCIETY OF GERMANY,
EXTERNAL MEMBER OF THE ACADEMY OF SCIENCE OF CONSTANTINOPLE,
ETC., ETC., ETC.

A VERBATIM TRANSLATION.

WITH PORTRAIT.

THIRD THOUSAND.

LONDON:
JOHN MURRAY, ALBEMARLE STREET.
1874.

TRANSLATOR'S PREFACE.

IT is not often that a Sovereign, at the completion of a tour, addresses his subjects in a personal narrative of his adventures, and of the attentions with which he may have been received by foreign potentates or peoples. Less frequent still is it that such a narrative, addressed by an Eastern Monarch to those under his rule, is laid verbatim before the distant nations whose guest he lately was.

The Shah's Diary of his Tour through Europe in A.D. 1873 is not the firstfruit of his royal authorship, nor was that journey the first of his travels. He had previously visited and inspected his own Caspian provinces of Gīlān and Māzandarān, having also journeyed beyond his own dominions, to the sacred shrines of Babylonia. Of each of these excursions he had published a narrative for the information of his people, therein following a praiseworthy example set by several ancient Rulers of his own original Turk nationality.

Those accounts, equally with the contents of the

present Diary, were communicated to the Persian public in the official part of the Tehrān Gazette, and are therefore more or less of the nature of what we daily read at home in the "Court Circular;" but with this difference,—that they are written in the first person, are personal communings of the sovereign traveller with his readers,—his subjects.

As Court Circulars, then, written day by day, they naturally contain a proportion of the merely formal notices that constitute this class of state documents. But, as personal narratives, they are written in the plain, unvarnished style of the private gentleman, much as any one of us may have used in letters sent home to gratify, inform, or amuse friends.

If the pages of the Diary, however, are thus entirely void of all the strained ornamentations of diction supposed to be inherent in all oriental compositions of literature, they are, on the other hand, brimful of enthusiastic expressions of the varied feelings called forth by the beauty or novelty of the scenes or manners witnessed, and by the genuine gratification derived from the splendid and cordial reception everywhere experienced.

The Shah's continued attention to the charms of natural scenery while pursuing his journeys, and to the splendid results of agricultural, commercial, or mechanical skill and industry, as also to the wonders of the sea and sky in his voyages, whenever the weather permitted, evinces great natural taste. His sustained pleasure in visiting the various zoological and botanical collections and museums, together with his remarks on these, and on the wild animals of the parks and forests, no less than those on the racecourse, show an especially keen talent of observation, and a discriminating acquaintance with animate and inanimate nature. His scrupulous conformance to every tittle of those ceremonious, but graceful observances that shape the personal intercourse of royal hosts and guests, bespeak the finished courtier; while the patience, the *bonhommie*, with which he admitted and recorded the sometimes fussy, but always kindly and respectful advances of every class with which he was brought into contact, give proof of a rare adaptiveness. His interest in armies and navies is a mere natural impulse in a sovereign; but his visits to factories, public establishments, schools, hospitals, &c., are witnesses to a strong desire for information; and several incidents of the tour have drawn forth spontaneous expressions of deep sympathy and kind commiseration, such as are the sure indicators of a humane disposition.

On the whole, a more interesting book of the kind can hardly be imagined. Even the mistakes occasionally made—and they were to be expected as inevitable—are easily overlooked by a candid mind, when the obstacles of languages, novelty of subjects, and press of time, are taken into consideration. The use of the first person plural, alternating with that of the singular, when the Shah speaks of himself, is in very common use by all in the East (to say nothing of the sovereign phraseology of the West), and is balanced by his employing the third person plural when mentioning other royal or illustrious personages; though this latter observance of courtesy, not unknown in several European languages, necessarily vanishes in our idiom. Another instance of attentive delicacy may be remarked, in the nicely poised modification of the oft-repeated, simple expression "men and women" into "women and men."

The translator wishes, and ventures to hope, that his effort to put the whole work into an English dress may give to its readers the same amount of pleasure he has himself felt in the performance. May he be further permitted to express a heartfelt trust that ever-strengthening ties of friendly and beneficial intercourse may be facilitated and multiplied, through the effects of this tour, between the Court and people of Persia on the one hand, and the Western Rulers and nations on the other,—some of them their not remotely allied cousins by race, as indicated by affinities of language,* and who are no longer personally strangers to their travelled Sovereign.

LONDON, *Nov.* 1874.

Note.—In pronouncing the Persian names mentioned in this volume, *a* should always be sounded short and surd, as in the first syllables of *above, aloft, alone;* ā long and open as in *father;* e as in *pen;* i as in *pin;* ī as in *caprice;* o or ō as in *go,* and *u* or ͨū as in *rule,* but shorter when without the long accent. Into modifications we do

---

* As instances, the following may be mentioned : padar, *father;* mādar, *mother;* birādar, *brother;* dukhtar, *daughter;* gāw, *cow* or *ox;* yūg, *a yoke;* tu, *thou;* du, *two;* marwārīd, μαργαρίτης, *a pearl,* &c., &c.

not here enter; and we prefer the use of this old Latin "long accent" to the "dash" used in some works, because every scholar knows the value of the old mark, and because the new one is based on the erroneous assumption that "in Italian" it marks a long syllable.

The simple consonants have their English values, excepting that *h* must always be aspirated, and *s* always be kept hard—never pronounced as *z*.

Compound vowels are not known; but of compound consonants (in English orthography only, being simple letters in the original), *ch* and *sh* sound as in English; while *kh*, as in *khān*, is the Scotch and German *ch*, in which it is far better to sound only the *h*, than only the *k*, until the true pronunciation be acquired. Neither the hard nor the soft sound of our *th* is used in Persian; but sometimes *t* is followed by *h*, even in the same syllable, both being then sounded separately.

Doubled consonants in a word, such as *Muhammad*, should be redoubled in pronunciation, as when we say *mid day, get two*, &c.

The apostrophe, ', has the same use as in English, that of indicating a suppressed vowel, as in Nāsiru-'d-Dīn. The pair of marks ' and ', adopted in imitation of the Greek "*spiritus lenis*'." and "*spiritus asper*," show the suppression of two different originally Arabic guttural consonants, the first soft, the second hard, both of a choking sound, for which European languages have no equivalents, and which are generally dropped in Persian conversational pronunciation, the preceding or following vowel alone being sounded. Like other consonants, they are both susceptible of being doubled, though no instance occurs in the Diary.

A few explanatory notes have been appended at the end of one or two chapters, and some others are interspersed, in parentheses, through the text.

The original meaning of the Persian word tūmān is—a myriad, ten thousand. It became the name of the gold coin of Persia because this coin, in matters of account, contains ten thousand *dīnār* (*the Latin* denarius), a mite, a pice. Its fractions are the hazār (thousand), otherwise called hazār-dīnar (thousand pice), and qirān (*short for* sāhib-qirān, Lord of the fortunate conjunction—*a title assumed by* Tīmūr-lang, Tīmūr the Lame, Tamerlane), of silver, ten of which equal one tūmān; and the shāhī (royal), of copper, twenty of which make one qirān. The tūmān is worth about eight shillings English, the qirān about ten pence, and the shāhī one half-penny. The gold and silver are without alloy, pure.

The correct name of the Prussian frontier station, towards Russia, mentioned in p. 68 as Aidgone, is Eydtkuhnen.

With respect to the weight of the guns and projectiles of Fort Constantine, mentioned in p. 57, I learn that the heaviest Prussian guns furnished for the forts of Cronstadt are of 26 tons, throwing projectiles of 250 kilogrammes. The Shah's 420 ass-loads may therefore possibly be for 520 hundredweights, exactly 26 tons, and the weight of the projectile may be about right.

I also learn that the number of hands employed by M. Krupp, as mentioned in p. 96, is even understated. The total amounts to 17,000, of whom 10,000 are housed or boarded within the estate of the works; and two hospitals, with 220 beds, are available for the sick.

The message sent by the Shah to the Contessa di Mirafiori (mentioned in p. 300), as an act of courtesy, was accompanied, in compliment to the King, by the presentation of a jewel with the monogram in brilliants of His Persian Majesty.

J. W. R.

Translator's Preface v
Preliminary Notice xix

CHAPTER I.
TEHRAN TO ASTRAKHAN ; 26 DAYS.

Leave Tehran, 1 ; reach Qazwin, 6 ; arrive at Rasht, 13 ; reach Enzeli, 16 : embark for Astrakhan, 17 ; accident to Russian Admiral, 20 ; anchor at Quarantine-ground off the Volga ; ascend river in boats, 22.

CHAPTER II.
RUSSIA ; 14 DAYS.

ASTRAKHAN. Aspect of the delta, 23 ; reach Astrakhan ; triumphal arch ; bread and salt, 25 ; palaces, 26 ; bath and fire-brigade, 27 ; theatre ; levée, 28 ; mosques, 29 ; museum, 30 ; leave by water for Tsaritsin, 30 ; aspect of Volga, 31 ; Tsaritsin, 31 ; railway to Moscow, 32.
MOSCOW. Arrive at Moscow ; lodged in the Kremlin, 35 ; Kremlin described, 36 ; theatre, 37 ; lower apartments and museum of the Kremlin, 38 ; Lazarof College ; ball ; fire brigade ; Ethnographic Museum, 40 ; leave for St. Petersburg by rail, 41.
ST. PETERSBURG. Arrive, 41 ; lodged in the Winter Palace, 43 ; theatre, 44 ; review, 55 ; Prince of Oldenburg, 46 ; ball of the nobles, 47 ; the Hermitage, 48 ; state banquet, 49 ; Michael theatre, 50 ; visits, 51 ; the Hermitage again, 53 ; bank ; mint, 55 ; state ball, 56 ; Cronstadt, 57 ; Peterhof, 59 ; fireworks, 61 ; Tsarskoi-selo, 63 ; leave for Prussia, 66.

CHAPTER III.

PRUSSIA, GERMANY, BELGIUM; 20 DAYS.

RAILWAY. "Hole in a mountain;" frontier reached, 68; Prussian station, 69; Königsberg, 70; Frische-Haff, 72; Custrin, 73; reach Berlin, 73.

BERLIN. Palace, 74; Potsdam, 76; Whitsunday; relics of Frederick the Great, 77; mill in ruins, 78; palace of Prince Charles, 79; state banquet; theatre, 80; Zoological Gardens, 81; cemetery, 84; the Empress, 82; Aquarium, 85; dinner, 87; theatre; coronation of the Emperor, 85; review, 88; dine with the Empress, 89; gala night at theatre; Sardanapalus, 89; lion of Holstein, 89; Order of Black Eagle, 90; Charlotte Pavilion; Orangery; Babelbrig, 91; Frederick the Great's tomb, 92; Crown Prince's house, 92; Parliament; the École-des-Cadets, 93; Prince Bismarck's house; Museum; visit of adieu, 94; Aquarium again, 95; leave for Cologne, 95; M. Krupp's factory, 96.

RHINE COUNTRY. Reach Cologne, 97; cathedral, 97; Botanical Gardens, 98; Zoological Gardens, 99; Coblentz, 100; Wiesbaden, 101; Mr. Blundberg's garden, 103; Prince Nicholas of Nassau, 104; Frankfort-on-the-Main, 105; the Palms, 106; Zoological Gardens, 107; tomb of the Duchess of Nassau, 108; the Kur-Saal, 108; Emperor of Russia at Darmstadt, 110; Heidelberg; Carlsruhe; Baden troops, 111; Palace at Carlsruhe, 112; Baden-Baden, 113; Chapel and tomb, of Prince of Roumania, 115; palace, 116; steam down the Rhine, 118; Coblentz, 120; Bonn; Cologne; by rail to Spa, 120; Aix-la-Chapelle; frontier of Belgium, 121.

BELGIUM. Spa, 122; Peter the Great; footstep of St. Mark, 124; procession of the Virgin; theatre, 126; Liege, 129; arrive at Brussels; the King, 130; arrival of the English Officials in waiting, 131; theatre, 132; cathedral; museum; Château of Laken, 134; Zoological Garden; Hôtel de Ville, 135; state banquet, 136; leave Brussels; Ostend; embark on board the 'Vigilant,' 137; cross the straits, 138; Channel squadron; arrive at Dover, 139; reach London, 141.

Contents. xv

CHAPTER IV.

ENGLAND ; 18 DAYS.

Visits of ceremony, 144 ; receptions, 145 ; banquet at Marlborough House ; ball at Stafford House, 146 ; visit to the Queen, 147 ; Order of the Garter, 148 ; drive to Virginia Water and back, 149 ; evening party at Guildhall, 151 ; Woolwich, 155 ; theatre, 157 ; Zoological Gardens, 158 ; Naval Review at Portsmouth, 160 ; concert at Albert Hall, 164 ; review at Windsor, 167 ; ball at Foreign Office, 170 ; Tower, 171 ; trip down the river ; the Docks, 172 ; Greenwich Hospital ; Lord Nelson, 173 ; Naval College ; Observatory ; return ; tides, 174 ; state ball, 175 ; to Liverpool, 176 ; emigrants, 177 ; Trentham Hall, 179 ; works at Crew, 182 ; Manchester, 183 ; Chiswick, 185 ; Richmond, 187 ; Lord Russell ; Whigs and Tories, 188 ; receptions ; Lord Stratford de Redcliffe, 189 ; fire brigade, 190 ; boxing, 191 ; Crystal Palace, 191 ; gymnasts, 193 ; beggars ; perambulators, 195 ; Tower ; St. Paul's, 196 ; Bank, 197 ; Parliament, 198 ; Westminster Abbey, 200 ; visit of adieu to Windsor, 201 ; Prince Consort's tomb, 203 ; Mme. Tussaud's, 204 ; Crystal Palace, 206 ; balloons, 209 ; Albert Hall ; donkey picture, 210 ; St. Thomas's, 211 ; Duke of Argyll's ; bagpipes ; sword-dance ; telegraph, 212 ; Albert memorial ; Drury-Lane, 213 ; leave London, 214 ; reach Portsmouth ; embark in the "Rapide"; reach Cherbourg, 216.

CHAPTER V.

FRANCE, SWITZERLAND ; 19 DAYS.

FRANCE. Cherbourg, 218 ; Caen, 219 ; reach Paris, 220 ; Jardin d'Acclimatisation, 225 ; Bois de Boulogne, 226 ; Diplomatists, 227 ; Versailles, 228 ; group of Apollo, 229 ; Canrobert ; Palikao ; Duc d'Aumale ; Prince de Joinville, 231 ; banquet, 232 ; the Invalides, 233 ; M. Crémieux ; M. de Rotñschild, 236 ; M. Lesseps ; M. Nadar ; M. Tardieu, 237 ; M. Larrey ; M. Cloquet ; M. Bouré, 238 ; review, 239 ; races, 240 ; illumination and fireworks, 243 ; circus, 244 ; Louvre 246 : Panorama, 247 ; Notre Dame, 248 ; École des Mines, 249 : Luxembourg, 250 ; Pantheon ; St. Sulpice ; Madeleine ; Palais Royal, 252 ; Mint, 253 ; river-baths, 254 ; Gobelins, 255 ; Louvre again, 256 ; Tuileries, 257 ; Sèvres porcelain, 258 ; the Assemblée Nationale, 259 ;

Jardin des Plantes, 263 ; party at the Élysée, 266; party at the Foreign Office, 267 ; Vincennes, 268 ; Sisters of Charity's school, 269 ; Circus, 270 ; cafés chantants, 271 ; Jardin Mabille, 272 ; leave Paris, 273 ; Dijon, 274.

SWITZERLAND. Geneva, 277; Lake of Geneva, 279; Vevay; King of Holland, 281 ; excursion into Savoy; 283; banquet; presents ; museum, 285 ; M. Favre, 286 ; Swiss system, 287 ; leave Geneva, 288;

FRANCE AGAIN. Aix-les-Bains ; Chambery ; Modane; Mont Cenis tunnel, 289 ; Turin, 291; Royal Family; 293 ; Superga ; Synagogue, 294.

CHAPTER VI.

ITALY ; AUSTRIA ; 19 DAYS.

ITALY. Turin Palace, 295 ; dinner-party ; royal presents, 296 ; theatre, 297; wild beasts, 298 ; illumination, &c., 299 ; the Countess di Mirafiori, 300; leave Turin, 301 ; reach Milan, 303 ; the Duomo, 304 ; banquet ; illuminations, 306 ; leave Milan, 307 ; Lake of Garda ; Peschiera ; Verona, 308 ; Valley of the Adige ; Ala, 309.

AUSTRIA. Franzansvest, 310 ; Innsbruck, 311 ; Rosenheim ; Trauenstein ; Saltzburg, 312 ; Schönbrunn of Saltzburg, 314 ; Lintz, 317 ; Emperor at Penzing, 318 ; Laxenburg, 319 ; Knight's Castle, 321 ; dinner at Schönbrunn of Vienna, 323 ; Exhibition, 325 ; shooting party, 331 ; screw-pump, 334 ; opera, 335 ; review, 337 ; the Empress : evening party, 339; leave-taking, 341; King of Hanover, 342; Saltzburg, 343 ; Innsbruck, 346 ; Schelleberg ; Gossensasse, 347.

ITALY AGAIN. Ala ; Verona, 348; Bologna, 349 ; leaning towers, 350 ; theatre, 352 ; library and museum, 353 ; leave Bologna ; Rimini ; Ancona, 355; Brindisi, 356; embark for Constantinople, 357 ; Corfu ; phosphorescence of the sea, 358 ; Cephalonia ; Zante ; Navarino ; Cape Matapan, 359 ; Cape Malea ; Cerigo ; Cape Sunium ; Zea, 360 ; Negropont ; Andros ; Psara ; Scio, 361.

CHAPTER VII.

TURKEY ; 11 DAYS.

TENEDOS ; Lemnos; Dardanelles, 363; Gallipoli ; Sea of Marmara, 366 ; Islāmbūl sighted ; steamers and Persians, 367 ; Princes' Islands ; walls, 368 ; Seven Towers ; Seraglio Point, 370 ; Bosphorus ; Beyler-

Contents. xvii

Beyi; the Sultan, 371; Palace of Beyler-Beyi, 372; Golden Horn, 376; receptions, 377; Gyūk-Sū, 378; breakfast at Chirāgān palace, 380; Chamlija (erroneously called Mount Boulgourlou on the maps), 381; Prince Yusuf; Aya-Sofiya, 382; Persian Mission; state banquet at Beshik-Tash palace, 384; receptions; trip to Princes' Islands, 386; Sultāna-Mother's vineyard, 387; steamers, 388; conflagration; palace of Chirāgān, 389; gardens; wild beasts, 390; bath, 391; conjurer, 392; visits of adieu, 395; leave for Poti, 396; accident to Eshref Pasha, 397; Sinope; porpoises, 398; birds from the land; Trebizond; coming storm, 399.

CHAPTER VIII.

GEORGIA; RETURN; 11 DAYS.

Storm, 401; transhipment, 402; land at Poti; Grand-Duke Michael, 403; Open-Heads, 404; railway; Kutaïs, 405; Tiflīs; palace, 406; Grand-Duchess; theatre, 409; storm at Poti, 410; Bahman Mīrzā, 411; banquet, 412; Tiflīs to Baku, 413; Ganja, 414; Nizāmi's tomb, 416; Kur ferry, 417; Aq-Sū—New Shamaka, 420; Shamakhi, 421; Baku, 423; embark, 424; storm for three days, 425; land at Enzeli, 427.

ILLUSTRATIONS.

PORTRAIT OF THE SHAH . . . . . . *Frontispiece.*
(By kind permission of the Proprietors of the *Graphic* newspaper.)

THE FAN-TAIL POSTURE IN DANCING xviii
MONOGRAM OR CYPHER OF THE SHAH, AS-SULTĀN NĀSIRU-'D-
DĪN SHĀH QĀJĀR xx

THE CHETR (FAN-TAIL) POSTURE IN DANCING.

(From a Persian painting.)

DIARY OF A TOUR IN EUROPE.

IN THE NAME OF GOD,
THE COMPASSIONATE, THE MERCIFUL!

PRELIMINARY NOTICE.

THIS is a Diary of the Tour in Europe, which we propose to write in auspiciousness and sanctification, under the will of God most high, the All-powerful, the Matchless, the Forgiving, the Beneficent, provided that health be accorded us.

The details of the country between Tehrān and Enzeli have been formerly given in the (account of my) journey to Gīlān, and therefore require no further elucidation here. I will, however, under the Divine will, note down the facts attendant upon our leaving Tehrān, our capital, and anything interesting that may occur on our road to Enzeli. Subsequently to that, from the day of our embarkation on board ship, the detailed adventures of the company will be noted in the diary of the ship, with the help of God, and His merciful aid.

DIARY OF A TOUR IN EUROPE.

CHAPTER I.

TEHRĀN TO ASTRAKHAN ; 26 DAYS.

ATURDAY, 21st *Safar*, 1290 (A.H., *i.e.*, 19*th April*, 1873).—We started from Tehrān in the intention of prosecuting our tour in Europe. It is now a whole year since information was given of this (intended) tour in Europe; and it is also some days that we have been suffering from a pain in the chest, and a severe cold in the head, so as to be very unwell, with sensations of fatigue and weakness; to so great a degree, that I have never experienced the like before.

Placing my trust in God, however, I sallied forth from my private apartments, my Grand-Vazīr, and others, being in waiting to receive me. We tarried awhile, and then started, mounting a carriage at the gate named Shamsu-'l-'imāra (Sun of the Palace). Crowds were assembled inside and outside the city, in the streets and roads, and elsewhere. We drove to the race-course, where to-day races were held. We went up into our pavilion. Masses of soldiery, and of private people, men and women, were assembled. They served breakfast, of which I took a little, though without the least appetite. Our master of the horse, Tīmūr Mīrzā, the Husāmu-'d-Dawla (Prince Tīmūr, the Keen Sword of the State), with Hājjī Aqā Ismā'īl, and others of our household, were in attendance. The Amīn-i-Huzūr (Lord Chamberlain, Comptroller of the Presence), who had been unwell for some days past, was to-day present on duty.

After breakfast, the horse-races took place. The horses of Murād Beg, Nā'ib (Lt. Murād, a Beg), which belong to the royal stables, carried off the four first flags. The horse of Wajīhu-'l-'lāh Mīrzā (Prince Wajīhu-'l-'tah) carried off also a first flag. Iqbāl Mahdī-qulī Khān (Gentleman of the Chamber Mahdī-qulī, a Khān) carried off the fourth flag in the last heat.

The races being concluded, the foreign representatives were admitted to an audience of adieu, the Grand-Vazīr and other officials being present. We then mounted a carriage and drove to the village of Kan, where the new tents of figured and brocaded silks were pitched on the bank of a stream. After a while the " Royal Maternal Household" came to Kan, and I had an interview with the " Shāh's mother," who remained there two days. A bitter wind was blowing.

Tuesday, 24th (Safar—22nd April).—Went to the royal palace at Kan; and this same day, mounting a horse, went out shooting in the rising grounds around the village, the Prince Regent accompanying me, as well as several of the officers of my household. The Grand

Huntsman had come out from town, and had found some game. Before breakfasting, I shot a buck of two years old, with slugs. Thanks be to God, all went off pleasantly, and I returned home in comfort. I am grateful that my health is perfectly restored, and no sense of weakness remains. It is now the season of new green plums, which are still very small, and not fit to eat. Green almonds and blossoms on the trees are well-nigh over; yellow and red roses are to be seen here and there. Mahdī-qulī Khān went to town for one night, and came back unwell.

Wednesday, 25th (Safar—23rd April).—Remained at the palace of Kan. Dr. Tholozan, and several of those who are to accompany me to Europe, arrived to day from town.

Thursday, 26th (Safar—24th April).—Proceeded to Quru-Chay (Dry-Brook), where we breakfasted. The brook was much swollen. Our chief photographer, and others of our attendants, were in waiting. Our sun-shade tent was pitched in a hollow, and the weather was very sultry. At the time of afternoon worship we returned to our station at Kan. The Anīsu-'d-Dawla (Familiar of Royalty; a harem lady) came from town, but somewhat in bad health.

Friday, 27th (Safar—25th April).—We were at Kan in the morning. A vast concourse of officers of the household, and others, came from town, the Grand-Vazīr being among them. This day, Munīf Efendi, the Ottoman Envoy, who has newly arrived, is to be received in audience. In this, our first station, they have pitched our tents of figured silks, &c. Four hours and a half before sunset we went to our tent, to which the Grand-Vazīr came. Five of our princes wore their swords at our levée. Thanks be to God, the wind is not blowing. The Envoy was introduced, with two Attachés; the Chargé-d'affaires, Nāzim Efendi, came with him for his audience of leave, as he has to return to his own country. Munīf Efendi speaks Persian and French, the former particularly well. He is of middle age. Āsafu-'d-Dawla has arrived.

Saturday, 28th (Safar—26th April).—In the morning we mounted, and proceeded on our journey to the pass of Sūlgān, where there is a fine waterfall on the left-hand side of the road, with water to turn one mill. They pitched our sun-shade tent there, and we breakfasted in that spot. The Prince Regent was in attendance, and several other princes also.

Sunday, 29th (Safar—27th April).—To-day several princes and others, the colonel of a regiment of our guards, and our Secretary for Foreign Affairs also, though a convalescent from illness, came to our camp and were received. Munīf Efendi, too, had another audience. Aqā Sayyid Ismā‘īl, the jurisconsult, of Bihbihān, came to visit me. The Lord Treasurer brought out the jewelled regalia that are to be taken with us.

(*Monday, 30th—28th April*, is not mentioned in the Diary.)

Tuesday 1st, Rabī‘u-'l-awwal (Former Rābī‘—29th April).—In the morning levee all the princes and others who had come out from town were received. The

Friday precentor of worship (a kind of equivalent to a bishop) came out and offered up a prayer for our journey. A son of the precentor of Ispāhān also came. Five Arab horses, brought for the royal stables, were led past our presence, and reviewed; and then we took our departure for Karj. On our road thither we were joined by the Grand-Vazīr from town, who had good news from Sīstān (the ancient Ariana or Drangiana), which he submitted. The Dabīru-'l-Mulk (secretary of state), too, mounted on a tall Turkman horse, came out with the Grand-Vazīr. The Prince Regent received permission to depart when not far distant from Kan, and returned to town. Several princes followed in our suite; one returned to town from Quru-Chay. M. Beger, the Russian Envoy, who is to accompany us to Enzeli, was of our party. We arrived at Karj four hours before sunset. We lodged there in the palace. Several of our household, our chief photographer, and Dr. Tholozan, came from town. Mahdi-quli Khān went out shooting, and brought in a female antelope.

Wednesday, 2nd (30th April).—Proceeded from Karj to Qāsim-ābād, a distance of five leagues. Weather very sultry; dust excessive. One of our princes took leave and returned to the capital; our Grand Usher is to accompany us to Enzeli. Some join us from the capital; others, taking leave, return thither. The duty of acting as scouts and sentinels to our camp as far as Enzeli devolves upon the 2nd regiment. Our Chief Groom-in-Waiting, Bīwak Khān, returned to town from Kan.

Thursday, 3rd (1st May).—In the morning mounted

on horseback, many of our princes and officers riding in our suite. The Grand Usher had purchased sixty horses for the artillery of Āzarbāyjān (the ancient Atropatene); he passed them in review in our presence. A troop of cavalry of Makrān (the ancient Gedrosia), commanded by Hājjī Aqā Beg, were also reviewed. We rode a certain portion of the way conversing with the Grand-Vazīr; after which we entered our carriage. Our station to-day is at Kāzrūn-Sang, three leagues' journey. We breakfasted there, where the camp had been pitched in a beautiful meadow, where all was green and luxuriant. Sari-Aslan (Yellow-Lion) came from town and was seen (by us).

Friday, 4th (2nd May).—Mounting our carriage early in the morning, we proceeded to 'Abdu-'l-'lāh-ābād, a distance of five leagues; weather sultry; dust abundant. On reaching the last outskirts of winter cultivation, we breakfasted; but, in the first place, taking our fowling-piece in hand, we sauntered about the environs, and shot a hare, a quail, and a yellow-hammer (or ortolan, *lit.*, yellow-belly). This day I have seen Dr. Dickson; and also Mr. Thomson, Secretary to the English Legation, who accompany me to Europe. Mīrzā 'Isà, governor of Tehrān, and another official of state, with Mīrzā Mūsā, paymaster of the forces, took leave and returned to Tehrān.

Saturday, 5th (3rd May).—To-day we arrive at Qazwīn; that is to say, they have pitched our camp at Hazār-Jarīb (Thousand-acres), near that town. The distance to travel is five leagues. Passed the village of

Khāk-i-'Alī (Ali's-land), and others. In the morning, as we mounted, the Grand-Vazīr brought to the side of our carriage the Russian Envoy, with his interpreter, Grebel, and we had some converse with him. A body of about three hundred irregular cavalry of nomadic tribes was drawn out. The Registrar of Āzarbāyjān was received in audience. Lt. Muhammad-Sādiq Khān, of Qarabāg, his aide-de-camp, was with him. Several princes detained at Qazwīn, several of the Doctors (of law and divinity), of the nobles and notables of the town, with the mayor and aldermen, &c., were presented to us in batches by Īlkhānī, the governor of the place. We breakfasted on the road; and afterwards a violent wind set in. Our Chief Groom of the privy chamber, who had remained behind, now joined our party, having ridden post from the capital. The cavalry, under the command of Asad Khān, of Qara-bāg, who is a member of the corps of couriers, had come out with the paymaster from Āzarbāyjān, on their way to the capital to be reviewed. The son of Asad Khān, who was in charge of them, is a nice youth. As we approached the town we mounted on horseback, and, conversing with the Grand-Vazīr, we reached our camp. He, with our permission, went to the town. A cold and violent wind was blowing; and, as we had passed the night before with very little sleep, we soon felt an inclination to take our repose.

Sunday, 6th (4th May).—To-day Aqā-Bābā is our station. It rained heavily in the morning; and, though it had already rained a certain while, it poured down afresh. This rain was of great advantage to Qazwīn.

Ílkhání brought and presented to us Mírzá Abú-Turáb, uncle of the late Mírzá Buzurg, the physician, a very aged man. After this, mounting, we passed by the outskirts of the town in conversation with the Grand-Vazír, and reached the high-road to Aqá-Bábá. The Secretary of State now left us to return to the capital. To-day, differently to what had hitherto been the case, the weather was pleasant, with a cool and refreshing breeze. The fields are one mass of verdure and blossoms. In the gardens of Qazwín we observed a species of thorn in bloom, with a flower like a yellow rose, very beautiful and pleasing. We gave orders that some roots and seeds thereof be taken to Tehrán and there planted. We took our breakfast in our carriage below the village of Mahmúd-ábád, so named after a late Shaykhu-'l-Islám. A bitter wind was blowing. Several of our courtiers were in attendance. We reached our quarters four hours to sunset, when an intensely cold wind was blowing with great violence, so much so that it tore down all the canvas fences and tents, and continued the whole night. No one could go out of doors, and all were benumbed with cold, so as to be incapacitated for any service.

Monday, 7th (5th May).—Have to reach Kharzán; but the cold wind and the frost is so intense, that even in the severest winter one does not see such, nor has such ever been heard of. We rode a couple of leagues in our carriage. Then, the road becoming very bad, we mounted on horseback and sent the carriages back. The country to-day is all verdant and in bloom; but the frost continues so severe that one could not admire, or even notice, the beauty and freshness of the landscape. In spite of my having put on a coat and cloak lined with fur, the cold was so penetrating that it seemed as if I was devoid of all clothing. Below the pass of Kharzān there was a valley with but little water in its stream; and there we breakfasted, several of my princes and officers, with Dr. Tholozan, being in attendance. After breakfast we ascended the defile. The mountain of Kharzān has no rocks or stones; it is all soft earth, and everywhere covered with verdure, flowers, and odoriferous herbs. In many places we saw cultivation without the aid of irrigation. The tribe of Giyāswand do the cultivation of this mountain. General Hasan-'Ali-Khān, one of those to accompany me, joined the party to-day. Conversing with the Grand-Vazīr, we ascended the steep. At the top I saw a village, which I took to be Kharzān. On enquiry, it proved to be Ismā'il-ābād, lately erected and peopled by Ismā'il Khān Giyāswand, chief of the tribe of Giyāswand. A beautiful spot has he populated, as its produce needs no irrigation. From thence we proceeded a league and a half to Kharzān. I saw some of our princes on the road, and spoke with them. They complained bitterly of last night's cold and wind, from which they had suffered much. Thanks be to God, we reached our station. There was then no wind, but a dense fog filled the air, with occasional showers of rain. The frost was so intense that the water froze as in winter.

Tuesday, 8th (6th May).—To-day we reach Lūshūn. Mounting our horse at daybreak, we set out chatting by the way with the Grand-Vazīr, Īlkhānī, and the Paymaster (of Āzarbāyjān). The road hereabouts has been somewhat improved by order of the Government. Cultivation goes on in the valleys and on the hills. Mahdi-qulī Khān had gone on ahead for a little sport after partridges, and he mentioned having found the yellow jessamine in flower in all the valleys. We went over the whole of the ground that he had explored. They had erected our sunshade tent. The Shāh-rūd (King River, which falls into the Safīd-rūd at Manjīl,) was very full of water, and extremely turbid. Many of our princes and officers were present. Breakfast was served. One of the attendants on Prince Wajīhu-'l-'lāh Mīrzā, who had plunged into the Kūfa branch of the Euphrates (when the Shāh visited the sacred shrines of 'Alī and Husayn at Najaf and Kerbelà in Babylonia), here also most bravely urged his horse into the stream. Truly it was an exhibition of courage. We remained there till the middle of the afternoon, and then proceeded towards our station. Below the bridge I noticed two carriages, very elegant, which a merchant of Shīrwān (in Georgia) was taking up to Tehrān to sell. We reached our station at sundown. They had pitched our camp in a wide valley at a considerable distance from the bridge. Thanks be to God, there was no wind neither. The Grand-Vazīr brought us soḿe dispatches from the Mu'tamadu-'l-Mulk, which we read.

Wednesday, 9th (7th May).—To-day we go to Manjīl. We started early in the morning on horseback. Prince Husāmu-'s-'Saltana joined us from the road to Bakandi, which he has recently purchased, and to which he had diverged from our camp at Aqā-bābā. We journeyed on, chatting with him, the Grand-Vazīr, and Ilkhānī. Contrary to what we had experienced for some days, the weather was warm, and the flies were numerous. The pathway was very bad, and we rode along out of the track until we reached the forest of Bālā-bālā. We reached the bank of the river at breakfast-time. At dawn to-day we had taken some quinine. After breakfast we again mounted and pushed on. During the journey we saw Mīrzā Ibrāhīm Khān, Governor of Rahmat-ābād, Ni'matū-'l-'lāh Khān of Rasht, and Nasru-'l-'lāh Khān, a Tālish-man from Gurgān-rūd (on the Caspian). The cavalry of this latter chieftain were very well dressed and armed. Nearing our quarters, his Reverence the Mullà Hājjī Rafī', a jurisconsult of Gīlān, had an audience. As it was not possible to pitch our camp on the same spot as in our former visit, at the foot of the cypress of Harzabīl, by reason of its having been laid under crops, we found it erected in a valley near to Manjīl, sheltered from the wind. In spite of this precaution, a high wind arose in the afternoon. It is one of the wonders and singularities of nature, that in this valley, at all seasons of the year, a violent breeze sets in every afternoon, so impetuous, and with such force, that all the olive-trees growing there lean over in one direction, according as the blast has impelled them. The whole of the lands of Manjīl and Harzabīl are under cultivation, so that the country has an aspect of fertility and joy.

Yesterday a snake bit one of the tent-pitchers, and Dr. Tholozan treated him; according to his report, the man's life is saved. Hereabouts snakes are very numerous (as was found by Marc Antony when he invaded the country).

Thursday, 10*th* (8*th May*).—Rustam-ābād is our next station. We started rather later than usual, and journeyed on, conversing with the Grand-Vazīr; also we had an interview with Mullà Rafī' the jurisconsult at the foot of the bridge of Manjīl, which spans the Safīd-rūd (White River), and over which they pass who journey to or from Gīlān. Formerly there was a wooden bridge here, the passage over which was very difficult for caravans; but a few years since a strong stone bridge has been built at the cost of the public exchequer, and under the superintendence of his Reverence Hājjī Mullà Rafī'. His Reverence is in the same state of robust health that he enjoyed when we first saw him, eight years ago. Passing his bridge, we pushed on to Fīl-dih (Elephant-village), and in the very spot where we had breakfasted several years before, in our journey to Gīlān, did we take our morning's meal to-day. The oranges are in bloom, and the pomegranates have just done flowering. The length of to-day's journey fatigued me. We reached our quarters three hours to sunset, and found the tents pitched on the riverbank. As we journeyed to-day we saw many swimmers and bathers amusing themselves in the river, along which our road lay.

Friday 11*th* (9*th May*).—We go to Imām-zāda Hāshim. Mounted at dawn, and journeyed conversing with the Grand-Vazīr. In some places the path was bad to-day; that is to say, that above Rustam-ābād some places were under water, and a distance of over a thousand feet was very deep with mud. In other places again rocks and stones abounded. Here and there I was forced to dismount and walk; and, as I conversed in one place with the Grand-Vazīr, the foot of his horse slipped in the mud, and he was thrown; fortunately, he was not hurt. It was reported, however, that one man had fallen from his beast; and, upon enquiry, I found it was an attendant of the Amīnu-'s-Saltana, who had fallen from a mule, and was killed. Some of our princes, &c., received permission to go on from this station to Rasht. A bridge (now completed) over the Siyāh-rūd (Black River) has also been built, under the care of Mullà Rafī‘, with the public money. There was, however, but little water in that stream, and a child might have waded across it. Sometimes again it runs with so full and impetuous a flood as to be unfordable by horsemen. We reached the mouth of this stream, where it falls into the Safīd-rūd, at breakfast-time. There was a pretty meadow, and we sat down in the shade of a tree, several of our household being in attendance. As we approached the end of our day's journey, the mountains were left behind, and we entered on a level country, where my droshka had been prepared for me. Mounting this carriage, I drove to the vicinity of our station.

Saturday, 12th (10*th May*).—To-day we arrive at the town of Rasht. Last night the air was very cold. Rising betimes, we rode a certain distance on horseback; then took our seat in the droshka, and drove on. The Russian Envoy, with M. Grebel, the interpreter, was waiting by the side of the carriage, and we had some chat with them. The sun was very hot. The nightingales every now and then sang in the woods. We passed the villages of Sarā-wān and Shāh-Aqāchi. Below this latter we saw the Muʻtamadu-'l-Mulk, who had come out from Rasht to meet us; and also the Sāʻidu-'l-Mulk, Mīrzā ʻAbdu-'r-Rahīm Khān, who had come from St. Petersburg with Prince Menschikoff, appointed to attend upon us. The Hakīmu-'l-Mamālik, commissioned from Tehrān to go and meet the Russian officials sent to attend upon us, also joined our party. We took our breakfast in the shade of some forest trees on the left-hand side of the road; and before we had gone very far forward from thence, we observed on the road a very handsome bazaar, entirely built of bricks and mortar. We were informed that the Muʻīnu-'t-Tujjār-i-Gīlānī, in partnership with some others, had erected this bazaar. From Lāhijān a large company of Doctors of law and divinity, &c., had come forth to meet us. Near to the town (of Rasht), Their Reverences Hājjī Mullà Rafīʻ, Hājjī Mullà Tāhir, and Hājjī Mīrzā ʻAbdu-'l-Bāqi, jurisconsults of the town of Rasht, formally met us. There we dismounted from the carriage and got on our horse, the Grand-Vazīr and the Russian Envoy being also on horseback, and conversing with us. A large concourse of women and men, inhabitants of Rasht, also came out to meet us. Six hours to sundown we reached the Nāsiriyya Palace, where a tent had been pitched for us. At one hour and a half to sunset Prince Menschikoff, in attendance on us, Colonel Bazāk, special aide-de-camp of the Emperor of Russia, the Russian Envoy, with his interpreter, M. Grebel, and the Hakīmu-'l-Mamālik, were admitted to an audience. Prince Menschikoff is a personage of distinction, one of the notables of the Russian empire, and a special aide-de-camp general of the Emperor; he is about sixty years of age.

Sunday, 13th (11th May).—In the morning we mounted our horse and started for Enzeli, passing through the whole of the town and bazaar (of Rasht). Multitudes were assembled along the road as far as Būsār. From henceforward we rode in our droshka. They have made the road to Pīra-Bāzār very nicely. At this latter place we breakfasted in front of the gate of the custom-house. Here they had prepared barges and man-of-war boats, &c.; and after breakfast we mounted a barge to go off to the small steam-vessels that were anchored somewhat far from the mouth of the river. One of these belongs to our own Government, and has been very nicely fitted up. Two others belonged to Russia. In one of the latter the Russian Envoy, Admiral Sivnikin, and Dr. Tholozan were mounted; in the other was a Russian band of musicians; while we embarked in our own ship, which by our orders had been recently built and despatched. Whatever is necessary as an ornament, whether plate-glass or sumptuous cabin furniture, is all present in this ship. It has a speed of three leagues per hour. After viewing and admiring her cabins, we went on deck, where an awning of embroidery in flowers upon broadcloth formed a shade. The Russian Envoy presented the Admiral in an audience. We remained a sufficient time for all our party to embark on board our vessel, princes and household officers. Orders were then given for the ship to proceed, and four hours to sunset we arrived at Enzeli. Immediately upon this, the Grand-Vazīr, the Mu'tamadu-'l-Mulk, and the Amīnu-'s-Saltana proceeded to the Russian ships that were anchored in the offing of Enzeli, in order to arrange the berths of each of our attendants and the stowage of our effects. Five ships had come by orders of the Russian Government; all men-of-war, acknowledged by the Russian State, but not fast ships. The vessels owned by "The Company" are more commodious than the men-of-war, and of greater speed. These men-of-war will not go with us, but will return (to their stations) from Enzeli. Our quarters are in a tower, built by our command by our Minister of Foreign Affairs when he was governor of Gīlān, and subsequently fitted up by Mīrza Muhammad-Husayn while he was acting as deputy-governor of Gīlān for the late Nizāmu-'d-Dawla. It still wants a little of completion, which the Mu'tamadu-'l-Mulk will see to. This tower is of five stories, and each story has a saloon and a balcony all round. It is entirely built of bricks, stone, and lime; excepting the balconies, which are of timber, painted. All kinds of needful furniture, as carpeting (or its substitutes, matting, floor-cloth, &c.), chairs, tables, candlesticks, &c., are there existing and ready. The view from this tower, on all four sides, is over the sea. Well; a cold wind was blowing, but the night was one of beautiful moonlight. It was settled that we should embark to-morrow. There was an exhibition of fireworks at Gāziyān.

Monday, 14*th* (12*th May*).—To-day, God willing, we embark on board ship, and, under the Divine favour, proceed to Hājjī-Tarkhān (Astrakhan, *lit.*, the Tarkhān, the pilgrim to Makka—a Tarkhān having been a kind of superior feudal baron with the Tatar and Mogul sovereigns, by one of whom probably the place was founded). We rose early in the morning. Looking out over the sea, we saw an unbroken line of boats and barges, conveying men and effects from Enzeli to the ships. The air was rather hazy, and a light wind was blowing on to the shore. This rather alarmed us. After awhile, however, the air cleared up, the haze disappeared; but, as the sky was somewhat threatening, it was judged better to hasten our departure. I sent therefore for the Grand-Vazīr, and ordered all my suite to embark. I then came down from the tower; and the jurisconsult, Hājjī Mullà Rafī', offered up a prayer for our voyage. A wonderful assemblage of all sorts and conditions had collected. In the first place I embarked in my own steamer, and in her proceeded to the "Constantine," sent on purpose for me. Prince Menschikoff and the others in attendance were on board. We waited another couple of hours while the baggage and our followers were being shipped, and then, five hours to sunset, the ship's anchor was got up, and we started. Three of the men-of-war present incessantly fired guns, and got under way, one ahead of our ship, one astern, and one on each beam. After awhile they stopped; and our ship then put on full speed. This vessel has beautiful cabins; all with embellishments, and sumptuous, and clean by rule. Servants were on board, specially sent from St. Petersburg, of the Emperor's household, with all the requisites for taking coffee, &c.

The following is the list of the personages who accompany us to Europe:—

1. Those on board the " Constantine," our own ship.

 The Grand-Vazīr.
 The Mu'tamadu-'l-Mulk.
 The 'Azdu-'l-Mulk (Privy Seal; cousin to the Shah).
 The Court Secretary.
 The Amīnu-'s-Sultān.
 The Sanī'u-'d-Dawla (Private Secretary to the Shah).
 The Amīnu-'s-Saltana.
 Mahdi-qulī Khān (a chamberlain).
 Dr. Tholozan.
 The Chief Photographer.
 Gulām-Husayn Khān.
 The Muhaqqiq (Court collector of information).
 The Chief Groom of the Privy Chamber.
 Farrukh Khān.
 Prince Wajīhu-'l-'lāh (cousin to the Shah).
 Ja'far-qulī Khān.
 The Chief Groom of the Coffee-Service.
 Aqā Rizà, Corporal.
 Mīrzā 'Abdu-'l-'lāh, (Groom of the Privy Chamber).
 Mīrzā 'Abdu-'r-Rahīm Khān, the Sā'idu-'l-Mulk (Minister Plenipotentiary at St. Petersburg).
 Prince Sultān Husayn Mīrzā.
 Hājjī Haydar, Special Barber.
 Aqā Hasan-'Ali, (Water-Bearer).

CHAP. I.]   *Tehran to Astrakhan.*   19

Aqā Muhammad-'Ali Jabbār, (Groom of Coffee-Service).
Three attendants of the Grand-Vazīr. Aqā Bāqir.

2. Those on board the ship " Baratinski."
The 'Azzu-'d-Dawla.
The I'tizādu-'s-Saltana (great-uncle to the Shah; Minister of Commerce).
The Husāmu-'s-Saltana.
The Nusratu-'d-Dawla (uncle to the Shah).
The 'Imādu-'d-Dawla.
The 'Alā'u-'d-Dawla.
The Īlkhānī (Governor of Qazwīn).
Hasan-'Ali Khān, (Minister of Public Works).
The Paymaster-General of the Forces.
The Hakīmu-'l-Mamālik.
The Ihtishāmu-'d-Dawla.
The Nasru-'l-Mulk.
The Mukhbiru-'d-Dawla.
The Shujā'u-'s-Saltana.
General Hasan-'Ali Khān.
Mīrzā Rizà Khān, (Aide-de-Camp to Grand-Vazīr).
Lt. Ibrāhīm Khān.
Mīrzā Ahmad Khān, (son of the 'Alā'u-'d-Dawla).
Two Equerries.
One groom.
Eight servants to members of the suite.
M. Dubeski, (Austrian Envoy).
Mr. Thomson, (Secretary of Legation of England).
Dr. Dickson, (Physician of Legation of England).

c 2

Names of the horses :—
The horse Julfa.
The horse Zillu-'s-Sultān.
The horse Jāfi.
The horse Sabāhu-'l-Khayr (*he with a " blaze " in his forehead*).
(The horse of) the Husāmu-'s-Saltana.

Dr. Tholozan informed me that the Russian admiral had been opening a bottle of soda-water, when the bottle burst and a piece of the glass flew into his eye, so as to make him blind of that one eye. I afterwards saw the admiral, who had put on blue spectacles. I enquired of him what had happened, and he narrated the same circumstances. I was grieved. Towards the middle of the afternoon, when I went up on deck, I saw the "Baratinski" was a full league distant. I slept in great comfort during the night.

Tuesday, 15th (13*th May*).—At sunrise we had reached the commencement of the promontory of Ābshārān (The Waterfalls; Cape Abcheran, of Black's Atlas; C. Aspheron or Shakoo, of General Monteith; the promontory of Baku). The more we advanced, the more and the better did the land of the promontory become visible. These coasts are arid and treeless, and are included in the district of "Bād-Kūba (Wind-beaten; Baku); many tamarisk-bushes were growing on them, and in some places rocks were visible. The ship hugged the shore so closely that the men and animals thereon were distinguished. On the central point of the promontory, a square tower is built for the purposes of a sea-lamp (lighthouse); and around it several houses of stone for the attendants of the tower. On our right there was an island (Sviatoi, of Black; Piralagai, of Monteith), on which we observed some large buildings. On enquiry I learnt that they were a manufactory for the purification of naphtha, but are at present unoccupied, there being no one on the island. From what was said, the proprietor had been ruined. Here they stopped the ship for a short time, while the Grand-Vazīr wrote some telegrams, which he gave to be carried to Bād-Kūba, to be from thence telegraphed to Persia and to Europe. The sea was calm until about two hours to noon; then, little by little, it became agitated, so that the waves rolled mountains high, and everyone on board was taken unwell, excepting ourselves, our Chief Photographer, the Sanī'u-'d-Dawla, the Corporal, and Dr. Tholozan. We were not cast down, but proved our self-possession. The whole of the officers and crew of the vessel were cast down also, with the exception of the admiral and a few of the sailors, &c. In fine, we should have been caught in a peril of great magnitude, but the Divine mercy encompassed our situation, and a favourable breeze sprung up astern, carrying us more quickly forward to our desired haven. All night, until dawn, the sea continued thus agitated and billowy; in spite of which, however, I slept a little. Rising at dawn and looking out at the sea, I saw it was still boisterous. I desired the admiral to be called, and with him I examined the chart that I might know our exact position. The admiral gave me an assurance that in ten hours' time we should arrive off the mouth of the river Volga, where there would be but four or five cubits (or ells, of forty-two inches each), of water, and that therefore the sea would be smoother. In the middle of the afternoon we saw some sailing vessels; and among them was one bound on a voyage to the coasts of Langarān and Māzandarān. We also saw a man-of-war steamer, named the "Iran." One hour and a half after nightfall we arrived at a place called the "Quarantine," beyond which large ships cannot enter. It was therefore necessary for us to leave our steamer and go on board a small vessel that would carry us to Hājjī-Tarkhān. Our ship anchored in that spot, and we dined. They who had been sea-sick and unwell gradually recovered. After dinner Prince Menschikoff brought and presented the Governor of Hājjī-Tarkhān, who was named M. Pipine, and who had every appearance, to one's eyes, of being a man of integrity and ability. He spoke French well. On leaving our presence he returned by night to Hājji-Tarkhān, so as to be in attendance on our arrival there. The small vessel that is to carry us to the city is named the "Coquette," and is very handsome. After the time of night Divine service, we went on board this vessel; another, similar to her, having been provided for our suite, and a small steam-tug taking us in tow. This night I enjoyed a delicious and comfortable sleep.

CHAPTER II.

RUSSIA; 14 DAYS.

WEDNESDAY, 16th (14th May).—Arrived at Hājjī-Tarkhān. At dawn I rose and looked around. Thanks be to God, we have escaped from the high sea, and have entered a large river named the Volga, which has a great charm. This stream is very wide; so much so, that the one branch of it which we were navigating is at least a thousand ells (about 1200 yards) across, and an ordinary musket-ball would not carry from bank to bank. Its waters are turbid, and flow with a rapid current, so as to raise waves like those of the sea. The banks are everywhere clothed with green forest-trees, common willows and Egyptian willows; the land is all grass and pasturage. For the most part these regions are inhabited by tribes of pagan Kalmuks, who pitch their felt tents by the side of the streams and rear vast herds of cattle, horses, mares, oxen, sheep, &c. We saw also some large villages, Russian villages, pertaining to the district of Hājjī-Tarkhān, and standing on the banks of the river. Seen from a distance, they appear to be of considerable extent and very populous. In each village a church has been built, very fine and majestic. The occupation in general of the people of these villages is that of fishing. As our vessel came opposite to each of these villages in succession, the inhabitants flocked to the river-bank, and cried out *hurrah!* They did not appear to have any gardens or sown fields, excepting in one instance where we saw a very large mansion and an extensive garden of trees in a village at a distance, belonging to the tribe of Sapogenikoff. They had shot down a good quantity of dead fishes into their vessels, and had made the banks of the river stink. Such fishes as they had not been able to salt and preserve, and which had consequently putrefied, they cast into the river. The water of the Volga is very light of digestion. We noticed many birds, such as magpies, crows, and cormorants (? *lit.*, great piscivorous starlings), flying in the air; we shot one of each of the latter as they flew past. We saw two small vessels with steam and sails, laden with merchandize. We thus continued our course, until about mid-day the mass of Hājjī-Tarkhān began to appear, the first building seen being the large church of the city, which is very lofty and majestic. The city is like an island encompassed by two or three branches of the river. One large branch skirts the town, and another branch passes through it, being spanned by many bridges, and its banks occupied by streets and houses. It has numerous mosques, the greater part of which belong to the Tatars, one very fine one belonging to the Muslims of Īrān (Persia). Well, we arrived at the town. Skirting the town were all kinds of craft, and windmills in abundance were seen. Astonishing multitudes of men and women were congregated, of various nationalities;—Tatars, Russians, Persians, Cossacks, Circassians, Kalmuks, &c., in groups on groups, were in the streets and thoroughfares, continually shouting hurrahs at each spot we arrived at along the course of the river, until we reached the landing-place and our vessel stopped. It then wanted four hours and a half to sunset.

This day, early in the morning, Mīrzā Malkam Khān, and Narīmān Khān, with Mīrzā Asadu-'l-'lāh Khān, our Consul at Tiflīs, and Mīrzā Mikā'īl, brother of Mīrzā Malkam Khān, had come down from Hājjī-Tarkhān and joined our party on board ship.

Descending from the vessel, we landed. The instant we put our foot on shore, the whole of the men and women assembled there simultaneously raised a loud shout of *hurrah!* It was an extraordinary crowd, a strange hubbub of voices. In the streets and thoroughfares men and women were standing, as closely packed as the space would hold. They had raised a triumphal arch of great altitude and of imposing appearance. A *triumphal arch* is customary to be erected on the arrival of sovereigns in a town. From the landing to the triumphal arch the passage was carpeted over. In conformity with a Russian custom, observed by them when the Emperor or a King, but no one else, arrives in a town, the mayor brought forward bread and salt. On the salt-cellar of gold, and on the gilt silver salver, on which the salt and bread were presented, the date of our arrival at Hājjī-Tarkhān had been inscribed. An open carriage harnessed with four handsome horses, and the coachman,

Russian fashion, standing with the reins in his hand, was in waiting. We made Prince Menschikoff mount this carriage with us. A troop of mounted Cossacks followed as our escort, and a crowd of men and women, old and young, ran along by our side shouting hurrahs. Dust and noise there were in plenty. Everywhere, by the sides of the streets, in the balconies, and on the roofs, were people standing to witness the spectacle, until we reached the Government House, in which they had appointed our quarters. A battalion of troops was drawn up in military order opposite the gate of the Government House, all handsome young men, dressed and armed in the most desirable manner. I dismounted and walked down their line. They saluted me with military honours, and shouted hurrahs. We then entered the house.

The edifice of the Government House is a very imposing and spacious structure, full of inhabited apartments. By the sides of the staircase by which one enters the house, and which leads to a great hall, numerous vases of flowers had been collected especially for our reception. The house contains many apartments and halls, reception-rooms, dining-rooms, bed-chambers, &c., all furnished and decorated. In most of these they had served sweetmeats, sherbets, fruits. The stoves of the establishment are the reverse of the ordinary Persian hearths,—that is, in a corner of a room a portion of the wall forms a kind of projection, which is tesselated with white glazed tiles, and behind this they light the fire. Tubes are arranged within this projection, and through them warm air comes into the room.

The bath of this establishment is on the ground floor, and one descends to it by a flight of many steps. The bath-room was elegantly fitted up with chairs, tables, couches; perfumes, flowers, and the like, were collected there in abundance of varieties. In one corner was a basin with two taps for water, hot and cold, so that the temperature of the water in the basin could be regulated and kept to any desired degree of heat. The floor of the bath was covered with a very soft mat. At a certain point there were a few wooden steps, with a kind of trap-door at the top; and whenever it is desired that hot air enter the bath-room, they open it. There were many taps for hot, cold, and tepid water, all round the room.

When I quitted the bath, M. Dubeski, the Austrian Envoy, and Mr. Thomson, Secretary of the English Legation, had an audience of leave, being introduced by the Grand-Vazīr; they precede us to Moscow. After them, the Governor of Hājjī-Tarkhān, Prince Menschikoff, Colonel Bazak, and M. Grebel, came and enquired whether we would feel an inclination to witness the practice of the fire brigade. We having signified our assent, the "alarm" was given—*i.e.*, the signal was given that a fire had broken out, and caused a general perturbation. This signal was displayed on a tower that dominates the town. Immediately, from every ward the firemen presented themselves with their wheeled fire-engines and their ladders, the horses of the engine of each ward being of a special colour. No sooner were they assembled in the square in front of our quarters, than their officer feigned that fire had broken out in a building that stood on one side of the square. Instantly did they direct the whole of their engines on that building, and incessantly did they discharge water upon it. They performed a very fine exercise.

In the evening there was an illumination in front of the house, and after dinner we went to the theatre, where the air was excessively hot. The theatre is small, and the crowded state of the audience was wonderful. The house has two galleries; no more. As soon as we entered the curtain rose, and various actings were produced. At first we might have imagined that the players were figures of pasteboard; but, little by little, it became evident that they were human beings. Thrice did the curtain rise, and three different plays did they enact. Each time the curtain fell, an interval of a few minutes elapsed ere it rose again. This interval was of sufficient duration for us to go from the pit of the theatre to an upper chamber by the side thereof, and to become somewhat refreshed from the heat, when we returned. Had it not been for the heat, the sight would have been something worth witnessing.

Thursday, 17th (15th *May*).—This is the day of the festival of the nativity of His Holiness the Seal of the Prophets (*i.e.*, of Muhammad; whom we vulgarly call Mahomet), upon whom, and upon whose household be salutations and benedictions. And to-day we have to start by water for Tsaritsin, from whence we shall proceed by railway.

Early in the morning we breakfasted, and then went to the state saloon to hold a levée, to which all the nobles and notables of Hājjī-Tarkhān, and all the officers of the regular and irregular forces in garrison there, came and were presented. The levée over, we mounted a carriage and drove to the mosque belonging to the Muslims of the Shī'a sect, the Precentor of which is Mullà Muhammad-Husayn, of Tabrīz,—a very agreeable man. Again, to-day, through whichever street we passed, the people ran by the side of our carriage shouting hurrahs. Rain had fallen in the night, and had laid the dust of the streets. The mosque is in the form of an upper chamber, reached by a wooden staircase. Arrived there, we found a great concourse present, of merchants and others, subjects of Persia, all being of the Shī'a sect. They were received in audience. The princes of our suite were there also. We there acquitted ourselves of our noon and afternoon service of Divine worship. After the service, Mullà Muhammad-Husayn, the Precentor, recited a glorious *Khutba* (discourse, sermon; *vide* Lane's 'Modern Egyptians,' p. 85, l. 26) in the Arabian tongue; following upon which, a certain Mullà Ahmad, of Rasht, a Licentiate of Law and Theology, recited some Persian verses of his own composition.

From thence I went to the mosque of the Tatars, where a large congregation of Tatars and of Doctors of the Sunnī (Traditionist) sect were assembled. Men of handsome form and features met my sight, who offered prayers for me. One of their Doctors ascended a pulpit, and recited a Khutba; he also presented me with a copy of the Qur'ān (*vulgarly known as the Koran*). The building of this mosque is similar to that of the Shī'a sect.

Next I proceeded to an establishment where are preserved various relics of Peter the Great, Emperor of Russia. I saw there two large boats built by Peter the Great with his own hands, and more especially one of them that is ornamented with very fine carvings. There, too, are portraits of Peter and Catherine. An immense glass tumbler was also shown, out of which it is well known that Peter the Great drank wine with Prince Menschikoff, ancestor of the very Prince Menschikoff who is in attendance on us. There was also a large chair presented by Catherine to the Governor of Hājjī-Tarkhān of her day: and further, a law book (*query*, charter), which Catherine sent for the inhabitants of Hājjī-Tarkhān. Again, there were the carpenter's tools of Peter—his saw, chisel, axe, &c., with which he built vessels. On the walls were certain ancient weapons and warlike instruments suspended, such as fire-arms, &c.; and outside the door, on either side, a pair of old bombshells. These are not devoid of some interest.

I now got into my carriage and drove to the steamboat named the "Alexander," belonging to "the Company," and embarked in her, my suite being already on board. She is a very handsome vessel, with excellent and spacious cabins, elegantly fitted up. Five hours to sunset she got under way. Besides her other good qualities, she is a very fast boat. On our passage we noticed several vessels on their voyage from Tsaritsin to Hājjī-Tarkhān, and with a numerous company of mixed passengers on board.

The river Volga, as before mentioned, is like a sea;

i.e., in some parts is so wide that the banks cannot be seen. Large islands are embraced in its channel; extensive villages are found on its banks. On the right bank of the river (in ascending) an enormous and beautiful temple was noticed, which belongs to the idolatrous Kalmuks. The whole of the banks of the river, where visible, are hilly, with grass and trees forming a pleasant aspect. Herds of swine, piebald and black, were pasturing on shore. The flesh of these animals is eaten by the inhabitants of the countries bordering on the river. No other river of equal magnitude and with equally beautiful sites on its banks was seen by us in those parts. I could not for one moment cease to admire them. The vessel never stopped. At nightfall we dined, and subsequently retired to rest.

Friday, 18*th* (16*th May*). — When I arose in the morning it was evident that it had rained heavily all night. The river banks are like those seen yesterday, but the number of villages is less. A telegraph from the Dabīru-'l-Mulk was received and read : " On the 16th of this month (Wednesday, 14th May,) a typhoon of furious wind occurred in Tehrān. The inhabitants of Tehrān were in a state of alarm lest this typhoon should have assailed us at sea." At three hours and a quarter to sunset we arrived at the town of Tsaritsin, from whence the railway commences.

Tsaritsin is built on an eminence on the bank of the river Volga, the length of the town following the course of the stream, and a branch of the river flows through it, dividing the town into two parts united by a bridge, over which people pass from one section to the other. Multitudes were assembled from the town and its environs. As soon as the vessel anchored, on board of which we were travelling, the railway train that was to carry us forward made its appearance. We performed our devotions, and then came out of the ship's cabin. The Governor of Saratov, within whose jurisdiction the town of Tsaritsin is situated, was presented. His name was Gavkin Varafski. He was a noble, pleasant-faced man, and had come a great distance. The Chief of the Nobles of Saratov, &c., and many officers of all kinds, were assembled and were presented. There was also an excellent band. The landing-place was beautifully decorated, and the Persian flag hoisted over a triumphal arch. After giving audience to these who had thus come to receive us, we returned to the ship's cabin, performed our devotions of sunset, and dined, proceeding to the railway one hour afterwards. The Governor of Hājji-Tarkhān here took leave and returned.

From the wharf, for a certain distance, the railroad was illuminated on both sides. Our railway carriages are a special train of saloons for the use of the Emperor, very handsome, spacious, and beautifully fitted up. They contained many different apartments, dining-saloons, sleeping-carriages, reception-saloons, all furnished with lamps, tables, chairs, sofas, and couches. They all communicated with one another, so that one could go and come from end to end of the train. Those of our suite who accompanied us on board the "Constantine" were placed in the same saloon with ourselves; our princes and the rest following in a separate train. This is the first time we travel on a railway, and very nice and comfortable it is: it goes five leagues in an hour.

Rising in the morning (17th May) it became evident that during the night we had been passing through a beautiful country; for, whichever way we looked out over the land, we saw green fields, meadows, flowers, grass, tented tribes, mares, sheep, swine, &c., and every two or three leagues a handsome, populous village. These parts are celebrated for their productiveness. Everywhere we looked we saw sown fields that required no irrigation, or else grass lands. We crossed a large and handsome bridge over a stream, full of water, that flows into the river Don. Every now and then we passed over smaller bridges in great numbers. At distances of two or three miles were guard-houses for the care of the road; and a few leagues apart were stations. A " station" is a place where the trains stop to have their wheels greased, and where the passengers take coffee and refreshments; so that it really is a post-house. These stations are prettily built; and at each of them there are always several carriages for the conveyance of passengers and merchandize. To-day we are passing through the government of Tambov; and at one of the stations we alighted from our carriage, and found a concourse of officers, troops, women, and men assembled. We walked down in front of the line and inspected the troops, who were all fine young men and well armed. This station was at the town of Borisoglebsk, the whole of the civil and military functionaries of which had come out to meet us. After receiving them we returned to our carriage and continued our journey. Our road now lay chiefly through forests of fir and pine. The pace of the train was such that we overtook the flying crows, passed them, and left them behind. Emerging from the forests, we again came upon cultivation, meadows, and open country. At this season the crops in these parts are not more than one finger-joint out of the ground.

We now arrived at Kozlov, where we found all the local authorities assembled, as well as a crowd of spectators. It is a fine town, and a handsome hotel of large dimensions was by the roadside, in which they had prepared a breakfast. The nobles and wealthy men of Russia have here a breeding stud, where very fine horses are reared. They brought several for our inspection. A few Russian generals and officials were presented in audience. After a stroll we returned to our train, and shortly proceeded on our journey. In less than every half hour we passed by a very large village. The night found us still continuing our onward course. Early in the morning (of May the 18th) we traversed a long bridge over a river (the Oka) that falls into the Volga, having passed Riazan about midnight; and two hours after daylight we reached the station of Faustovo, where our train was made to wait until the other, with our princes, &c., should come up. We then all of us put on our state dresses for our entry into Moscow. Prince Dolgoruki, the Governor of Moscow, an old and venerable man, full of honours and dignities, had come here to meet us, and was admitted to an audience in our carriage. M. Gamasoff, the interpreter of His Most Exalted Majesty the Emperor, was also introduced to our presence, having been sent by the Emperor. He is a very old man, and has visited Persia.

We now proceeded till the city of Moscow appeared in sight. The cupolas of its churches—all gilded, the magnificent houses, the gardens, the parks, the summer residences, the manufactories, were well seen. We arrived at the station—the terminus, where the train stops, and where an immense multitude of men and women were assembled. We alighted from the train. The Governor of the city, the Generals, the Civil Functionaries, were all there. The crowd was beyond all calculation. A carriage and four, with escort, and with footmen in the splendid liveries of the Emperor, awaited us. The Grand-Vazir, the princes, the officers of our household, and the rest, were placed in other carriages, forming a cavalcade behind us. In this manner did we pass through the streets; everywhere marvellously thronged with women and men, until we reached the gate of the citadel-palace of the Kremlin, which is one of the grand palaces of Russia—nay, of all the Franks. It has a brick wall of great height and ancient construction, being situated on the top of a hill-like elevation, and so overlooking the city of Moscow. The arsenal and armoury are also within this palace, and we passed near them. There is a very large gun placed in the entrance to the palace, such that few so large will be seen. The bell of the church of Moscow, which fell down in times of old and was broken, is near the Arsenal. No bell of its size is visible in any other place. Cannon captured from the first Napoleon in the battle of Moscow are collected in the Arsenal.

At length we reached the steps of the palace. Count Lensdorf, Marshal of the Palace and Intendant of the Parks and Domains of Moscow, a pleasant-looking young man, who speaks French extremely well, showed us the way, and explained the details of the palace. I really cannot undertake to write a description of the Palace of the Kremlin. We went up many stairs, so constructed as to be mounted with the utmost comfort. In the corridors are huge columns of porphyry and other stones. The middle part of the staircase and corridors is carpeted. As one goes up the stairs, one sees on the right hand a picture representing a battle between the Russians and the Moguls. Thence one enters a large saloon, and from it passes into the still vaster Hall of the Knights of St. George, *i.e.*, of those who are decorated with the insignia of the Order of St. George, the names of every one of whom, ancient or recent, is inscribed in this hall, which is very spacious and lofty, with large candelabra and chandeliers. Thence one passes to the Throne-Room,—also a very large, oblong, and lofty hall, on a dais in which the throne is placed, embroidered with a crown, seated on which the Russian Emperors are crowned. Still passing on, I entered two or three other rooms, and from thence to the sleeping apartments. From the hall there is a door leading to a kind of terrace, from whence the whole city of Moscow and the surrounding country is visible, and where I walked about a while.

In this palace they have executed some surprising works in the art of converting lime (or plaster) into stone, so that the plaster is as lustrous as a mirror, and as hard as stone. There are some beautiful columns in these rooms; for instance, two columns of porphyry, lofty monoliths, in the bed-chamber; while in the hall there are many columns of malachite. All the stairs are of marble. The number of apartments in the palace, upstairs and downstairs, is so great that a stranger would lose himself among them, and that one cannot inspect them all in a day. There are large numbers of crystal and china vases in it; also a small winter-garden, like the orangeries (conservatories) of Tehrān, contiguous to it, and filled with strange exotic flowers, brought and cultivated there,—very pretty. The palace has a picture gallery,—an oblong hall, filled with ancient paintings in oil,—very fine pictures, and set off with rows of large china vases.

After dinner, a meal partaken of before the sun had gone down, we started for the theatre. Crowds were in all the streets. Arrived at the theatre we went upstairs, passed the crush-room, and took our seat in a box fronting the stage,—the place where the acting is performed. The theatre is of large size, and was built by the Emperor Nicholas. It has six tiers of seats, and all of them were crowded with women and men. A large chandelier is hung in the middle of the theatre. Prince Dolgoruki, the Governor of Moscow, sat in our box. The curtain rose, and a strange world made its appearance. A large number of dancing-women set-to dancing.

This dancing and performance is called a ballet, *i.e.*, a performance and dance without speaking. In its course they both dance and perform in various ways, which it is not possible to describe. Opposite the audience and below the stage there were also a great number of musicians who unceasingly sounded their instruments. Every now and then a light, produced by electricity and variously coloured, was thrown from the corners on to the stage; this had a very pleasing effect. The dancers, too, every now and then changed their costumes. Such dancers as danced well were applauded by the audience clapping their hands, and crying "bis," *i.e.*, "encore." At the conclusion of one act the curtain fell; and after a quarter of an hour, when people had reposed somewhat, the curtain again rose and another act was performed. At the end of one act, I went to another box near to, and looking on to, the stage. Our princes and attendants were seated in our first box. Five times did the curtain rise, and five times was a different kind of play brought out. It lasted till midnight. The theatre was extremely hot. We went home. The name of the director of the theatre was Gavelin.

Tuesday, 22nd (20th May).—We remained at Moscow. This day we visited the lower apartments of the Kremlin, where the jewelled regalia, ancient crowns of the Emperors, &c., are collected; and these we inspected. It is a magnificent edifice, apartment within apartment, being both an armoury and a crown-jewel office. All the various articles are tastefully arranged in glass cases; ancient porcelains, gold and silver utensils, objects of curiosity and virtu, spoils taken in battles, &c.; and all were pointed out to us by the custodian and registrar, whose name was Soloviessa. Among them were some things taken from Charles XII. of Sweden by Peter the Great at the battle of Pultawa; especially the litter on which Charles, after being wounded, caused himself to be carried about as he gave directions for continuing the fight; also some of the flags of that king. There were about ten crowns,—crowns of the old sovereigns down to the time of Peter the Great, most of them set with fine precious stones in gold of old-fashioned workmanship: there were jewelled sceptres, and one without jewels that had been used by Peter the Great; there were old royal robes and dresses, and others more recent; also the furniture of the chamber of Alexander I. and of that of Peter the Great. I saw two thrones set with turquoises and gold and other precious stones, which had been sent as presents to the sovereigns of Russia by Shah 'Abbás, the Safawí (*i.e.*, of the race of the Shaykh Safí or Safiyyu-'d-Dín, who lived in the days of Tímúrleng, and whose descendant in the sixth degree, his great-great-great-great grandson, Sháh Ismá'íl, founded the Safawí dynasty of Persia in A.D. 1501; the title of Sofi, or Sophi, attributed to the kings of this dynasty by European writers, being an ignorant corruption of this word Safawí). I also saw two saddles, with their equipments, jewelled, sent by the Ottoman Sultan ('Abdu-'l-) Hamíd Khán to the Empress Catherine; also the boots of Peter the Great and of Alexander I.; and furthermore, a colossal marble statue of Napoleon I. There were also some ancient carriages.

From thence I went to visit the Lazarof College, a beautiful place of education, where Armenian, Muhammadan, and Russian youths are taught the Oriental and European languages. The name of the superior was Delianof. Returning from the college, the generals and military officers stationed at Moscow were received in audience. The General commanding-in-chief the whole of the forces in Moscow, a tall old man, was Gildenstol. In the evening I went to the theatre, and saw some nice acting. From thence to the house of Prince Dolgoruki, to a ball. As his wife was dead, his niece, daughter of his sister, did the honours of the evening.

23rd (*Wednesday, 21st May*).—In the morning I mounted a carriage and for a space drove about the streets of Moscow. The companies of the fire-brigade went through a portion of their exercise; and afterwards I went to the Ethnographic Museum, a fine building, in which they have collected wax images of all the different tribes and nationalities subject to Russia, each dressed in its special local costume, so as to look like living men. There I also saw the arms and implements of the savages of America and Africa, which are exhibited as curiosities. There is also a library said to contain two hundred thousand volumes. Whenever the Emperor visits Moscow, he resides in the apartments on the ground-floor of the Kremlin; and these too we went through. They are beautiful rooms; and nothing can be conceived finer than the furniture there seen, the porphyries, the balustrades of marble, the tables, chairs, looking-glasses, and couches. In the Emperor's own room there were the skins of two bears shot by himself and serving as rugs in front of couches. Having finished this survey, I drove to the Nicholas terminus, the end of the railway to St. Petersburg; as, under God's will, we go to-night to that city. The streets were illuminated all the way from the Kremlin to the terminus, and vast crowds of citizens lined the road and showered upon me the extremest tokens of respect and reverence.

The population of Moscow is three hundred and fifty-one thousand souls. The Order of my Portrait was conferred upon the Governor of Moscow. Our princes were put into my own carriage, in which I dined and then lay down to sleep.

24th (*Thursday, 22nd May*).—Awaking in the morning, I saw that both sides of our road was a forest of firs. We crossed two iron bridges of great length, carried over two wide valleys, of which the one was waterless, the other possessing a stream. After a while the road passed over a large river named the Wok, which is spanned by a very long iron bridge that carries the railway over. This river forms numerous backwaters, among which are large numbers of villages. We proceeded until we came to a station where we alighted amidst an immense crowd, and some officials of the Ministry for Eastern Affairs were presented by Stramakof, the Under-Secretary of Prince Gorchakof, and an elderly person, but very shrewd, able, and diplomatic. We had a little conversation, and then, re-entering our carriage, we continued our journey.

Nearing St. Petersburg, we put on our state costume, ready for our arrival. When the train stopped at the terminus, His Most Exalted Majesty the Emperor, with the Nawwāb¹ the Heir-Apparent, and his other sons, as also the whole of the princes of the Imperial House, the Commanders-in-Chief, and Generals of the army, were there. His Most Exalted Majesty the Emperor Alexander II., Autocrat of all the Russias, received us with the perfection of warmth and friendship. The Nawwāb the Grand Duke Nicholas, Commander-in-Chief of all the Russian forces and brother of His Most Exalted Majesty the Emperor, handed in a state of the forces stationed at (St.) Peter(sburg). The Nawwāb the Grand Duke Constantine Nicholaïevich, another brother of His Most Exalted Majesty the Emperor, was also present. In short, giving our hand into the hand of the Emperor, we walked forward on foot. Very many officials in uniform lined the passage, and we thus reached the head of the street known by the name of Newsky, which is a very wide and long street, with houses three and five stories high on both sides. On each side of the streets there are stone pavements, while the middle is of wood, which makes no noise when carriages pass over it. Whenever a vehicle passes over a stone pavement, a disagreeable sound arises therefrom; but they roll along over the wood noiselessly and with great comfort.

At length we took our seat with the Emperor in an open carriage, the air being serene and the sun shining. Both sides of the road, the balconies, and the roofs, were full of men and women, who shouted hurrahs. Incessantly did we and the Emperor bow to the people. For a while we drove on, until at length, passing beneath an arch and a lofty gateway we entered the square in front of the Winter Palace. In this square there is a very tall and stout column of stone, a monolith, bearing on its summit a statue in metal of the Emperor Alexander I. Leaving the square we entered the palace, and went upstairs with the Emperor. Decidedly there were at least a thousand officers and generals on the steps and stairs, and in the halls. We passed through rooms, each one more sumptuous than the other, and more perfect. Beautiful paintings, columns of porphyry, tables of choice stones, chairs, vases, and other articles of furniture impossible to describe in writing, (did we see); especially a vase of malachite was there, at the head of the staircase, most choice. The Emperor pointed out the rooms one by one, until we reached the apartments allotted to us. There the Emperor took leave and went to his own residence. The Emperor is a man tall of stature and majestic, who speaks with great gravity, and walks with a stately gait. We sat down a while, and then Count Alderberg, Minister of the Court of His Most Exalted Majesty the Emperor, and a very pleasant man, of robust frame, came and brought to us from His Most Exalted Majesty the Emperor, the Order of St. Andrew set in diamonds, with its blue riband,—the most noble of all the Russian orders. After the lapse of a minute or two we went to return the Emperor's visit. He was standing in his own chamber. Taking each other's hand, we sat down, our Grand-Vazīr and M. Gamazof, the Emperor's interpreter, being present. A long and pleasant conversation ensued. The Emperor has two very handsome black slaves, dressed in the costume of Constantinople, who waited on us. In a few minutes we rose and returned home. After an interval we set out to return the visit of the Nawwāb the Heir-Apparent. The residence of the Heir-Apparent is at a distance from the imperial palace. The Nawwāb the Heir-Apparent is a young man of graceful form, and about twenty-five years of age. His wife is the daughter of the sovereign of Denmark. Having sat there a little while, we took tea, chatted considerably, and returned home to dinner. About the hour of sunset His Most Exalted Majesty the Emperor came to our quarters; we mounted a carriage together and drove to the theatre. The air was so cold that we stood in need of a wadded cloak. The way was long. We alighted at the door of the theatre, mounted many steps, and took a seat in a box facing the stage. In this box were the Emperor, I, the Heir-Apparent, the wife of the Heir-Apparent, the Grand Duke Constantine, the rest of the Emperor's sons and of the imperial family. The pit was filled with officers, generals, &c. This theatre has six tiers of seats, and every tier was full of women and men. The Persian princes and others of our retinue were present. The chandelier hung in the middle of the theatre was lighted with gas, which burnt beautifully. But the theatre of Moscow was larger, and its players were better than here. As soon as the curtain fell the first time, we went to another box. Here we saw the French Ambassador, a very old man, named General Le Flô; also the Ottoman Ambassador, Kyāmil

Pāshā. When the curtain was again raised we went with the Emperor to a lower box nearer to the stage. Two acts were played here, after which we returned home.

25th (Friday, 23rd May).—In the morning Prince Gorchakof, the Russian Prime Minister, came to us, and with him we had a long conversation, M. Grebel acting as interpreter. Prince Gorchakof is a man of great intelligence and shrewdness, and is seventy-five years old. After he had left, His Most Exalted Majesty the Emperor came, and we went together in a carriage to the Champ de Mars, *i.e.*, the parade ground, where more than twenty thousand troops were drawn up, infantry and cavalry. Crowds of spectators, women and men, stood around the square. A tent somewhat like a sun-shade tent was pitched in one part of the ground, in which were the wife of the Nawwāb Heir-Apparent, the foreign representatives, and our princes. After going down the whole of the lines of infantry and cavalry with the Emperor, we came to the vicinity of that tent and took up a position, sitting on horseback. The troops then marched past us. Two buglers on horseback, posted behind the Emperor, conveyed his orders to the troops by notes of their bugles. First came a company of Mussulman cavalry of the Guards; next the regiments of Foot-Guards in various beautiful uniforms; then the other troops followed, artillery and infantry; and, lastly, some squadrons of cavalry, all handsome young men, with choice uniforms and powerful horses all of the same colour.

The review being over, we went as we were, on horseback, to the house of the Prince of Oldenburg, where we became his guests at breakfast. His house looks on to that square. The daughter of this prince is the wife of the Nawwāb Grand Duke Nicholas, brother of His Most Exalted Majesty the Emperor, and she was our hostess and mistress of the house. She is a lady princess very much venerated. We went upstairs; our princes, the Grand-Vazīr, and others were present. At this breakfast members of the imperial family alone were invited. Before breakfast we saw the maidens that study at a college, under the protection of the Empress, and also their teachers. The Empress herself is not at (St.) Peter(sburg); having a chest complaint, she is gone to Firangistan (Europe). We now sat down to table. The wife of the Nawwāb Grand Duke Nicholas, mistress of the house, was on my right, and His Most Exalted Majesty the Emperor sat on my left. The Emperor conversed with Dr. Tholozan. I too conversed in French.

Breakfast over, we mounted our carriage at the same time with His Most Exalted Majesty the emperor, who went to his house at Tsarskoi-selo, one of the imperial summer residences outside of the city, by railway; for he has to return to town and be present at a ball given to-night in the club of the nobles. We took a little turn in the museum of the Hermitage, which adjoins our quarters. It possesses some splendid jewels and various objects worthy to be seen. I made the resolution to visit them in detail on another occasion, if God so will.

About midnight I went to the ball of the nobles. The chiefs of the nobles met me at the foot of the staircase. The Emperor had come there beforehand and was awaiting us. He came forward; we took each other by the hand, walked about a while and then sat down. There was a numerous assemblage of women and men. The following is the arrangement of this edifice: In the middle there is a very large hall, which is the place for dancing; around this and looking down on the hall is a gallery where people walk about or sit down. After a while I went home.

The river Neva flows from the north of (St.) Peter-(sburg) in a direction between south and east; and is a very large river. Large steamers navigate it. Every day many pieces of ice like mountains are brought down by it from the north, which are extremely pure and beautiful, like the ice in ravines of the Alburz mountains. It is said that the water of the Neva is not wholesome; and the Emperor cautioned us against drinking it. On one side of the stream is the palace in which we have our quarters, and on the other side is the old fort built in the time of Peter the Great, within which there is a church with a high tower and spire of gold. The tombs of the sovereigns of Russia are in that church. The mint of the Government is also within the fort. The streets of St. Petersburg are lighted with gas.

26th (Saturday, 24th May).—Arose in the morning, and after a while the foreign representatives came and were received in an audience. Four were Ambassadors, who were introduced singly in a private chamber, and on retiring remained in the hall (of audience), to which we followed. There I spoke to each of the representatives, enquiring after their health. They then presented the members of their establishments. Our princes and others were also present. It was a grand ceremony. The following are the names of the four Ambassadors : General Le Flô, Ambassador of France, an old man of sense; Lord Loftus, the English Ambassador; Kyāmil Pasha, the Ottoman Ambassador; the Prince of Reuss, the German Ambassador. Ministers and Chargés-d'Affaires from most of the states of Europe, America, and Greece, came to the audience. After seeing them, I came back and breakfasted. The Prince of Oldenburg, at whose house I breakfasted yesterday, came also to pay a visit; and then His Most Exalted Majesty the Emperor came. We had a little friendly chat, and he went to a parade of troops. We, however, having arranged to visit the Hermitage, did not go to this parade. The fire-brigade went through their manœuvres to-day at the foot of our palace, which we witnessed from a window. We now went to the Hermitage. The director, a M. Kidianof, who is also the director of the theatre, and is an old man, was presented, and one by one pointed out the various objects,—rooms full of pictures, of marble statues, large and small water-basins of rare stones from Siberia and elsewhere, the most part of their columns being monoliths from Finland, tall and stout; tables of stone enriched with mosaics in colours, tables and vases of malachite, which is a Siberian stone, and many strange and wonderful things worthy to be seen. More especially, there were marble statues in the form of men, women, and children, standing, or lying down, at which one marvelled. One standing (figure of a) woman was most graceful, so that one could have admired it, seated before it for three whole days. To see every picture and every statue in every room would require ten days or more; as we merely looked on them for a moment, we really comprehended nothing about them. We incessantly strolled from room to room and from hall to hall, and then descended by a great number of steps, by the sides of which were tall and stout columns of porphyry, to the ground floor, where also many ancient statues from Egypt and elsewhere were seen, which the director had himself gone for, purchased, and brought there. There was one colossal statue of a man sitting, as large as an elephant, but with all the limbs and parts in due proportion. There were ancient coins, vessels of gold, &c., dug up in the Crimea out of the earth, or out of graves. All these were in glass cases. The pictures were by old masters, English, Italian, or Spanish,—most beautiful pictures, more beautiful than which cannot be imagined. After a long inspection, we returned home, rested a while, and then dressed for the banquet to which we were invited by the Emperor, for the middle of the afternoon.

At the proper time we went. One hundred and seventy individuals were invited,—members of the Russian imperial family, with our princes and officials. It was a numerous assembly. We first went to a private chamber, where the Heir-Apparent, his wife, and others were. We sat there a while, and then, proceeding to the banquetting-hall, we took our seats at the table. The Emperor was on our left, the wife of the Heir-Apparent on our right. The dinner was eaten. In the middle of the dinner the Emperor arose, upon which we all got up. He drank a glass of wine to my health; and at the very instant guns were fired from the fort. After a minute or so I rose, and again all rose; I drank a glass of sherbet to the health of the Emperor. At length the dinner ended; it had passed pleasantly.

We now went to the apartments of the Emperor's mother and walked about. The Emperor presented his ministers and some generals. We then retired, and the Emperor also returned.

An open carriage was ready; mounting it, we drove about the city and passed near to a statue of the Emperor Nicholas, in cast-metal of large size, and seated on horseback. It is opposite the church of St. Isaac, which too is a grand structure entirely of stone, its domes being gilt and its columns of porphyry tall and stout in large numbers. The air was cold; so we returned home.

In the evening we went to the Michael theatre. The Emperor did not come, being at Tsarskoi-selo. Our Grand-Vazīr and the Russian Lord Chamberlain, &c., were there. We sat in another box. This theatre is smaller than the one first visited, but is very pretty and nicely decorated. It has six tiers of seats. Women and men were there in crowds. We were extremely near to the stage. In this theatre they act comedies, *i.e.*, they talk. One Swedish woman performed well on the tight-rope. Some individuals performed wonderful feats. For example, one man brought forth from a locked wooden box a lad, a graceful woman, and another human being, after having opened it to show it was empty. Another stood upon a large globe, and walked about with it, at the same time casting knives,

&c., into the air with both his hands and catching them during a considerable space of time. Again a fat woman clothed in tights, with naked bosom and legs, mounted a three-wheeled velocipede and went along at a rapid rate; then, a black man brought many wine-bottles and placed them on the floor which was covered with cotton-wool wetted with spirits of wine; this was set fire to and the woman then urged the velocipede about among the bottles at a high speed; ultimately she fell over from the vehicle to the floor, and her skirts took fire. It was a great piece of folly. Again, they several times represented a tableau-vivant, which was a very strange and pretty sight. Several women, children, and others, stood or sat motionless in beautiful postures, which were exceedingly interesting, and like the pictures of a painter. While motionless they were turned round and round by a rotating floor, so that they might be seen in various aspects. When all was over, we returned home and went to bed.

News has come from Paris that M. Thiers, President of the Republic, has resigned, and that they have made Marshal MacMahon president, who was Commander-in-Chief of the army.

27th (*Sunday, 25th May*).—When I rose in the morning it was raining heavily. The Emperor is at Tsarskoi-selo, and it had been arranged that to-night there should be a display of fireworks at the islands. This was put off on account of the rain. We paid some visits to-day. We first went to the house of the Grand Duke Constantine, brother of the Emperor, and an admiral. He has a very fine house, with many rooms, all full of things; especially, there is a room fitted up Constantinople fashion. Here we sat. Water flowed into basins from the walls and from taps. Around the room were written verses from the Kur'ān (Koran), the blessed name of ('Alī) the Commander of the Faithful, with those of the Imān Hasan and the Imān Husayn, upon each of whom be peace. The names of the Caliphs (Khalīfa) were also there. It was a small circular room very cheerful; and there I smoked a qalyān (a Persian huqqa, hubble-bubble, or water-pipe). We then rose and went to see the other rooms. There were many models of naval appliances, of ships, of guns, &c., also a library and a museum. We went upstairs, and there too were many things. The Grand Duke Constantine leaves to-morrow for the Black Sea, where a ship has been built which he is to launch.

Returning thence, we went to the house of the Grand Duke Nicholas, another brother of the Emperor, who was not at home. His wife, the daughter of the Prince of Oldenburg, and his son, a handsome youth, tall in stature, were in. Daughters and sons, small and grown up, of his family, were also there. He has a fine palace. We sat a while, took tea, left, and went to the house of Prince Gorchakof, which is his official residence. We sat down in a back room, after ascending many stairs, and we had a little conversation with him. Returning from there, we proceeded to the quarters of Barinyotiski, which are under our own residence. This person is the friend of the Emperor, and was at one time the Governor of the Caucasus. He it was who brought to a close the war with Shāmil, and took Shāmil prisoner. He was lying on a bed, with a coverlet drawn up over his face, so that no part of him was visible but his head. He is an old man. It was merely because he was a great man, respected, and unwell, that I went to visit him. He shaves his chin, but his cheeks have whiskers. He spoke in French. We sat down awhile. His wife, who is a native of Georgia, was received. Then I returned home.

After an interval, I went to the jewel-office of the Hermitage. There was a golden peacock there, which they wound up, and which then spread its tail beautifully. There was also a golden cock, that crowed as the domestic fowl. We walked about a considerable time, arrived at the back door of the building, and then went up a staircase to where are kept the Emperor's crown, the Lazarof diamond, which is mounted on the top of the Emperor's sceptre, and the jewels of the Empress. All these we saw. The large diamond is a fine stone. The crown also is set with many fine brilliants, with a large ruby on the summit. There was also a small crown in diamonds, with a necklace of very fine brilliants, belonging to the Empress. There were also other jewels. We now returned home again.

In this palace there are eleven hundred rooms, the greater part of which we went through.

At night, after dinner,' we went to the great theatre, where we found the Emperor, and had a long conversation. We sat in a lower box near the stage. The Grand-Vazīr, Alderberg, the Grand Duke Constantine, &c., were also there. The acting lasted a long time in different modifications. When the curtain fell we went with the Emperor to a small room and there smoked a cigar. In one of the intervals between two acts we went on to the stage with the Emperor, where there was a great crowd. The girls threw themselves down and kissed the Emperor's hands. Our princes, &c., were in a box opposite the stage. All being over, we mounted our carriage with the Emperor and went home. Praise be to God for all things!

In Hājjī-Tarkhān, Moscow, and (St.) Peter(sburg), multitudes of pigeons walk about the streets and city, without taking flight for fear of man.

Monday, 28th (26th May).—In the morning rose, breakfasted, and dressed. To-day the Grand-Vazīr had an audience of His Most Exalted Majesty the Emperor, and afterwards we drove with the Emperor in an open carriage to the parade-ground, where two or three thousand regular cavalry and Cossacks were drawn up to be reviewed. The sky was cloudy, and it began to rain, so that our clothes were wet. Arrived on the ground, we mounted our horses, and the troops were put through some manœuvres. The rain ceased awhile. After their evolutions, the regular cavalry dismounted and fired volleys like infantry. The artillery also opened fire. Afterwards the Circassian, Cossack, and Muhammadan horsemen of Qara-Bāg, to the number of over a hundred, went through their equestrian feats in our presence, discharging their muskets and pistols. Some of them had severe falls, the ground being very muddy. After this I got into my carriage and drove home, the Emperor proceeding by railway to Tsarskoi-selo.

Arriving at our quarters, we reposed a while and then drove to the fort and the State Bank. We first reached the bank, which is a wonderful place. In reality, it is the treasury and storehouse for the cash and for the gold and silver of the Government. There were altogether to the value of at least two crores of Persia (500,000 tūmāns each; *i.e.*, 1,000,000 tūmāns, at eight shillings per tūmān, is 400,000*l.*) in cash and ingots of gold and silver. The ingots were made in the form of half bricks of Tehrān, and laid on the floor. The Russian Home Minister, whose name is Reiterne, explained all to us on the spot.

Leaving the bank, we mounted and drove a considerable distance, passed over a great and long bridge that crosses the river Neva, and entered the fort. The governor of the fort is a very old general who shakes with palsy. His name is Karsakof. We proceeded first to visit the tombs of the Russian sovereigns, in a place like a church. The marble sarcophagi over the imperial tombs are collected in the corners (*or*, in chapels). From Peter the Great to Nicholas, all are buried here.

From thence we went to the mint, which is within this fort. Gold imperials and silver coins are struck here. After looking on a while, we proceeded on foot to the place where medals are struck. They struck a large gold medal in memory of us, on one side of which is the profile of the Emperor, extremely resembling, and on the other side, in Persian characters, the date of our arrival and visit, together with our name. We now returned home.

To-night there is a ball at the Emperor's palace. In the night we went to the ball, again passing through those saloons and long halls. Our princes, court officials, &c., were present. First we went to the apartments of the second son of the Emperor to return his visit. After sitting there a short time, I went to the Emperor's chamber, the Heir-Apparent and others being present. The Emperor invited me to proceed to the ball-room, where was a numerous assembly of men and women, officers, and generals. Our own suite were also present, with the exception of the I'tizādu-'s-Saltana and the 'Alā'u-'d-Dawla, who had pleaded indisposition. The entrance to the ball-room was in this wise. In the first place, I took the hand of the Heir-Apparent's wife and walked in advance, and then the Emperor, taking the hand of the wife of Prince Alderburg, followed behind. The women and men had formed a circle. Two complete rounds did we walk in this fashion, and then stood still. The foreign Ambassadors—the Ottoman, the English, the German, and the French—were all present. The women and men of the imperial family and others set-to dancing, and all danced much. We sat with the Emperor a while, we stood up a while, we went to another room and reposed a while, incessantly conversing with the Emperor, the Ambassadors, and others. After the dancing, again in the same manner did I take the hand of the wife of the Heir-Apparent and went to the supper-room, a large hall lighted up with many lamps. Numerous date-palms in vases were beautifully arranged in the hall, and around each palm-vase were collected a table and many chairs, food being placed ready. The Emperor led us to the large middle table, placed the other people at the other tables, and he himself walked about. Every individual present at the ball sat down to a table. According to the number of persons were there palm-trees. So many flowers, roses or hyacinths, were there collected or scattered about that it is impossible to imagine more. The musicians also played. Around our table were seated the Ambassadors, the Heir-Apparent's wife, the Grand-Vazīr, and others. After supping I again took the hand of the Heir-Apparent's wife and returned to the ball-room, where I stood a while, and again they danced. This finished, I went home. All passed off very pleasantly.

Saturday (Tuesday), 29th (27th May).—To-day I have to visit Peterhof and Cronstadt. The air is very clear, with a beautiful sunshine. All my suite accompanied me. Mounting our carriage, we went to a landing-place which they had constructed. Alighting at this landing, we went on board a small steamer, in which the whole party was collected. We started towards the sea and Cronstadt. As far as Cronstadt the sea is very calm and smooth. The air was very cold. We breakfasted in the steamer. In an hour and a half we reached the tower and forts of Cronstadt. It has several very important forts. They have built some turrets and batteries of stone, with several tiers of embrasures for guns. The most important work is named Fort Constantine, which is above the town of Cronstadt by a space of a thousand ells or more. Alighting from the steamer, we first went to see an iron man-of-war steamer named the Kremlin, and went all over her, above and below. She has about ten guns of very large size. The crew were put through their exercise, and a few shots were fired from the upper tier of large guns. We then descended, and mounting a small steam launch, we went to Fort Constantine. The foundations of the batteries and fort are of stone. About twenty large guns are placed in two batteries, such that each gun weighs 420 ass-loads (of one-third of a ton; *i.e.*, 140 tons)², while each shot is of the weight of 70 maunds (of $7\frac{1}{2}$ lbs.; *i.e.*, 525 lbs.). These guns are of Prussian make, and are breech-loaders. They bring the shot on a truck, lift it with a mechanical apparatus, and then pass it into the gun. The loading of a gun occupies a space of five minutes. There is another battery and turret, named Fort Menschikof; and yet another, named Fort Alexander; but these are small. Again, another turret was seen in the distance. Leaving the fort and mounting a small vessel, we pushed off. On reaching the landing-place of the town, we alighted amid a great concourse of women and men. Our suite followed after us. The Governor of the town of Cronstadt, named Kazakevitch, with the mayor, aldermen, and notables of the place, as also the military officers, had brought a gilt tray and a golden salt-cellar, with bread and salt. We walked a little way and then mounted a carriage. Everywhere were we surrounded with men and women on both sides of the streets. Passing over the bridge of the dockyard, we went to the workshops for iron, where two ships had been built, but not yet finished. The port of the town was full of merchantmen and other craft. This town carries on commerce with Denmark, England, the coasts of Russia, Prussia, Sweden, and Norway. In the works they had cast a large slab of iron; with certain apparatus established in the upper part of the shop they brought this slab, red-hot as it was, under a press and bent it somewhat. It is an important (establishment for the) casting of iron. After going about a while we turned back, mounted our carriage and went to our steamer. The town of Cronstadt is very beautiful. Its inhabitants are all sailors, or soldiers, or artificers. It has a public garden, fine houses, and a population of thirty thousand. Thence we proceeded to Peterhof.

In half an hour we arrived there. The Governor is an old man of robust form, and named Bomgarden. Numbers of officers and of men and women had come to the landing-place. From the very seashore it is a park with avenues, the end of which cannot be discovered. The carriage-drives are covered with a red earth, as soft as collyrium, while beneath the trees all is greensward, lawns, and flowers; but the trees are not yet in leaf, nor the flowers in bloom. We mounted a carriage and our suite followed. The Governor went before us in a carriage, and led us from avenue to avenue, from pathway to pathway. Everywhere *jets-d'eau* were methodically disposed in order. Children besieged us in our carriage, and ran after us everywhere. It is really impossible to give a written description of the parks, avenues, fountains, which must be seen with one's own eyes. There are four hundred *jets-d'eau*, all lofty and large, their source being very elevated and distant. Whenever they wish, they can in one instant set them all playing at once, or turn them all off. These fountains are of different kinds.

There was a stone colonnade without a roof, and very elegant, out of every part of which a *jet-d'eau* spouted up. Some of them play together, like one mountain of water; others separately from one another. Some are like waterfalls; in some places the water fell from the roofs of buildings. After a long drive, we went to the house of Peter the Great, which is in a park, is very pretty, and full of things. There were many articles that had belonged to Peter himself. Returning thence, again we mounted. In one place there was the Emperor's bath, a spacious enclosure without a roof, in four walls. Numerous fountains sprang from the interior of the basin of this bath, like a white mountain. It was a place like paradise. At times the Emperor there takes a cold bath. Diverging from this, we saw a fountain like the mass of a Pyramid of Egypt, of a conical shape—a beautiful fountain. Next we visited the middle palace, which is better than the rest, and has two façades; two hundred *jets-d'eau* play in front of it. Statues of men and other figures, of cast metal, are there arranged, out of the mouths or orifices of which the water runs. One of the fountains threw its water to a height of twenty ells (70 feet). The water of these jets becomes a cascade, flowing down a succession of steps. In front, too, there is an avenue and a long basin of water, with jets on either side. The sea even enters into the view from this palace. To say the truth, a description of the palace and its abounding contents does not admit of being recorded. The palace is one of the buildings of Peter the Great and Catherine. Descending thence, we again drove on to the palace of the Emperor and to that of the Heir-Apparent. In fine, there was no end to this visiting of palaces and of drives; besides which, we had not the time; so, with the utmost reluctance, we turned back, and getting out of our carriage near to some magnificent and numerous fountains, we walked about a while. The wonder is that in this vast park and ample space such neatness and cleanliness were maintained, that not a leaf from a tree, not a chip or a straw was seen on the ground. The trees are all forest trees, but planted out regularly, and made to interlace over the avenues. There are also avenues of firs and yews.

We at length regained our steamer, and paddled away back to the islands of Ilakin, which are near to the city of (St.) Peter(sburg), where to-night there is to be an exhibition of fireworks.

Crossing the sea, we arrived at the mouth of a stream, both sides of which are occupied by houses and by green and pleasant trees. On the right-hand side of this river the preparations for the fireworks were ready; while on the left tents were pitched. Passing a little farther up, we landed at the stairs on the left hand. Here were collected great numbers of officers, of women, of men, and of carriages in which the people had come out from the city to witness the fireworks. The arrangement of the ground, trees, and avenues was the same in this place as at Peterhof. We walked on until we arrived at a very handsome house, where we found the wife of the Heir-Apparent, the Heir-Apparent himself, the princes, and others. We sat down a while, and the Emperor came. Salutations and conversation ensued. Remaining still a little space, we then mounted our carriage with the Emperor, the wife of the Heir-Apparent, the Heir-Apparent, the wife of Prince Alderburg, and the other children of the Emperor, setting out for a drive to pass away the time until darkness should set in and the hour for the fireworks come. Our suite followed us in other carriages. The air was exceedingly cold. Driving about in a devious manner, we went about a league. Numerous detached houses and innumerable avenues, neat and cleanly, were seen. We then turned back to the same house from whence we had started, stopped there a little, mounted again, and went to the tent we had noticed before. An assembly of Europeans and of Īrānis was in the tent, and a crowd of spectators was in ships, in boats, and on the river-banks. We sat down within the tent. The fireworks were excellent, with a novelty. They had written our name in Persian characters, with the device of the "Lion and Sun." It was plainly legible. After the fireworks, we mounted a carriage with the Emperor and drove back to the former house. Tarrying there awhile, our carriage was announced. We then left, and driving by many a pretty place and beautiful summer residences, in front of the mint, and along the fort, we crossed the long bridge, and reaching home, dined, and retired to rest.

The admiral that accompanied us to-day from (St.) Peter(sburg) was a short man, who had lost an arm by a shot at the battle of the Alma in the Sebastopol campaign, and his name was Skolkof.

1st *Rabī'u-'s-Sāni* (*the Second Rabī'*; *Wednesday, 28th*

May).—Rising in the morning from sleep, we dressed in state to receive Prince Gorchakof, with whom we had a lengthened conference, and then drove to a photographer's. Dismounting at his door, we went upstairs. His name was Levitski—a fat, bulky man, with a certain wit. He possessed good and numerous apparatus, and spoke French well. He took several negatives of us, which were extremely good. After concluding this business, I returned home, performed my devotions, and took some tea. This evening we are invited to dine with the Emperor at Tsarskoi-selo, a special palace and park of the Emperor's, rather less than four leagues from town, which are got over in half an hour by the railway.

At the appointed time we drove to the station, where a great crowd had gathered, and took our seat in an elegant and comfortable carriage, special to the Emperor. Starting thence, we reached the first buildings of Tsarskoi-selo in half an hour. It is a beautiful town, nicely situated, and with a large population. Its streets are all straight and clean. Alighting, we mounted a carriage, and our suite were placed in others; thus we reached the palace, which is very grand and beautiful. There is a church adjoining it, and special to it, with four or five gilded cupolas. We passed along by beautiful and spacious avenues like those of Peterhof; we then turned back, alighted at the steps of the palace, and went upstairs. It is impossible to imagine a more delightful residence. All these improvements are from the time of Catherine. The Emperor had not arrived, so we sat down a while in an apartment that had been specillay designated for us until he came. We went together to stroll through the rooms, and we saw numerous and charming halls and saloons, which cannot be described. Exquisite pictures, the works of old and modern painters, were there. One room was visited in which the whole of the walls were inlaid with amber; *i.e.*, infixed piece by piece. It was truly a magnificent room. These pieces of amber were sent by Frederick the Great, King of Prussia, to Catherine II., and she had them set in this room. I visited the rooms separately, one by one; all were beautiful. At the back there is a private chapel for the Emperor, with gilded cupolas—a very attractive fane. This place of worship is on the ground-floor, and above it are windows and an outlook over what is below. We then returned through the same chambers to the first one, in order to take our dinner; and we passed through a marvellously beautiful hall—impossible to describe—and thence to a room where we stayed a short time with the Emperor, after which dinner was announced. The Emperor, the members of the imperial family of Russia, the great officers of state, and others, with our princes, the Grand-Vazīr, and others, were present. An exquisite dinner was served, during which a band played. Then, rising, we walked about for a time with the Emperor on a terrace overlooking the park; and afterwards I retired to my own room. Standing there a short time, the Emperor came to join me, and, with two of his sons, we got into a carriage and drove for some time about the avenues of the park. Many women, on foot and in carriages, went also about the park. Everything here resembles the park at Peterhof, but there are no fountains. There are some handsome barracks for the military, cavalry and infantry; and never is any untidiness seen in this park. Some ancient ruins were seen; and all these buildings, ruined or inhabited, are from the times of Catherine. At length we returned to the palace, and the Emperor told me he had a winter apartment on the ground floor, inviting me to see it. We alighted and entered. There were there two large dogs of the Emperor's, the one black and the other yellow. In this apartment were all sorts of things that could be imagined, such as Kurdish lances, Turkmān spears, muskets, and pistols, and swords, and other implements of the Red-Heads (old Persian militia of the Safawī dynasty), bow-horns and quivers, skins of lions and tigers, daggers and the like set with precious stones and sent by the Khān of Bukhārā, china coffee-cups with holders of gold, and a scrap-book, bound in gold covers, enamelled, sent by the late Prince-Regent ('Abbās Mīrzā, grandfather of the Shah) after the peace of Turk-mān-Chāy, were all collected there. It was a collection well worth seeing; but, alas! there was no time. Issuing from hence, we again went to the palace; and after an interval, mounting in carriages, we all went together to a theatre in the park. I and the Emperor, with the wife of the Heir-Apparent, went to a box near the stage. It was a pretty theatre with three tiers of seats. The Grand-Duke Nicholas, the Prussian Ambassador, with other officials and notables, were in the pit on chairs. The curtain rose, and the play of *Don Quixote* was acted. They had got up a Don Quixote and Sancho Panza,

F

his servant, that were very funny and suggestive. In the meanwhile, maidens in very pretty costumes danced. When all was over, we departed. The sky was brilliant as though it were day. We also saw the new moon of the second Rabī', and we returned many thanks unto God. We next got into the train, returned to town, descended, mounted our carriage, and went home.

This night his Imperial Majesty the Emperor presented to every one of our suite, to each according to his rank and dignity, either an order, a ring, a watch, or the like; I, too, presented to the Emperor my Jāfī horse, and to the wife of the Heir-Apparent my Julfa horse.

Mīrzā Aḥmad, Aide-de-Camp to the Grand-Vazīr, who had been sent from Tehrān to Constantinople, was received in audience at (St.) Peter(sburg).

2nd (Thursday, 29th May).—To-day I have to go, God willing, *viâ* Wilna, a Russian town, and Königsberg, a Prussian city, to Prussia and Germany. To-morrow, also, the Emperor, with the Heir-Apparent, the wife of the Heir-Apparent, and others, is to start for Firangistān (Europe).

As I rose from sleep in the morning the Emperor came. After expressing our adieux, we mounted together in an open carriage, and started. A great concourse was collected on either side of the way, who cheered. Many manufactories were seen at a distance on the outskirts of the city; and so we arrived at the terminus of the railroad to Prussia. Alighting with the Emperor, we again mutually said good-bye, and then passed down the line of troops drawn up at the station. We then took our seat in the train, but again said good-bye to the Emperor, and started with our suite. This was the very same train of carriages in which we had travelled from Tsaritsin to Moscow.

Again every spot on the plain was green and smiling, with forests of fir and yews, &c. We passed several bridges. About sunset we dined. At the station of Pskow, which is the seat of an important government, we made a stay of about fifty minutes, and the Governor was received in audience. Then again we sped along; and every now and then halting a few minutes, we continued our journey until night. Rain also fell. This day we have seen a good deal of cultivation and signs of population. The farther we went the warmer did the air grow. The trees in these parts were in flower and in leaf. During the night we slept with difficulty, through the motion of the carriage.

Of the things frequently seen in Russia were the abundance of carriages in (St.) Peter(sburg), many tramways of iron in the streets, and also many beautiful dogs, large and small.

---

[1] This title of Nawwāb (Nabob) is never used in Persia, but is imitated from expressions probably used by English officers from India, and is intended to represent " Son Altesse Impériale," or " Son Altesse Royale," &c.—J. W. R.

[2] The weight of 140 tons for a gun is evidently a confusion of weights. If we take the Persian "ass-load" here to stand for the Russian "pood," of 36 lbs., the 420 ass-loads become 135 cwt., or nearly 7 tons, which may be the true weight.—J. W. R.

CHAPTER III.

PRUSSIA, GERMANY, BELGIUM; 20 DAYS.

3RD (*Friday, 30th May*).—In the morning, on arising, they told me immediately that we were on the limits of the government of Wilna, and that the Governor, named Patapoff, had to come and say adieu before returning. There was a halt until he came and left. We then passed over a very long iron bridge, which they have built over the river Niemen. In the morning, whilst I slept, as they said, the train passed through a "hole in the mountain" (tunnel), of about 400 ells (470 yards) in length. After a short interval we came to another "hole," of a thousand four hundred ells (1633 yards) long, and as dark as night It occupies six minutes to traverse it. We now went on till we reached the frontier place between Russia and Prussia, named Aidgone. At the station of the Prussian town we alighted. There were many soldiers, officers, and peasants, men and women, present. The officials sent by the Prussian Government to be in waiting on me all came into the carriage and were presented. The chief official in waiting was a general of distinction, aide-de-camp (to the Emperor), and named Boïen. We passed down in front of the troops, and then retired to a room in the station. The rooms of this station and their furniture are plain. A breakfast had been prepared for my suite, of which they partook. They transferred our luggage from the Russian to the Prussian train. We had to wait a considerable time. I was in a small room with the officers of my household, and for a while I wrote up my Diary. A great crowd of spectators, men and women, scrambled up to the glass of the windows to have a look, and they squabbled with each other. The liberty (or licence) of this place is very much more than what was seen in Russia. When they dispersed we went and seated ourselves in our carriage. The Prussian train, unlike that of Russia, has carriages that do not communicate with one another; so that, wherever one takes one's seat, you have no knowledge of the rest, excepting at intervals when a halt occurs for a minute or so.

Prince Menschikof and General Bazak came and took leave; and at length we got in motion. The pace was several degrees swifter than that used in Russia. My carriage was spacious and handsome. On either side there was a small coffee-room. In these regions everything became changed,—the men, the country, the carriages, the food, &c. The populousness and cultivation in the land of the Prussian are greater than in Russia. Whenever I looked out there were villages, houses, men, horses, oxen, mares, sheep, meadows, sown-fields, water, and flowers of all colours. We crossed many rivers. Human improvements of charming aspect came in sight, near and afar. And so we came to a station. The train stopped; the Grand-Vazīr came to our carriage. The Prussian telegraph officer handed in a number of telegrams from Tehrān, and these were perused. Thanks be to God, they conveyed good tidings.

Again we started. As the Prussian trains travel very fast, it was but two hours and a half since leaving the Russian frontier before we arrived at Königsberg, a city of Prussia, and very near to the Baltic Sea. A large river passes through this city, which is named the Pregel. Merchant steamers come up from the sea to the middle of the city, and return in like manner. It is a small city, but pretty; its population is 95,000 souls. We have to-day seen in the Prussian territory the cultivation of rape, which has a yellow flower of a very charming tint. It is sown for its oil (colza oil), which is much used for the lubrication of machinery on railways, and the like. It was very extensively cultivated, and it gave a peculiar charm to the landscape. Naturally, the whole country is a meadow, with forests of fir and yews, though in much less quantities than in Russia.

We reached the station, where there was a large body of troops and officers, all very handsome young men, with helmets on their heads, and beautiful clothing on their bodies. They were a very pretty soldiery. The Prussian kingdom is all soldiery. The bands here, like those in Tehrān, have all drums and fifes, whereas in Russia this kind of fife was not observed. Infinite numbers of men and women lined both sides of the streets everywhere. I mounted an open carriage and drove off.

Crowds of children ran by its side. It was a curious hubbub. A long street was passed down. The houses are all of three or four stories, small, and narrow. We arrived at an ancient palace, built five hundred years ago; dismounted at its gate, and went up many stairs. It is an old structure. The whole of our suite, princes, household officials, &c., all came there. As the people of this city had never seen a Persian, they were much surprised at sight of us. The name of the Governor of the city is Vivekler. The carriages of this place, and the horses in the carriages, are not so numerous nor so beautiful as those in Russia.

Black-tailed tumbler pigeons, and others, swifts, storks, and magpies, appeared very numerous in this country; windmills are in great plenty.

In the night several bands of music stood beneath the palace and played a long time, *i.e.*, they beat the retreat on the drums. The harmony of the fifes of these bands, and the tenue of the men, were excellent. A great military drum, too, was fastened to a large dog, with a truck beneath it, which the dog drew. Heavy rain fell, but great crowds congregated.

4th (Saturday, 31st May).—This day, God willing, we are to go to Berlin. This city (of Königsberg) being near the sea, the air was extremely cold. The palace contains some small pictures by old masters, which are very good. On the ground-floor is a very large oblong hall, with a low-pitched timber ceiling, in which the kings of Prussia are crowned. We had to wait some little while; then mounted a carriage, and by the very same road we had followed in coming did we return. It was early morning, so that the congregations of people were less than yesterday. We reached the station; we all took our seats, and started. The train went at an extremely rapid pace, and in an hour-and-half's travelling we came in sight of a lake (the Frische-Haff) on our right, which must be twenty leagues round. Its environs were all populous, with trees, while sailing-vessels and others were on it. On both sides of our road everywhere we saw villages, towns, cities, populousness, forests, numerous trees, firs, yews, and others. Here the forests of firs are more frequent than in Russia. Some parts of the forests were hilly and elevated. Many very pretty avenues of willows and great poplars were seen, which are places of promenade for carriages and pedestrians. We passed many streams, large and small, but all bridged over, and so went by the town of Marienburg, through which the Vistula, a great river, flows. Numbers of vessels ply on this stream. It has an iron bridge over it of very great length. At the stations and guardhouses along our line of road we saw very pretty gardens, and cultivations, and many pretty flowers. The jasmine of Shīrwān, called by the Franks the lilac, was everywhere in flower. As far as the eye could reach, all was cultivation, human improvements, rivers, guardhouses, hotels, avenues, forests, flowers, meadows. Many oxen were seen, resembling those of Māzandarān.

And thus we sped on our way, until, in the middle of the afternoon, we arrived at a station to breakfast.

They brought me a little food in the carriage, of which I partook; the rest went out to breakfast, and then returned. Again we proceeded, and reached a large town with very strong fortifications, named Custrin, where a salute of cannon was fired. We stopped; the Governor of the city, and the General of the place, were received in audience. Women and men in crowds were collected. After an interval we went on, and arrived at another station, where we had to put on our state costume, being near to Berlin. Our suite did the same. We then drove on a long way, and ultimately reached the outskirts of the city. Our train was taken sometimes over a bridge, sometimes up and sometimes down, and then again turned back, like a horse, the bit of which is in the hand of a man. This was to us a source of wonder. Many lines of railway are laid down in every direction. Carriages and engines without number were seen on the lines, and many trains passed us on the road to-day.

At last we reached the station, and alighted. His Most Exalted Majesty, the Emperor of Germany,—William, the Nawwāb the Heir-Apparent,—his son, the Nawwāb Prince Charles,—his brother, Frederick-Charles, —son of a brother of the Emperor and captor of Metz, together with other princes of the royal family, such as Prince Hohenzollern, a youngster, and the very prince respecting whom the war between Germany and France occurred, as the French were not willing that he should become king of Spain; also Prince Bismarck,—the famous Chancellor of Germany, Marshal Roon, the Minister of War and Premier of Prussia, and General Moltke, now

Marshal and Generalissimo, very celebrated, and much spoken of, and other generals and officials, with a battalion of the Guards, a band, a cavalry regiment, and others, as also a concourse of people beyond all compute on the roads, were there to receive us. They gave us a most cordial reception. Taking the hand of His Most Exalted Majesty, we mounted an open carriage, and drove along a wide street, bordered on either side with ancient trees and white cluster roses in flower, everywhere paved with stones, and spacious, with houses the whole way. The crowds were great, and shouted hurrahs. I saluted them all, together with the Emperor. We conversed together in French, until we reached a place like a gateway, where the trees ended. It was a wide street, with sumptuous palaces on either side, of several stories. We noticed a column recently erected in commemoration of the victory over France, and not yet completed. A statue of Frederick I., *i.e.*, of Frederick the Great, cast in metal, was in our path. We passed by the University, a great place of instruction where two thousand students are taught; by the Arsenal, which was on our left hand; while on our right was the Emperor's own palace, in which he has resided from the days when he was Heir-Presumptive until now. Next we passed the palace of the Heir-Apparent, and so reached a square with two basins of water, from which sprang lofty jets-d'eau. On our right was a royal residence, that was assigned to us. There was a crowd up to the very edifice. We alighted. Veteran troops in beautiful uniforms, who are the guards of the palace, were in the rooms; patrols of cavalry, all handsome young men, with good figures, and well dressed, were at the gate, with officers of the household, &c., all stationed. We went upstairs. The middle of the square in front of the palace was laid out in beautiful beds of flowers and shrubs, lilacs, and the like. There were also two statues of horses, of cast-metal, each held by the mouth by a man.

The Emperor showed me all the apartments. There are some beautiful paintings and portraits in this palace. I presented the Grand-Vazīr, the princes, and others; the Emperor also at the station had presented his princes and servants. Next we went to a private apartment with him, and had some conversation, at which the Grand-Vazīr was present. When the Emperor left, I waited a short time, then mounted my carriage, and drove to his residence. He came to the foot of the stairs to meet me; we went in; we sat down; a conversation ensued; and after a few minutes I returned. The Emperor is seventy-six years of age; his brother seventy-three. Both of them, however, are perfect in bodily health and strength. Prince Bismarck is fifty-eight; Marshal Moltke seventy-five. The Nawwāb the Heir-Apparent is of the age of forty-two.

This evening I went nowhere. The city of Berlin is lighted with gas; the lamps being more numerous here than at (St.) Peter(sburg). Opposite our palace, on the other side of the square, is the establishment of the Museum of Berlin. On one side is a church, and opposite it, the Armoury. In the centre of the square is a raised platform, with steps all round, on which is a cast-metal equestrian statue of Frederick the Great. The exteriors of the buildings of Berlin are coloured ash-colour, which takes away somewhat from the appearance of the city; on the contrary, at (St.) Peter(sburg) the edifices are of all colours. The river that flows by one side of Berlin is named the Spree, a branch of which runs through the middle of the town; but it is narrow, and its waters very filthy. To-day we travelled eighty leagues distance in eleven hours or less.

5th (*Sunday, 1st June*).—To-day we went to the town of Potsdam, which is outside of Berlin. Mounting our carriage, we drove along the same track, and through the very gateway that we had traversed yesterday, passed by many avenues, noble forest trees, beautiful houses with exquisitely pretty flower-gardens in front of them, and basins of water with fountains and jets-d'eau, so arriving at the station. We took our seat in the train, started, and in half an hour's time, getting over the journey, arrived at that town.

It is a small place, with forty-two thousand inhabitants, for the most part regular troops. The Governor of the town, &c., came to receive us. We alighted. There is also a large river here, named the Havel. We mounted a carriage, and passing by the houses, &c., of the town, we entered an avenue. The parks, avenues, &c., here are similar to those in Russia. Of the two palaces, one is called Potsdam, and the other Sans-Souci; both built by Frederick the Great. The quarters of the Heir-Apparent are in that of Potsdam. We drove in our carriage to that palace; he was not at home. We then drove for a promenade, and passed through magnificent avenues in beautiful parks. The parks here are great forests, like those of Māzandarān. To-day being Sunday (Whitsunday), the whole world was out for a promenade, and great crowds were in the avenues. We came to a large fountain, the water of which spouted thirty ells (105 feet) high. Statues of marble, very beautiful and antique, were seen around the gardens and the basins. In short, this fountain is one of the wonders of the world. Its head is due to steam power, by the force of which the water is raised. Through the thronging of the people, we were somewhat impeded in going about. Lilacs abounded. Nightingales and wrens sang in the trees. It was a world of delight. We next went into an avenue opposite that fountain, at the end of which was another basin, the jet-d'eau of which was very lofty, but not equal to that of the first. We then got into our carriage, and went to the palace of Sans-Souci to visit the Queen Dowager, wife of the former Sovereign of Prussia, who was a brother of the reigning Emperor. The first Lord-in-Waiting, and the Chief Usher of the Queen (Dowager) and others received us. We went to the apartment of the Queen (Dowager); she rose and came outside of the apartment. She is a woman seventy years of age, or even more of her life may have elapsed. We sat down, and conversation ensued. We then arose and passed on. This is the special palace of Frederick the Great. The very room in which he died was seen by us. The chair in which he expired, his writing-table, a timepiece, and other effects of Frederick, were all there. Some things were placed on chairs merely from veneration, and the hands of the timepiece have remained since his death in the very same position to a minute, never having been set since then. There were many beautiful paintings, left from that time. They told me that when the first Napoleon took possession of this town, he tore the cloth on the table of Frederick, and that it has been so preserved since, torn. There were beautiful rooms, and many relics of antiquity.

We then descended. In front of the palace there is a lofty terrace. In front of the eminence there are very beautiful gardens, with small basins of water. From the top they have arranged statues, from the mouths of which water flows into basins. The view from this terrace and this eminence has not its equal in the world. That lofty jet-d'eau is opposite to this eminence. In short, the fountains, the parks, and the beautiful avenues were numberless. We walked about a while; we then mounted our carriage, and drove to a place where we saw a ruined mill, which has remained from the time of Frederick the Great, and has a date on it. From this we gathered that when Frederick wished to build this place, he was unable, do what he would, to content the proprietor of the mill, and induce him to sell his property, so that the park might not remain incomplete. He would not consent; and, as an instance of equity, the mill has been preserved in the same condition ever since.

We next went to the hot-houses and orangeries (conservatories), which are constructed with brickwork, glass, and other appliances; but we did not enter them, the whole of the flowers and shrubs having been brought out of doors. In front of the conservatory there is a garden, a basin of water, and a terrace, which have beautiful parterres of flowers, with statues of marble. From hence there are many steps, as they have arranged very beautiful parterres range upon range. Here we walked about a bit; and then, mounting our carriage, we drove to the palace and summer residence of the wife of Prince Charles, a sister of the Queen of Prussia, *i.e.*, of the wife of the Emperor, and is mother of Frederick Charles. It has a pretty courtyard, with statues and ancient stone figures and carvings, of Egypt, Syria, Nineveh, Mawsil (Mosul), &c., such as a leg, a head of a shoulder, an arm (or hand), of the figure of an animal or man, large or small, imperfect or whole, collected therein of every kind, and fixed to the walls in an artistic manner. It became evident that Prince Charles and his wife are persons of learning and taste.

In short, most beautiful gardens, fountains, lawns, and the like, were there seen. We went upstairs and sat down a while in a room. The wife of Prince Charles offered many excuses, and expressed great chagrin that notice had been given to her late, saying: They telegraphed to inform me that you would not come today. She brought out a book, and we inscribed our name therein. She is an aged woman.

Rising from thence, we took our seat in our carriage to go to the residence of the wife of Frederick-Charles. She was not at home. In front of the avenue leading to the gate of Frederick-Charles, there were two statues of stags lying down, on the top of the railings, most beautifully executed. We drove on; we passed some charming spots; and we came upon a small pavilion most beautifully placed, which belongs to the Emperor. It has some pretty gardens, and a charming prospect over a large river.

We then went to the station and returned to the city. On our passage we remarked a singular pastime which they had devised. They had fitted up a kind of gypsey-tent, and around the tent there were pasteboard carriages and horses, on which people's children rode, while the tent revolved incessantly, causing the carriages, the horses, and their riders to go round also.

We reached home. This evening the Emperor gave a special banquet in this very palace where our quarters are. Our princes, the Prussian princes, our Grand-Vazīr, Prince Bismarck, Marshal Moltke, Marshal Roon, and others, were present, as also Marshal Wrangel, with whom we conversed. He is a short and very old man, ninety years of age, but full of mental vigour. He served everywhere in the wars of the first Napoleon.

After dinner we went to the theatre, a beautiful house with five tiers of seats, about the size of the Michael Theatre at (St.) Peter(sburg). The audience was crowded. The play was a ballet this evening, and they danced well. The dancers wore strange costumes. I and the Emperor went on the stage and looked about a little. We then returned, and another scene commenced. They danced, and represented some interesting situations. Prince

Charles, the Emperor's brother, also was present. When all was over we went home.

On the day when we came away from (St.) Peter-(sburg), the Mukhbiru-'d-Dawla remained behind to see his son, who is to come to (St.) Peter(sburg).

6th (Monday, 2nd June).—After our breakfast the foreign representatives came to an audience. The French representative did not come, because, M. Thiers having resigned, he had no credentials. We then went to another chamber, and spoke to each of the representatives, one by one, enquiring after their health. Subsequently Prince Bismarck came, and with him a long conversation ensued. Next Marshal Roon, the War Minister, came; and then Marshal Möltke, with whom we conversed a little.

After this, changing our (state) costume (for a private one), we mounted our carriage and drove to the Zoological Gardens. To-day also (Whit-Monday) was a festival of the Franks, and the whole population of the city were in commotion. There was an enormous crowd, and numerous equipages in the road, and on both sides. Bands were playing in the gardens. There were many ponds, and various species of aquatic fowl in the ponds. Next we came to beautiful separate large cages, in which the various kinds of beasts were kept apart. Different birds of prey,—eagles, a pair of condors, which are a well-known bird of prey brought from the New-World (America). It is a singular creature, of a dusky black colour, and of great ferocity; but its talons are not like those of the eagle, since it belongs to the class of feeders on carrion.

There were various kinds of cranes from Africa, India, the New-World, and other parts; much more wild and beautiful than the common crane of Persia. All the different species of birds produced in the whole world are there collected together, so that it is impossible to mention them all. What we had formerly seen pourtrayed in books, we here saw living.

We then entered the corridor in which are the cages of the carnivorous quadrupeds,—the beasts of prey. Here were wild beasts that cannot be imagined, maned-lions of Africa,—which I had not hitherto seen, save in books,—huge in bulk, terrible in appearance, with very thick black manes hanging down, their heads as large as those of elephants, or larger; with glaring eyes especially terrific; with graceful bodies resembling velvet. The keeper raised high a piece of flesh; the lion rose on his hind feet and seized the flesh. His stature was from three to four ells (10½ feet to 14 feet). The flesh was placed on a truck, and so conveyed from den to den and given to the beasts.

The compartment which looks out on this corridor, and is subdivided to hold the different beasts, has a door of stout timber that can be raised by a chain. The other side of the door is where the animals walk about. When the door is raised, the beast goes to that other side; the door is then quickly lowered, and the den is swept clean. The compartment is floored with timber very carefully. No one is allowed to go near these creatures; and the flesh is given to them through the interstices of the fronts of their cages.

I was extremely tempted to stay and observe these lions a long while; but, through the thronging of the crowds of spectators, this was impossible.

I saw several enormous tigers, African and Indian; two black leopards, from Africa, very singular and terrific. Also some other lions; one, a maned-lion, of a good size, though his mane was not as yet so large as those of the two lions first seen. There was a lioness that had given birth to several cubs in that very establishment, her cubs having grown up. There were many leopards, various chetahs, strange-looking hyænas from Africa that made curious noises. In short, I saw numerous cages, in each of which were animals of many kinds, various monkeys, and the like. There were two elephants; one very large, that had been brought from India; the other from Africa. The African elephant is very different from that of India, its ears being much broader and larger. There were three giraffes, and a zebra, *i.e.*, a wild horse, the body of which is in stripes, and very beautiful. Also many bisons,—the wild buffaloes of Africa and the New-World; and large and small buffaloes (yaks?) of Tibet, from the sides of which so much wool hung as to trail on the earth; they looked very ferocious. Llamas, an animal between the camel, ox, argali, and other species, and which runs very fast, were kept in spacious gardens enclosed with railings. There were argalis, mountain-goats (chamois or ibexes?), and antelopes, from India and Africa; for instance, there was one argali as big as a horse, with long, thick, sharp horns, having no resemblance to the argali of Persia. Also various kinds of swine and wild boars: curious animals, too, of other species, and in such varieties, were collected in that place as cannot be computed. Every animal, wherever it may naturally exist, was to be found there, and are there fed with all care and cleanliness. Various parrots, peacocks, golden pheasants of Australia, that are very pretty, were there; also many kinds of birds with magnificently-coloured plumage flew about, played, and amused themselves in very large aviary cages. The name of the director of these Zoological Gardens is Doctor Bodines, a learned and distinguished man.

We now returned home, and somewhat later took a drive through various streets of the city. One place attracted my attention as being a park. I alighted and entered; then I saw that it was a cemetery. But it was a charming place, where there were many nurse-maids with infants and little children. These flocked around me.

Again mounting, we arrived at a circular open space surrounded by buildings, and having pretty flower-beds in the middle. Here, too, we got down and strolled about for a while; thence returning home again.

The official in attendance upon us, whose name is General Boïen, was also in attendance on Napoleon during his captivity and seclusion; as also upon the Sultan of Turkey while in Prussia.

7*th* (*Tuesday, 3rd June*).—To-day I wish to go to the Aquarium, a place where they keep marine animals and plants as a spectacle.

In the morning, on rising, we went to visit the Empress

Augusta, who had newly arrived. As the Emperor was unwell, we did not see him, but went to the apartments of the Empress, which are in the Emperor's palace. She is an elderly woman, seventy years of age. We sat and conversed; then, leading me away, she showed me over the apartments, which are nicely furnished.

Next we went to the residence of the Heir-Apparent to see his wife, a daughter of Her Most Exalted Majesty the Sovereign of England, and her firstborn child. We sat and conversed a little. She has three sons and two daughters by the Heir-Apparent, her eldest son being fifteen years of age, and her eldest daughter ten. The Heir-Apparent's house is plain.

Keeping in mind the Aquarium, we rose, mounted our carriage, drove there, alighted at the gate, and went upstairs. The Heir-Apparent and a large assemblage of people were there. We were taken to some very strange and marvellous places,—dark corridors and caverns, hills and dales, cascades, fountains, all constructed of rocks from the mountains in such a manner that at first one cannot comprehend that he is not really in a cavern of a mountain, but is in the midst of a city. It is a curiosity of design, and is one of the things in this world worthy to be seen. The director, whose name is Hermess, explained all to us. They have placed various kinds of fishes, with other marine animals and seaweeds, in tanks covered over with large sheets of plate-glass or common glass; and the water is incessantly renewed. From the spot where we stood the bottoms of the tanks were seen; so that the fishes, the other animals, and the plants appeared to us in their natural states, as though actually in the sea. Some were asleep, others in motion. There was one kind of animal like a bunch of flowers, roses, or lilies, full of filaments of various colours, and attached to a rock or to a plant, without the least visible movement. Never could it be known that this is an animal endued with life; but when the keeper of this place conveys down into the water a worm, and then lets it go, so as to fall into the midst of this bunch of flowers, then it moves, draws to itself the worm, and eats it.

There were many sorts of strange fish, of all colours, some large, and others small; there were numerous shellfish, various crabs of many colours, frogs, and other things extremely interesting. Descending some more steps, we reached another place, the roof of which was equally of rocks from the mountains, having no difference from a natural cavern. Here were varieties of aquatic birds, parrots of all colours, one kind of large white parrot (cockatoo) that has a voice extremely like that of a man. There was an inclosure (aviary) like a cage, in the middle of which a fountain was playing, and around which again were compartments like cages, in which artificial trees or shrubs were arranged; and every kind of bird that can be imagined in the world, from cold countries and from tropical places, are there to be found. All the forms of birds that I had seen in books, there, colour for colour, did I witness them. To all of them, with the utmost cleanliness, do they supply food and water. All these birds would at one time cry out together, at another would play or fly about; and the contemplation of them inspired me with the utmost amazement.

There was another pair of animals, male and female, very curious, for which they had constructed in one corner apart a small house to them alone, which had an extremely small hole for an entrance, by which they both went in together. They are of a yellow colour. Their head, mane, shape, and tail, are like those of the African maned-lion; but their hands and feet resemble those of man and the monkey. Besides, they have a finger like the spur of a cock, at the end of which is a claw like the talon of a hawk. They were very tame, had a singular cry, and were fed on worms. (*Mr. Bartlett, of the Zoological Gardens, Regent's Park, concludes from this description that the animals seen were Silky Marmosets, or Lion Monkeys*, midas rosalia, *natives of Brazil, which have more than once bred in the Society's gardens. I see they are also mentioned by the names of* Marikina *and* jacchus rosalia.)

Again two other animals were noticed, exceedingly interesting; but these were said to be also visible at the Zoological Gardens. They are called "Sloths," and resemble melancholy, sorrowful men, are very inoffensive, and continually utter a cry like the chirping of a cricket.

In short, I witnessed many wonders, and then returned home.

In the afternoon we were the Emperor's guest at dinner in the upper story of this very palace in which we are quartered. All the wives and lady princesses, all the princes of the Prussian royal family, all our princes, the

Heir-Apparent, Prince Bismarck, Marshal Roon, Marshal Möltke, and others were present. A band played. This upper palace is very magnificent, having many pictures, with sumptuous halls and apartments.

After dinner we descended, and in the evening went to the city theatre, which is small, and has four tiers of seats. The Heir-Apparent, the Grand-Vazīr, and others were present. We sat in a box near the stage. They gave a beautiful entertainment, the last scene representing the palace and gardens of Versailles, with the coronation of this very Emperor. The representatives of the Emperor, of all the leaders, of Marshal Möltke and Prince Bismarck, were dressed exactly like those personages. It was a beautiful scene; *i.e.*, it was not a picture, but a collection of men dressed up. At the conclusion we returned home.

8th (Wednesday, 4th June).—To-day I have to go and see a review. Having breakfasted, I mounted my carriage, the Grand-Vazīr, my princes, and others with me. We went to the outskirts of the city, where a large concourse was assembled. The parade-ground was a beautiful piece of grass-land. Descending from our carriage, we mounted the charger of the Husāmu-'s-saltana (sharp sword of sovereignty). The Empress, the wife of the Heir-Apparent, and others were present. The Emperor is still unwell. The battalions of infantry, together with the cavalry, were about eighteen thousand strong. We slowly went down in front of the line. The Heir-Apparent, the whole of the officers, and the Prince of Wurtemberg, who was in command, and is an old man, tall of stature,

Frederick-Charles, Prince Charles, and others accompanied us. We then took up our position, and the troops marched past, the infantry, cavalry, and artillery, in beautiful uniforms, and well armed, being reviewed. After the ceremony, we remounted our carriage, and returned home.

We were invited to dine with the Empress in the evening. We went; all were there; dinner was eaten; and we returned home. From thence we went to the theatre. This evening was a gala evening at the theatre. All the women wore magnificent costumes; all the men were in court dresses. We, the Empress, the other women, the Grand-Vazīr, the Prussian princes, and our princes, sat in a large box fronting the stage. It was very hot. They brought out some pretty scenes. They danced nicely. After two acts, we went for a little space to a large saloon and had some conversation, and from thence to a box near the stage. The last scene enacted was of a king of Mawsil (Mosul, for Nineveh; the king, Sardanapalus), who, after being vanquished by his enemies, cast himself, with all his effects and family, into the fire. It was a magnificent scene. From thence we came home.

To-day, while returning from the review, we visited the Arsenal, *i.e.*, the armoury. On the lower floor they have collected specimens of the cannon taken from the French and Austrians, with those of ancient artillery. In the middle of the court of the Arsenal there was a colossal figure of a lion in metal, which had been cast and set up in Holstein by the Danish Government, in memory of the conquest of Holstein from Germany. When the Prussians retook the two provinces of Schleswig and Holstein, they brought away this lion, and placed it here. It is as big as a mountain. We went to the upper story, which is very spacious, and where they have collected an enormous number of muskets. Of every model, ancient, modern, or otherwise, were muskets to be seen there. The general in charge of this Arsenal was a tall man, of the name of Treh, who spoke French well. His left arm had been carried away by a French shot in the battle of Gravelotte, the last that was fought.

It is worthy of remark that in this city the noise of carriages never ceases from evening until morning, nor from morn to night. One evening the Fire-Brigade came with torches and went through their practice at the foot of the palace.

9th (Thursday, 5th June).—This morning I started by train and went to Potsdam with all my suite, excepting the I'tizādu-'d-Dawla, who remained in town, as they have completed the telegraphic wires to Tehrān, and he is talking with them. The Order of the Black Eagle in diamonds, with its yellow riband, &c., was sent for us by the Emperor through General Boïen, who is in attendance on us.

Well; we arrived at Potsdam, alighted, and at once went upstairs. The Empress, the wife of the Heir-Apparent, with others, were there. The garrison of this place is to be reviewed to-day. The whole of the troops were drawn out in a parade-ground at the foot of this palace. When the review was over, the Heir-Apparent and others came upstairs, where breakfast was prepared. As I had no appetite, I excused myself to the Heir-Apparent, mounted my carriage, and went for a drive to the Orangery. It has a very handsome and cheerful hall, well lighted, its roof being partially of marble, like a vault. Paintings, marble statues, and beautifully furnished apartments there were. It is one of Frederick's buildings. From thence we went driving about, and alighted near a large fountain, sat down awhile on the steps, and contemplated the jet-d'eau. Again we drove about. In the park there is a mansion, which is magnificent, named the Charlotte Pavilion. It was the residence of Dr. Humboldt, so celebrated, who died ten years ago. It has a grassy terrace, a fountain, a basin of water, some small rooms, full of curiosities, preserved like those of a museum. It had a curator, who could not speak French. At the top of the steps of this building there was the figure of an antelope, which had been cast in metal, of a very graceful form.

From thence we again returned to the Orangery, performed our devotions, and towards the middle of the afternoon went to the palace of Babelbrig to dine by invitation with the Emperor. It was a long way off. Passing over a long bridge across the river Havel, which separates the town of Potsdam from this palace, and through many a charming site and beautiful avenue, we reached the gate of the mansion. The Empress, the Heir-Apparent, Prince Bismarck, Marshal Roon, the Prussian princes, our princes, with others, and the lady princesses, were all present. The building is very fine, and was erected by the present Emperor. It has handsome basins of water, good prospects, lawns, flower-gardens, all very beautiful. We had dinner, and conversation ensued. After dinner we took a walk on the lawn. There was a fountain that rose from the middle of the river to a very great height, and of great volume, that caused great pleasure to see. The Empress was in a carriage with the Heir-Apparent. He alighted, and we walked together for a space. Then I mounted with the Empress, and we went to the residence of the Heir-Apparent. He and the others followed on foot. There we alighted, and I, with the Heir-Apparent, set off to visit the tomb of Frederick the Great. We now repassed that bridge over the river, and entered the town of Potsdam, so reaching the door of the mausoleum, which is a building like a church. Flags taken from the French and others were there seen. Two tombs were in the mausoleum, one of Frederick, the other of his father. After standing there a space, we returned, and again went to the Orangery, where we spent a short time, and then the Heir-Apparent went to his own mansion, that was now illuminated. Later, we followed him to his mansion, which is a charming place. All the Diplomatic Corps, women, princes, and others were there. The park opposite was illuminated in colours. The fountains threw up red water, which was very beautiful; but there were no fireworks. The wife of the Heir-Apparent wore the Order which I had conferred on her, with its riband. Later, the Empress took my hand and led me downstairs; we sat a little, and we walked about a little;

then went to a long room where a *buffet* was laid out, *i.e.*, where they had spread many kinds of food on a table. The lady and gentlemen guests all sat down at the table, and eating of the viands was achieved. We then took leave of the Heir-Apparent and others, and went to the station.

In that place one beautiful saloon was seen, that was of the time of Frederick, the whole being inlaid with mother-of-pearl, haliotis, and similar shells in beautiful designs.

The train started, and we arrived at the city station, which is a noble work, with many chandeliers, all of iron and glass. Thence we proceeded home, driven in our carriage.

10*th* (*Friday, 6th June*).—In the morning, after breakfast, went to the Parliament, *i.e.*, to the Council-House of Germany, which is in an outskirt of the town. We sat in a gallery. There were about a hundred deputies present, the rest of the chairs being unoccupied. Prince Bismarck was in his place, to the right, and below the seat of the President of the Council. The name of the President of the Council is Simpson. The Under-Secretary of War was standing below Prince Bismarck, and was speaking to the deputies, and refuting, on the part of the Government, the proposal of the deputies about the maintenance of the École des Cadets. He delivered a long speech. This École des Cadets is a college in Potsdam for young nobles and the sons of living and deceased officers. The excellent officers of Prussia issue from this college. The Heir-Apparent was himself educated there. One day the Heir-Apparent brought those students in front of our palace, where they went through their exercise. The students are seven hundred in number. As the expense of maintenance is heavy, the nation is dissatisfied; but Prince Bismarck wished to augment it.

We soon rose from there and went to the residence of Prince Bismarck to return his visit. He was at home, and came to meet us. His house is small and simple. His wife and daughter were seated in a room. A long conversation ensued.

We then left, and proceeded to the Museum, which is opposite our palace. The Director, an aged person named Lepsinius, came (to receive us). On the walls of the staircase of the building there are designs and scenes, very beautiful and old, drawn on the surface of the plaster. Going upstairs, we walked about. There was a crowd. Plaster figures, small and large, all imitatively prepared after the works of Greek and other artists, were there in great numbers. Other objects also, in porcelain, crystal, ivory, amber, wood, &c., were seen. We went about a while, and then returned home.

Before long we set out again to go and pay a visit of adieu to the Emperor. The Emperor's wife was present. This day, on the bank of the Rhine, Prince Aldeberg (Adalbert), cousin of the Emperor, and Director of all the war-ships of Germany, has died; the aged grandmother of the Emperor also is dead; and for this reason a concert, instrumental and vocal, appointed for this evening, is put off. Well; the Emperor came in also, sat down, and we conversed. The wife of the Emperor presented me with a china vase as a gift.

We then went to the Aquarium, walked about a bit, and to-day have examined attentively that slothful animal (the sloth ; cholœpus didactylus; bradypus didactylus). On its front paws it has two long claws like those of an eagle, and on its hind paws three such. Wherever it attaches itself, it is with difficulty that it is separated. Went home.

11th (Saturday, 7th June).—We have to go to the cities of Cologne and Wiesbaden. Rose early in the morning. There was a violent wind, the weather being cloudy and cold. We dressed in anticipation of the arrival of the Heir-Apparent. When he came, we mounted a carriage and drove to the station in an outskirt of the city; there got into the train, said good-bye, and started. Much as we wished to sleep, it was impossible. As soon as my eyes closed, we would arrive at a station, talking and discussion would ensue ; there was nothing for it but we must dress and hold ourselves in readiness until the governor of such a town, or the commander of such a fortress, should be introduced by the Mu'tamadu-'l-Mulk and took himself off again.

Mirza Malkam Khān has remained in Berlin to settle with the Prussian Government a contract for the purchase of muskets.

Well ; the appearance of the country, the grass-lands, the trees, the forests of fir and yews, the flowers, the rivers, the populousness of the villages and towns, everywhere, were just the same as those seen when we were coming to Berlin. We passed the city of Hanover, which is very pretty, and then the cities and regions of Westphalia, which are charming spots. Here we saw a few mountains and high hills, and crossed numerous rivers, one very large,—and at an hour to sunset we arrived at the works of M. Krupp, who came himself to the railway (to meet us). He is a tall, thin old man. He has himself, in a certain space of time, created the whole of these works. The cannon of every government does he furnish from hence. Guns of every description, such as large cannon for forts, cannon for ships, and cannon for field use in campaigns, are all manufactured here. His plant and workshops, of which steam is the motive power, resemble a mighty city. He employs 15,000 workmen, for the whole of whom he has erected houses and lodgings, paying them salaries and wages. After deducting his expenditure, his own yearly income amounts to 800,000 tūmāns (320,000l.).

We went to the shop of the steam hammers. They are singular hammers, like mountains; and, worked by steam, fulfil the office of forging cannons. They make these of any pattern they desire. When the hammer strikes the gun, the earth floor of the workshop emits a sound and trembles. It was a marvellous thing. We went all over the works, and they turned out some large and some small cannon. We then went to a house which he had prepared, and there we dined. He gave us an excellent dinner. In the conservatory of this house we saw a tree, the leaves of which were two ells (seven feet) long, and half an ell (twenty-one inches) wide. The steam-hammers, in spite of their great distance from this room, made the earth shake here as though in an earthquake. M. Krupp made us a present of a most magnificent breech-loading six-pounder cannon, with all its appliances.

We now went back to the railway. It was night. I lay down. Sleep overtook me. It was two hours' journey to the city of Cologne. All at once we sprang up from sleep; I heard the sound of music, and of voices speaking. I knew that we had reached that city, and that the authorities were waiting to be received in audience. I dressed; I stood up; the authorities came up; then I alighted and inspected their troops. Now we mounted a carriage again and entered the city. There was a great concourse. A beautiful city appeared before my sight; it has a large, lofty, well-placed church, which they say is the first in Europe. I went to an hotel, a cheerful building, and there we took up our quarters. After awhile I again slept.

12*th* (*Sunday, 8th June*).—This afternoon we have to go to the city of Wiesbaden. In the morning on arising from sleep we breakfasted, mounted a carriage, and drove to the Botanical and Zoological Gardens, which are near the city. The wealthy of the city have supplied the funds, and maintain these two gardens for their own amusement and that of the people. We passed by at the foot of the great church. It is a most imposing edifice. It is more than four hundred years that they have built it here, and they are still busy working at it, as it is not yet completed, the cranes being on the spot.

At one side of it is a very magnificent structure, into which we did not go, but we examined it all round. It has many conical domes. It has so many openings and apertures, and is so vast and so high, that many crows have therein made their nests.

Thence we passed on, and saw a very long iron bridge that spans the river Rhine. The river flows through the middle of the town; but the bulk of the populous part of it was on one side of the river, where our quarters were. We arrived at the Botanical Gardens. It has a building, in front of which are beautiful beds of flowers, basins with fountains, and lawns. They had laid down an india-rubber tube, which incessantly revolved in the water, and from its orifice water flowed to all parts of the lawn. Some had two tubes; they revolved like the catherine-wheels of fireworks, and so scattered the water. Well; we entered the room and the hall of the plants, where we saw some flowers, some date-palms, and others; we passed on into a small hot-house to which they had given the temperature of India, and in which they had reared African, American, and Indian plants. There was a plantain-tree, which has large leaves. One tree was seen, the leaves of which were narrow, but were five ells (seventeen feet six inches) long.

Coming out from thence, we entered a fish-house (aquarium), which was small. As at Berlin, the fishes were behind sheets of plate-glass. We surveyed them and came out again. We sat down awhile. From the other side of the glazed windows the people looked on in great numbers. The weather was very cold, with rain falling at intervals. Red roses were newly come into bloom.

We now went to the Zoological Gardens, which are very beautiful and grand. Such animals as we had seen at Berlin, such as maned-lions, black leopards, &c., we found here also, though in somewhat less numbers. The small, beautiful, many-coloured birds were few; but there were many strange and wonderful large birds, of charming plumage, that I did not see at Berlin. A large crowned pigeon (gaura coronata) from the Molucca Islands, which is a splendid bird; various kinds of turkeys, crested, with fine plumage, but strange-looking, there were in numbers; the condor was there; also two ostriches. The feet of the ostriches had two toes, of an unusual form. Large black bears, white polar bears like snow, diminutive horses, one white male camel in heat, were there. It is very strange that a camel should be in heat during the summer season. There was a humped ox from India (zebu, bos indicus); the horns and every other particular of which are similar to those of ordinary oxen, but which is of the size of a sheep. A kind of male argali—bearded argali (aoudad, ammotragus tragelaphus) was seen, brought from Morocco, the head, the colour of body, and the horns of which were like the vicious rams of Persia, but the hair on the breast of which was yellow and very long, and from the knees to the soles of the feet of which hung a thick fringe of hair. There were so many kinds of birds and quadrupeds that one became bewildered. As a pen for the argalis and antelopes, a kind of artificial mountain was formed, with fountains of running water, that had caused grass and flowers to spring up on the stone pavement,—all most surprising.

We then remounted and drove over the bridge. It had two roadways, one for ordinary horse vehicles, the other for railway trains, between which an iron network acted as a partition. The bridge must be a thousand feet in length. It is all of iron. The river Rhine is a mighty stream, very wide, clear, and pleasing. Large steamers ply thereon. Merely for a drive, we went to the further side of the city, and again returned to Cologne over the bridge, and by the foot of the dome and of the great church. There were beautiful shops, magnificent houses of wealthy men.

Now we went to the station and took our seat in the train. The Hakīmu-'l-Mamālik and Mr. Thomson both started to-day for London. Every place in the country was beautiful, populous, full of cultivation, trees, woods, and forests; through such did we pass till we reached the city of Bonn. Here the train stopped, and we alighted. A regiment of hussar cavalry, special to the Emperor, was drawn out on foot, the colonel of which is the Prince of Reuss, brother of the German Ambassador at (St.) Peter(sburg), whom we had seen there. He was received in audience. There was also an old marshal of distinction, retired from service, and residing here, whose name was Hervard Bitenfeld. We next reached Coblentz. The train stopped; the Governor of the place, with others, came to an audience. The guns of the town fired a salute. It is a large place. We crossed the

Rhine by a bridge, the river here being narrow, with hills on either side. The bank of the river is all villages, towns, cultivations of vines, cherry-trees, and the like. The cherries were ripe and the trees laden with fruit. Each vine was bound to a stout stake. The whole hillside and the plain is one continuous vineyard, the famous Rhein-wein being produced from these very vines. On either side of the river is there a railway, and continually do the trains run. There are also roads for carriages, waggons, and pedestrians, well made and kept. The whole region is a garden. All the mountains and plains are grapevines, fruit-trees, flower-gardens, and avenues; with towns and cities at frequent intervals. One wonders, and is never tired with admiring. Every now and then a beautiful solitary pavilion, with large and small summer-houses, in the best taste and of the most graceful forms, are seen erected on the river's side, or up on a hill overlooking the stream, like a paradise. Some ruins of old castles were also noticed on the mountains and on the river bank. The going and coming of the trains, the buildings, the verdure and flowers, whether natural or artificial, put one beside one's self. For several leagues our road was (through a country) similar to that witnessed on our first visit to the land of Gīlān and the river Safīd-rūd. Sometimes our trains passed over the tops of the roofs of houses in streets of villages. In fine, it was indescribable. After awhile the mountains and valleys terminated, and the river flowed on our right. By degrees we left the river at a distance, and we turned in the direction of Wiesbaden, where at length we arrived.

There was a crowd of all denominations. As this city possesses hot mineral springs, strangers flock to it from all quarters. We mounted a carriage with the Grand-Vazīr and the General (in Waiting), and drove to our quarters, a palace belonging to the Government. Our own apartments are in the middle story, the others being lodged higher up. The windows of our room look out on a street and a square where there is a church of great height; the spire thereof, being the spire of the clock (tower), rises to an extremely acute point. At the four sides of the church, there are other four constructions with sharp-pointed spires.

In the evening a band played, a large crowd collecting. In niches and apertures in the front of the church, electric lights and Bengal lights were exhibited. They had improvised, by means of a pumping-engine, a very lofty jet-d'eau in front of the church, with a great body of water; and this was made to assume various colours, according to the nature of the light thrown upon it, which was very charming to behold.

To-day we saw Nazar Aqā, our Minister Resident at Paris, and also Mīrzā Ahmad, son of Mīrzā Muhammad Ra'īs, who had both come here from Paris.

13th (Monday, 9th June).—We rose in the morning, and having taken breakfast, mounted our carriage and drove out to the town of Schierstein, near the river Rhine, where there is a manufactory of champagne, a variety of wine. Quitting the city (of Wiesbaden), we followed a very delightful avenue, for the space of about an hour. This avenue is arranged as a carriage-drive, and is exceedingly beautiful. The weather was cloudy and cold. We passed through a village and a town where there was an assemblage of people. Quitting this, we drove along the river-bank at about the distance of five hundred feet from the water. Passing by some pretty sites, a charming garden attracted my attention. It had a low wall, and an iron gate that was closed. We there got out of our carriage, and on knocking (or ringing; *lit.*, making a noise), the gardener came and opened the gate. There were several Prussian officials with us, who entered the garden likewise. It was a sweetly-pretty place with nice walks and delicious spots, lawns, red roses, &c. The Rhine in prospect, with its surroundings, resembled a paradise. The mansion was magnificent and tastefully built; its little hot-house, very pleasing; its trellises in decussated work, for the support of vines, were constructed in the best style. In it there was a wooden hive for the honey-bees, which was quite a novelty. There were basins with fountains, the source of these latter being in a high turret built of stone, to represent a natural hill, from whence the water was brought to the fountains, through pipes, &c. There were edible cherries of very fine sorts. The doors of the rooms were locked, but the interiors of those on the ground-floor were visible through the plate-glass windows, each being furnished with chairs, tables, looking-glasses, carpets, and various numerous articles of embellishment. This house was the property of a man of consideration, named Blundberg, but he was himself away at (St.) Peter(sburg), and his wife in Wiesbaden; they were consequently not presented. It is a most charming summer residence, and he bought it for thirty-five thousand tūmāns (14,000*l.*). There was also in a cage within this garden a handsome monkey, the tip of the nose of which was of a light blue colour. There were also several elderly damsels, who brought us tea, bread, sweetmeats, and the like. We walked about here a considerable time, and I then mounted my horse "Blaze," the others got into the carriage, and we started for the town of Biebrich (Biberich), which is of some importance.

On the bank of the Rhine we noticed a large park and mansion belonging to the Duke of Nassau, who was, a few years ago, the independent sovereign of this region. He is now in Vienna. His brother, Prince Nicholas, was riding in the park with his wife and her brother. The prince wore spectacles and a long yellow beard; his wife was from Russia, and wore a black riding habit as she rode. We conversed together a while. I then galloped my horse about a bit and again mounted my carriage, when the prince, with his wife and her brother accompanied us on horseback for the space of half an hour. They then left us, and we entered Biebrich.

This town is populous and very flourishing, has good shops, many houses, and considerable traffic. Passing through it, we fell into an excellent avenue, and drove towards Wiesbaden. This avenue had three roadways— the middle one for carriages, very wide; on one side was a ride for horsemen, and on the other a path for pedestrians.

When, on quitting the town and garden first mentioned above, we turned to proceed to Biebrich, we observed at a distance, as we went along, the bridge and town of Biebrich coming into view. It is a place of some importance, and has regular fortifications.

We reached home in the middle of the afternoon. In the evening there was an illumination, with performances of legerdemain in a garden within the city; but as it was not a befitting place, we did not go to see it. The prince, Wajīhu-'l-'lāh Mīrzā went, and was loud in his praises of the conjurer. The Grand-Vazīr, the princes, and the rest of our suite have all visited the place. We did not go out for a promenade this evening, but retired to rest.

14th (Tuesday, 10th June).—Rose in the morning and breakfasted. Mounted a carriage, leaving the Grand-Vazīr and others behind at Wiesbaden, and drove to the station. Got into a train and started for Frankfort-on-the-Main, taking with me all our princes, &c., excepting the I'tizādu-'s-Saltana, the Nusratu-'d-Dawla, and the Il-Khāni. The distance to Frankfort is about the same as that from Tehrān to (the village of) Karj. We did it in an hour or less. Every part was populous and cultivated. We went by the side of the city of Mayence, of which the chief part is on the other side of the Rhine.

We reached the station (at Frankfort), alighted, mounted a carriage amidst the usual military honours, and drove through the streets, where crowds were collected. The cities of Firangistān (Europe in general) all resemble one another. When one has been seen, the arrangement, condition, and scale of the others is in one's possession.

We went a little way outside the town and arrived at a suburban district, where we remarked better and more beautiful detached mansions than those within the city. The whole environs of the town are full of parks, avenues, and flower-gardens. We came to a garden known by the name of "The Palms." It is now three years that this garden has been established with funds contributed by the wealthy inhabitants for the pleasure and pastime of the public. There was a large concourse of men and women assembled. Troops of the line were drawn up, their bands playing. We alighted. It was a garden exquisitely laid out in flower-beds with many kinds of flowers. There was a basin of water in the midst, a fountain from which spouted to the height of five ells (seventeen feet six inches). The Director of the garden came forward and made a speech. We passed on among the women and men, went up some steps into a building covered over and laid out in beds of flowers. Further on we entered a covered park, which is the palm-house. The roof is arched and glazed, so as to be protected from frost in winter. There were some tall and handsome palm-trees, but they never yield dates. There were also various American plants, a fountain, and further on a cascade, from which the water fell over rocks, as in a natural mountain. There were a number of private women and men, with great numbers of officers. We went to the upper story of the Conservatory. This building has been constructed solely for the purposes of instrumental music, eating, and drinking wine. The band played. There was a nice view over the city and the garden. We sat there awhile, descended, mounted our carriage, and drove to the Zoological Gardens. Although this establishment was not equal to that at Cologne, it was not bad. It possessed many animals;— white and black bears, some argalis, a ram and ewe of a certain kind (mouflons), from the island of Sicily or Sardinia in Italy, like those of the regions of Persia, but somewhat blacker; also parrots of various plumage, in cages hanging from trees. There was one kind of very handsome parrot, small; a large maned-lion, a lioness, a panther and two tigers. There was a big elephant, to which they brought a large musical box (an organ), the handle for playing which the elephant turned round rapidly with his trunk, so playing it, while he himself danced to the tune. The keeper then brought to him a different instrument, that children and others play with their mouths; the elephant took it unhesitatingly in his trunk, and began to play it and to dance;—which was very singular.

We now returned by the train to Wiesbaden. After a short rest they brought our carriage, and I went out for a drive. Leaving the city behind us, we got into avenues and gardens, where the notables and others have beautiful detached mansions with nicely laid-out beds of choice flowers. Flocks of women and men were taking the air in these walks, where we drove about for a time, and then went further up to an eminence with many trees and knolls, that overlooks the city. Still, every spot was full of avenues and carriage roads. The tomb of a niece of the Russian Emperor Nicholas, wife of the Duke of Nassau, was there, erected on a mountain, she having died when only nineteen years of age. She was buried here, in this country, and the Russian Government has built this tomb of stone and marble in a most beautiful manner. It has more than one gilt dome. Her own statue, recumbent as in the throes of death, beautifully carved in marble, is placed over her grave. She was a daughter of (the Grand-Duke) Michael, brother of Nicholas, and her husband was the former sovereign of this country, who is still alive, and resides in Vienna.

This country is called Nassau, and Wiesbaden is its capital. It is now possessed by the Prussians. The city of Frankfort, also, to which we went to-day, formerly was part of it; but, after the war with Austria, it was conquered by Prussia, and a heavy fine was imposed upon it.

We now returned home, dined and again mounting our carriage, we drove to a very fine building (the Kur-Saal), in front of which was a square with a garden and trees. There was a fountain playing in the middle, and all around were shops. They had prepared a display of fireworks here, and in the upper story of the building they had arranged chairs. Here we sat down, with the Grand-Vazīr, the princes, and the rest. There was also a large concourse of women and men in the balcony and in the square. The fireworks were very successful.

This over, we walked round the rooms and halls of

the building, which are very sumptuous, with many chandeliers and other furniture, being now the property of the State. In some of the rooms they still play at chess; in others there are large tables, and the newspapers of the whole world are brought there for people to read, and thence to acquire information. From thence we went out into the garden, and sat down by the brink of the basin. A daughter of Malkam (Sir John Malcolm), the English Minister Plenipotentiary to the Presence of the late Khāqān (Fath-'Ali Shāh, great-grandfather to the author), of pious memory, was seen here,—a fat old woman with a very pretty daughter, both of them being presented to us. We conversed; they are now residing in Prussia. The wife and daughter of General Boïen were also presented. We then returned home.

Mīrzā Malkam Khān, who had remained behind in Berlin for the purchase of muskets, rejoined us this evening. Dr. Tholozan will go to-morrow to see M. Krupp about the purchase of cannon.

Of mornings the wives of villagers bring in on carts fruit, vegetables, and the like, to sell; and form a market for these commodities opposite our quarters around the church. After a time, when all are sold off, they go away.

Saddle-donkeys are much in use; especially the women hire them and ride on them.

15th (*Wednesday, 11th June*).—God willing, we have to go to Baden-Baden, and to be the guest for one night of the (Grand-) Duke, whose wife is the daughter of the Emperor of Germany. He is free and independent;

coin is struck and prayer is read in his name, which is Frederick; that of his wife being Louise.

In the morning, therefore, we rose, breakfasted at home, and then proceeded by train, the Grand-Vazīr, the princes, and all the rest of my suite accompanying me, excepting the Īl-Khắni, who, with a few others, remained behind at Wiesbaden.

We passed the city of Mayence, which is strongly fortified. This very general who is in attendance on us is the Governor of the place, in this sense, that he commands the forts and the garrison, whereas the Administrator of the Finances and such like is appointed by the Duke of Darmstadt. The town is the property of the Duke, and the Prussians have forced the garrison upon him.

Passing by Mayence to Frankfort, and from thence to the city of Darmstadt, we here fell upon a curious coincidence. At the very moment of our arrival, we saw a train come in and go past us, when it stopped. We were informed that it was the Emperor of Russia on his way from Vienna to go to the hot-baths at Ems. We sent the Grand-Vazīr to make enquiries after His Majesty's health; upon which, the Emperor himself, his Heir-Apparent, his Heir-Apparent's wife, Alderberg, and others, came (to see us). They were all dressed in plain clothes, not in uniforms. We alighted, went (to meet them), and shook hands. We had a very affectionate interview. Afterwards, the brother of the Empress of Russia,—a tall man, and independent ruler of this country, over which Prussia exercises no rule, and also his wife, were presented; as also a daughter of the Sovereign of England, wife of the son, or grandson, of this ruler, whose child lately fell from a window and died in consequence, for whom she was still in mourning,—the full details of which have been previously given.*

After taking leave, we again joined the train and arrived at Heidelberg, the first place within the dominions of the Grand-Duke of Baden. Here the train stopped, and a few individuals—the Governor and some Professors of the Colleges of Baden—were introduced. One of the Professors made a speech in Persian. Then we proceeded to the city of Carlsruhe, the capital of the Grand-Duke of Baden. He himself, with the whole of the grandees of his State, Ministers, Commanders, and others, was at the station (to meet me). I alighted; military honours were observed, there being a band, and a company of the (Grand-) Duke's troops drawn up, which we inspected. The nature of the uniform, the musket, the cap, and everything else, of these troops of Baden, were similar to those of the Prussians; only their caps bore a distinguishing mark for Baden. In the French war the Baden contingent showed great firmness; twenty thousand men having been furnished. Now, in time of peace, they are but ten to fifteen thousand (under arms).

Carlsruhe, the capital of Baden, is a beautiful city and prosperous. Its population is thirty-seven thousand. Its streets are long and straight. All the produce of this region is independent of irrigation.

---

* No such details are in the printed work. They were probably struck out, without attention to this reference to them. —I. W R,

I and the (Grand-) Duke mounted together in a carriage and drove off, being followed by the others. The weather is always cloudy. Women and men in great numbers stood on both sides of the horseway in the streets, very respectful and quiet. The (Grand-) Duke himself is a very handsome, noble, and courteous man. He has a yellow beard, very long and thick; his face is fair and rosy; his eyes are large, his body robust. We talked together for a while in French, until we arrived in a square fronting the ancient, ancestral palace of the (Grand-) Duke. The square was very pretty, with flower-gardens and fountains. Some regular cavalry marched before us. We alighted in front of the palace; the wife of the (Grand-) Duke came forward, to whom we gave our hand. The wife of the (Grand-) Duke's brother, who is a Russian lady princess of distinction, by name Marie, and niece or cousin of the Emperor of Russia, was also present. She wore magnificent jewels on her head. We shook hands with her also; and then went upstairs. It is a beautiful palace, full of ornaments and furniture, &c. The (Grand-) Duke led us away to a private chamber that was specially assigned to us. We rested awhile and changed our costume, going thence to the dining-room, where all were assembled. The (Grand-) Duke was seated on our right, and his wife on our left. We had an excellent dinner; after which we walked about a bit, and then went down to the lower garden of the palace, which contained some beautiful flowers. All were there with us; we again walked about a little, and then, mounting a carriage with the (Grand-)

Duke, we drove along the road by which we had come, went to the station, got into a train, and started for the city of Baden-Baden. The (Grand-) Duke returned home, to come on to-morrow.

As we passed by Darmstadt, everywhere to our left the mountains and forests were near at hand; while to our right was a level country. But at first the mountains to our left were like hills and had not much forest. As we went further and got near to Baden (-Baden), the forests were denser and the hills somewhat higher. The whole surface of the plains and mountains here was green with grass, and the climate very cool, like a summer mountain-station. We arrived at the town of Baden-Baden after sunset. It is a town in a valley, having mountains all round, with meadows, woods, and green crops, exactly like the mountains of Kalārdasht in Māzandarān. The weather was cloudy and misty, very cold, and every now and then heavy rain fell; which is very similar to the climate of Ashraf and Safī-ābād in Māzandarān. Wealthy people from Firangistān have here built detached residences of great magnificence and beauty; for, during the summer season, the greater portion of the pleasure-seekers congregate here. It has a climate like that of Paradise; a river, like that of Shahristānak, that issues from a valley and flows through the town. In verity, it is not a town with the contemplation of which one can tire. For lovers, pleasure-hunters, sybarites, it is a capital nook. Pretty women and graceful ladies continually promenade about its avenues, lawns, and hills, on foot, on horseback, and in carriages. In truth, it is a

I

fairy abode. It has a fine church for those of the Roman faith, and there are those who are Protestants. The whole town is lighted with gas. There are mineral hot-baths and others. To the very tops of the mountains there are winding, tortuous carriage-roads everywhere, as well as avenues by which carriages travel in every direction. Prince Menschikoff, who was in attendance upon us in Russia, has here a beautiful seat, a wife, and all the appliances of life. He was here himself. He came, and we conversed. The wife of the Prince, too, was presented. In short, our quarters were in a very charming hotel.

We alighted and went upstairs. Crowds of women and men, spectators, looked on. In the evening, after dinner, we went downstairs for a stroll. A band was playing. Light rain fell from time to time. In the neighbourhood there were some handsome shops and a very pretty square, all grass and flowering shrubs. We entered the shops and bought some pretty things. Everywhere women and men, spectators, collected in numbers. Our purchases took up much time. We returned home; fireworks were exhibited; we went upstairs; we sat a while, and then retired to rest.

16th (*Thursday, 12th June*).—In the morning we arose and dressed. Prince Gortchakof, the Russian Premier, had also arrived here yesterday for travel and pleasure. He came to an audience, at which the Grand-Vazīr was also present. We sat and had a long conversation. He left, and I went to a bath. It was a beautiful bath; with a stove, &c., had they made it warm. It had a small basin of marble. We went into the water; came out; dressed; and went home. After a short interval had elapsed the (Grand-) Duke arrived. Mounting an open carriage together, we went for a drive. The General likewise was with us. The weather was cloudy and very cold; rain also fell occasionally. I had come out of the bath in a state of perspiration, and had not put on an overcoat. As we drove about I was very cold. We went about, up hill and down dale, passing through charming sites, until we arrived at the summit of an eminence where there was a church. Here we alighted and entered the church. It was an edifice erected by the former Prince of Roumania, *i.e.*, of Wallachia and Moldavia, in memory of a young son of his who had died. The Prince and his wife now live in this town. They have had a beautiful marble statue of their son executed, whose tomb is in one corner of the church, and a marble group is over his tomb. Opposite to that is another tomb which they have prepared for themselves, that they may be buried there after their deaths. Statues in marble of the prince and of his wife are placed upon this tomb, that of the prince pointing with its hand to the tomb of the son. The church is built in coloured marbles, and is a beautiful edifice. Its cupola appears to be gilt outside, like that of the tomb of the daughter of Michael, the brother of Nicholas, Emperor of Russia, that we had seen at Wiesbaden.

Coming out from thence, we again mounted the carriage with the (Grand-) Duke and the General, went over ascents and descents, through many a delightful vista, but the rain came on heavily. We returned to town, passing in front of the residence of Prince Menschikoff, through a handsome avenue; saw a beautiful fountain on the bank of the stream, around which they had arranged stones after the fashion of a single natural rock, and from the fountain the appearance of a cascade was produced, which flowed down into a basin. The (Grand-) Duke pointed out to me the house which the English Sovereign, Napoleon of France, the Emperor of Russia, and others, have occupied on the occasions of their visits to these parts. As we drove along in the rain, I and the (Grand-) Duke were seated alone in a close carriage, and so we reached home.

After remaining a short space, we again mounted with the (Grand-) Duke, and drove to his own palatial castle, a very ancient structure, built on an eminence, the work of his ancestors, and possessing a most extensive lookout over the town and its environs, the forests, and the hills. We arrived at the gate of the castle. A crowd of women were there. We alighted and went upstairs. On the first floor a breakfast was laid out. There were beautiful rooms, grand and sumptuous, with chandeliers and other furniture, pictures and fine portraits; more especially those of the ancestors and of the parents of the (Grand-) Duke, hung up on the walls. After a while we went to the table, the Grand-Vazīr, the princes, and others, being present. The air, tempered by the rain, was very cool and pleasant.

After breakfast, we enjoyed for a while the prospect afforded from the windows of the palace over the country, the hills, and the town. The effect was splendid. The mountains and former frontier places of France, sites which, before the war, had been included in the French territory, were there in sight; but now that the provinces of Alsace and Lorraine have been taken from France by the Prussians, the French frontier is removed to a distance from hence.

When we had viewed this landscape for a little time, the (Grand-) Duke led us to the upper story of the palace, and showed us the pictures, painted of old and hung on the walls, of the various birds and beasts hunted in this country. In particular, there was one bird, called "coq de bois" (cock of the woods, mountain cock, capercailzie, capercaillie, auerhahn, tetrao urogallus), *i.e.*, the jungle-cock, which is found in these woods. Its head and shape are like those of the pheasant; but it is larger, and its tail is not long like that of the pheasant, but resembles that of the "umbrella-bird." It is a beautiful animal, and none of the kind are found in Persia. These woods give shelter to the red deer, the "shūkā," the wild boar, and have in them large numbers of this kind of bird, and of others also.

We now came down stairs, got into a carriage, and drove to the station, where we had to wait a little. Prince Gortchakoff, the Russian Minister, Prince Menschikoff, and a numerous company, were there. At length we took our seats in the train, the (Grand-) Duke and the Grand Vazīr being in front of me; and so we started.

Between Baden-Baden and Carlsruhe there is a celebrated town and fortress named Rastadt, one of the strongest and most famous in all Europe. We saw it at a distance. In the (Grand-) Duke's castle there was a very large looking-glass, five ells (17 feet 6 inches) in height, by more than two ells (7 feet) in width. I was informed that it was manufactured at the plate-glass works of Mannheim, in the territory of this very state of Baden.

When we reached Carlsruhe, the (Grand-) Duke's capital, we took leave of each other, and he left. We continued travelling by the line over which we had passed in coming, and arrived at Wiesbaden by nightfall. The distance between Baden-Baden and Wiesbaden is about thirty-five leagues, and this is got over by rail in five hours.

The (Grand-) Duke has three sons by the daughter of the Emperor of Germany, his eldest son, seventeen years of age, being his designated successor to the Grand-Duchy. To judge by his looks, the (Grand-) Duke himself is about forty.

17th (*Friday*, 13th *June*).—To-day we have to go to the town of Spa, the first place in the territory of the kingdom of Belgium. Rising early, and having dressed, we mounted a carriage with the Grand-Vazír and the General in attendance upon us, and, by the road that leads to Biebrich, we travelled and arrived at the wharf. Troops were drawn out, whom we inspected, and then went on board a steamboat. The deck was furnished with chairs, and decorated with shrubs and flowers in vases. We took a seat. The weather was very cold. My suite and luggage were all put on board this vessel. Her cabins were on two decks, very long, and very handsome. The upper cabin was a dining-room, where the princes and our other attendants took their breakfast. The lower one had been designated for our use; but we were on deck most of the time, going below now and then only. When we embarked, the Amīnu-'s-Sultān and Gulām-Husayn Khān had lagged behind, not having kept up with us, (and did not make their appearance) until we had cast off and got under way. Then they arrived at the wharf and made all kinds of signals, took off and waved their caps, but no one paid attention. Ultimately a person was sent with instructions to bring them by rail to the city of Cologne; and we went on.

The river Rhine is like a paradise. On both sides of it, everywhere, there were castles, pavilions, populousness, cultivation, railroads; and trains incessantly ply backwards and forwards. Numerous steam-ships, like the one in which we were sitting, navigated it upwards and downwards, carrying passengers and travellers, goods and merchandize. The depth of the river is as much as ten ells (35 feet). Each of its banks is hilly, with ridges and peaks; but there are no high mountains. The whole of the hills are covered with woods and vineyards, and one is never satiated with gazing on them. At each moment some new feature, some new castle or palace of a different style of architecture, comes in sight, which have been built by men of wealth as summer-residences, where they take their pleasure and enjoy life. Truly, for the purposes of a promenade, no place could be better than these regions. Some of these structures are perched on the very tops of eminences, on rocks, or in forests; and in front of them are orchards, flower-gardens, and the like, which surpass all powers of description. We saw many towns, villages, and manufactories carrying on their respective operations.

And thus we arrived at Coblentz, where our vessel passed under an enormous bridge of iron, of three arches, over which a railway crosses. On both sides the river is a very strong fortress; but the greater proportion of the inhabitants of the place live on the left-hand side. From the fortress on our right hand, which stands on rocks and hills, and which is entirely constructed of stone, a salute was fired. It was in this city that the Ottoman Sultan, during his tour in Europe, met the Emperor of Germany, and was a guest for three nights. All round the city of Coblentz there are very strong forts.

We left it behind, and reached Bonn, where our ship was taken alongside a wharf, and our suite and luggage were landed. They went to the station, and at length we followed. There were crowds of men and women. We reached the station. Our train had been changed. We took our seat in a car, started, and arrived at Cologne. Here we turned our faces in the direction of Belgium, and again were on our way, the whole country being verdant, with meadows, and populous. We went through a "hole in a mountain" of about five hundred ells (583 yards) in length. Hereabouts the greater part of the region on both sides of our road was hilly, and the railway is in a narrow gully (a cutting). This is why to-day the greater part of our road was beneath mountains, and before reaching Spa we traversed fifteen "holes," six of which were long, varying from two to three and four hundred ells (233 to 350 and 470 yards), the rest being from fifty to seventy or eighty ells long (60 to 100 yards), not more.

We passed by Duren, a Prussian town, and arrived at Aix-la-Chapelle, a city belonging to Germany. Here troops were drawn out. We alighted, inspected them, and again returned to the train. After proceeding a short space of time we reached a station near to the Belgian frontier. The train stopped. General Boïen, in waiting on us, came into our presence and took leave, returning with all those of his suite. The interpreter Grebel, and one Russian officer, who had accompanied us until now, received their congé at this station also, and left us.

We then went on, and shortly reached a small stream with a little bridge over it, which forms the frontier between Belgium and Germany. But what a difference has the All-Wise and Almighty Creator placed between the two nations and the two countries! Man's mind is lost in amazement thereat. In one moment a total change came over the people, the language, the religion, the appearance of the land and water, mountains, and plains;—all were different, nothing here resembling what is in Germany. The mountains are rather more lofty and more wooded, the air is colder, the tongue of all is French, the people more tranquil, the arrangement and uniform of the troops and citizens utterly different. The whole population of Belgium speak French, but have a special dialect of their own; they are chiefly of the

Romish faith. This nation has more liberty than is enjoyed in Germany. Their sovereign is King Leopold II., and their capital is named Brussels. From Wiesbaden to Spa, by boat and by rail, we travelled in a little more than eight hours.

Proceeding now over hills and dales, through forests and other scenes, we arrived at Spa. True, we were not yet officially arrived (in Belgium); but still, the Governor and notables of the town, with some regular cavalry, and a large concourse of spectators and others, had come to meet us in the station and streets. We alighted from the train; the Governor made a speech, to which we pronounced a reply. They are nice people. The Governor's name was Henri Peltzer. We mounted a carriage and drove into the town, which is small, but pretty, and is situated in a valley and on the hills, its environs being hilly and full of trees. Everywhere we saw crowds, until we reached the Orange Hotel, which became our quarters, we ourselves having our apartments on the ground-floor, while our princes and officers were upstairs or downstairs.

After dining, we sallied forth with the Grand-Vazīr, and others, going about the streets for a walk. Immense crowds of men and women now collected around us, hemming us in, and following us about wherever we went. They had illuminated the streets. The name of the street is "Seven-o'clock," and a fine street it is. We entered the shops and bought some articles, such as desks, dressing-cases, pictures, and the like. They had very nice wares. The fronts of the shops are of single sheets of crystal (plate-glass), so that all the goods are visible behind these. We continued our stroll to the end of the street, where there was a basin of water with a fountain. This was lighted up with the electric light, and by means of coloured glasses they caused the water to assume various hues. They had also constructed a sort of two-storied pavilion, and illuminated it. There a band stood and played, singing songs and catches also, very charmingly.

We now retreated by degrees to our hotel. The Amīnu-'s-Sultana and Gulām Husayn Khān rejoined us. They, too, had embarked in a steamer after our departure, had arrived in Cologne, and thence came on by train. At Biebrich, where we left them, a person of Austrian nationality from the States of Hanover had turned up, who spoke Persian, and who rendered them his assistance.

In Germany the women are very much occupied in business and at work; especially at agriculture and in gardening do they labour much more than their husbands. The ears of the carriage-horses, and others, are covered over with red and other coloured cloths, as a protection against the flies. In Berlin, and in other towns, the little boys fasten soldiers' knapsacks on to their own backs, run about the streets, and play on fifes. How excellent is it that they, from infancy upwards, thus learn to be soldiers. They pave their streets with stone most artistically. They cut the stones into small squares, and do the work with these, joining them together very closely. The bricks of Firangistān are not like those of

Persia, large and square, but are of the shape of the cut bricks of Tehrān.

Spa is a small town, with only one good street; the rest are all of an inferior class.

18*th* (*Saturday, 14th June*).—We awoke in the morning at Spa. We took breakfast, and then mounted a carriage for a drive about. The Governor also was seated in a carriage, and preceded us, showing the way. From the street we drove up-hill to a bath which we were informed was the establishment where Peter the Great, when unwell, was treated with the mineral waters. We mounted the ascent a little further, and the town terminated. Carriage-roads and avenues now commenced. Ibrāhīm Khān, with another groom, had brought out our horses after us. We pushed on until we arrived at a place where there was an hotel, with two basins of mineral water; *i.e.*, these were springs flowing out of the earth, with steps to go down to them. At the bottom of the steps there stood a woman, who had some tumblers, in which she gave of the water to the people. Invalids who suffer from weak stomachs, or who are thin and meagre, and especially women, come here before breakfasting, drink of the water, sit down on chairs, call for food from the cook of the hotel, and eat. Strangers, and particularly the English, travel to this place. I drank a little of the water, which tasted very nasty. On the outside of the basin there was a large foot-print on the surface of a stone; of which the Governor said: "This is the vestige of the footstep of St. Mark;" which saint is one of the holy men of the Franks. "Whatever woman, when childless, comes here and places her foot in this vestige, conceives (and bears children)." This is a very surprising thing. In Persia such beliefs are rife.

We drove off from thence and entered a different avenue to reach another hotel with another mineral spring. Several Frank men and women followed after us in another carriage. I mounted my horse "Blaze," and took a canter in the woods and along the avenue; and so we reached the hotel, and the other mineral spring, which was worse-tasted than the first. At a distance I espied two Frankish individuals, urged my horse, and came up in front of them. I conversed with them a bit in French. He was an English nobleman, who had generally resided in India at Allahabad, and was recently returned to Europe. His wife was reading a story-book. I took the book and looked at it a little. I then rode off by a narrow path, by the side of which a rivulet ran, with about water enough to turn one mill-stone. They took the carriages round by another road. Rain came on. We then made off for another hotel, sat there, and again went on.

Arrived at home, I became quite unwell,—all through that bath at Baden-Baden, from whence I had issued in a state of perspiration, had gone on a drive with the (Grand-) Duke, and had taken cold, which now showed itself. I shivered a whole hour; a headache seized me; Dickson came. Tholozan, likewise, who had gone to see M. Krupp, returned in the night. We went to bed; slept through the night; and, thank God, my health returned.

19th (Sunday, 15th June).—On rising in the morning, I was all right again. The weather is cloudy, and rain is falling. The sun is never seen in these parts. To-day is a festival of the Franks. A body of damsels and women, after passing along the street that faces our hotel, went into the church. They had stuck up lamps in all the streets; also, bringing out many shrubs grown in vases, and strewing the streets with fresh-cut grass, they escorted the chief priest with many honours to the church. About two hundred pretty maidens, all engagingly dressed in white, with white head-dresses, and carrying each a nosegay of flowers,—followed by another company of younger girls to the number of two to three hundred, each holding in her hand a stick with a nosegay attached to it, and by a third company of charming little children, girls and boys, nicely dressed, and each carrying a stick with a taper bound to it, or a gold-embroidered velvet banner, —carried the portrait of Her Holiness Miryam (the Virgin Mary), on whom be peace; and sang with a sweet melody, repeating litanies. Behind these was an ornamented wooden frame, with the figures of Jesus and Mary on it, upon both of whom be peace, and with the space below it unoccupied. Meanwhile, the priest walked out on foot, and four individuals took up this frame and supported it over the priest like an umbrella.

In the evening we went to the theatre on foot, which was very near to our hotel. Many women and men were congregated. The theatre is very small—less even than the one at Ḥājjī-Tarkhān, but very pretty, with three tiers of seats, and with a handsome chandelier lighted with gas. The curtain rose. A number of men and women conversed in French, representing love, love-making, and the like. Afterwards an astonishing conjuror came forward,—a young man of short stature, who had a very graceful wife. His name was Kaznow. In French jugglery is called "prestidigitation." He performed some astonishing tricks, so that one became dumbfoundered.

For example. He took the people's watches out of their fobs, and without interfering in any way with their regulation—without even laying them down—he showed that all of them pointed, for instance, to three hours after sunset. He then opened them and showed them, when one watch pointed to four, another to eight, a third to two, and so on.

He opened a large padlock. He then locked it, and gave it to the Mu'tamadu-'l-Mulk, who was sitting in a box near to him. The Mu'tamad again locked it himself, and essayed to force it open, but could not. He then passed the lock on to a stick, and gave the two ends of the stick to two persons to hold. He next asked of the Mu'tamad: "How many do you wish that I shall count, and that the lock shall come open as I name that number?" The Mu'tamad said: "Twelve." The juggler counted this number out, one by one; and when, on his pronouncing the word "open," in the place of "twelve," the lock opened.

He performed also some surprising feats of hocus-pocus. The Mu'tamad wrote down something on a piece of paper, which the conjuror burnt in the presence of all.

He then went and fetched a packet that was carefully sealed with wax, which he gave into the hands of the Mu'tamad. He broke open the packet, and found therein a second packet similarly sealed up, and so on until twenty sealed packets had been broken open. Enclosed within the last was the paper with the writing upon it which the Mu'tamad had written.

He placed four large coins one by one in a small box, and consigned this into the hands of one of the company. He then placed a table at some distance, on which stood a china vase. He now ordered the coins to come into the vase; and one by one, as they passed from the box and fell into the vase, we heard them chink. When the box was empty, he went and fetched the vase from its place, and the whole of the coins were found in it. Before placing the vase on the table, he had shown to the company that it had nothing in it. He performed also many other tricks, which I cannot here narrate.

He now brought forward his wife and seated her on a chair. She was a very pretty woman, and elegantly attired. He put her to sleep by sundry rubbings with his hands. When she was asleep, his wife gave information of absent things; as for instance, the Mu'tamad wrote down: "This is a fine evening." The conjuror asked his wife what had been written, and she, in the most charming manner, repeated the very words.

20th (Monday, 16th June).—To-day, God willing, we are to proceed in health and safety to Brussels, the capital of Belgium.

I saw Khanikof, the Russian, at Spa, where he had an

audience. Twelve years ago I had seen him in our camp at Sultāniyya (a town or village about half way between Tabrīz and Tehrān). He is now younger-looking and stouter. He is a member of the Academy of Sciences of Russia, but is staying at Paris.

To-day, thanks be to God, I feel quite well. We mounted a carriage with the Grand-Vazīr, and drove to the station. They had brought there for us the railway-carriages of the King, which were extremely handsome. We took our seat amid a great concourse of people. We also perceived the wife of last night's juggler. The Grand-Vazīr and Dr. Tholozan occupied seats in our carriage. We started. The Belgian train is very comfortable and pleasant, not jolting much, and travelling very swiftly. In a short time we reached Liege, where there are extensive manufactories of fire-arms and railway rolling-stock. The whole road, so far, was hill and dale and forest. We passed through three or four "holes," one of them being about three hundred ells long (350 yards); but from Liege onwards the country is flat.

At Liege we stopped; a most extraordinary crowd had assembled. The Governor and notables of the town had come. We alighted from the train. Troops were drawn up clothed in broadcloth, with a band playing. The throng was to such an extent that there was no passing. After we had walked down (the line of troops), they forced the crowd back, we remounted our carriage, and again got in motion.

The town of Liege is very large and handsome. The whole place is up-hill and down-dale, upon hills and in

K

valleys. It has very handsome parks and flower-gardens. The whole of the carriage-roads in Belgium are paved with stones. The whole country is green and smiling, under cultivation, and populous. In these roads, as far as Liege, there was a profusion of a kind of yellow flower, extremely beautiful, and resembling the flower of the bean (the laburnum being probably meant).

At length, after four hours, or perhaps three hours, after leaving Liege we arrived at Brussels, the capital of Belgium. At the station His Most Exalted Majesty King Leopold II., together with his brother, the Count of Flanders, the whole of the military officers, the civil functionaries, and others were present. The mutual gratulations of etiquette were gone through. The King presented those of his suite; we also presented those of ours. Taking our seats in an open carriage, we drove off, I and the King conversing together. On both sides of our road a large concourse of people stood, and incessantly did I and the King salute them. In return they shouted hurrahs, and ran along with us. We came to a royal palace situated in the centre of the city. We went upstairs, where, on the first floor, the King, having shown us our apartments, retired to his own residence in the back apartments of this same palace. I sent the Order of my own Portrait to His Majesty, and shortly followed myself to return his visit. The King's wife came forward to meet me, and we sat down; after a space I returned to my apartments.

The King is a man thirty-eight years of age, tall, somewhat thin, and with a long yellow beard. During the period when he was Heir-Apparent he travelled to India, to Constantinople, to Egypt, and to the Syrias. He is the grandson of Louis Philippe, the former King of the French, whose daughter was the King's mother; and he is cousin to the actual Sovereign of England, son of her maternal uncle. He has three daughters, but has no son; and his brother, the Count of Flanders, is his Heir-Presumptive, who is somewhat younger in years than the King. The wife of the King's brother is a lady-princess of Prussia, while the King's wife is an Austrian lady-princess, being a Hungarian by birth.

The Kingdom of Belgium is very free, the ordering of all matters being in the hands of the Parliament, where the Deputies meet together and give judgment. The Parliament House is a sumptuous edifice, and is in the city. It was in active session (when we arrived), the members being assembled. The editors of the public papers in this country are extremely free. Whatever they may write, they are in fear of no one. The population of Brussels is of about a hundred and seventy-two thousand souls; that of all Belgium, ten crores and a fraction (five millions odd). Its income is about thirty-seven crores; its army in time of war, one hundred thousand. Formerly, the whole of this country was subject to Holland, but forty-two years ago, the kingdoms of England and France, with others, combined and separated it from that State, giving it to Leopold I., the maternal uncle of the Sovereign of England, and making him King.

Lāransūn Sāhib (General Sir Henry C. Rawlinson, K.C.B.), Kambal Sāhib (Colonel Sir Arnold B. Kemball,

K.C.S.I.), Tāmsūn Sāhib (Ronald F. Thomson, Esq., Secretary of Legation, Tehrān), and a few other Englishmen, who had come to be in attendance upon us, were here received in audience and were conversed with. Twelve years ago Lāransūn was Minister (Plenipotentiary) at Tehrān; now he is somewhat aged.

After breakfast we indulged in a little quiet. They have made a small garden in this palace, with plants grown in vases, and have covered it in overhead with glass. It had chandeliers with gas, a basin and fountain, small but very pretty, from which the water flowed like a bubble. The flowers were of various sorts and kinds. I walked about there.

Before the palace is a square, around which are very beautiful gardens for the public to walk in; but I did not go there. There is also a private garden belonging to the palace. The city of Brussels is extremely handsome; its streets are straight and wide, but the town is up-hill and down-dale, the streets and houses being now low down, now high up; and there are hills and valleys in it. It possesses a very ancient and grand church, which does not fall short of that at Cologne.

In the evening we took a seat in a carriage with the King and the King's wife, and went to the state theatre. It was a long way off, and the people had formed a prodigious throng. We arrived at the theatre, and went upstairs, being there seated in a special box with the Grand-Vazīr and the wife of the King's brother. Our princes and attendants, in state costumes, were in other boxes, with the whole of the Diplomatic Corps. There were about three thousand men and women present. The theatre is large and has six tiers of seats, the whole being lighted with gas. It is not inferior to the large theatre at (St.) Peter(sburg). The play was an opera; *i.e.*, they sang pieces, and an orchestra played beautifully. They sang very melodiously. After much singing and dancing, they gave a ballet. Women danced. It lasted very long. At length, the curtain having fallen, I arose. The King and his wife again rode with me in the carriage, and we went home. We said adieu, and they went away. I went to bed. The greater part of our attendants are quartered in an hotel. This palace, in which I have my apartments, is a very handsome palace, ornamented with beautiful pictures and portraits; though it is small, but well designed. It has many handsome and large chandeliers, its furniture is rich, and it is well supplied with tables, chairs, and the like, all good. The street lamps are lighted with gas and are numerous.

21*st* (*Tuesday*, 17*th June*).—Remained in this city. In the morning after breakfast the Diplomatic Corps were received in audience. There is a Representative here from every State. The Belgian Ministry came also, and were followed, after their departure, by the King, with whom we mounted a carriage and went out for a drive. We passed along the streets and came to an open space where a statue of the father of this present Sovereign has been placed on a high column. Here we had a beautiful view over the city and its environs. We here came in sight of the princes of our suite, who were taking a walk on foot. I told them to accompany us. We now drove to the large church, alighted, and entered the fane, which is a magnificent building, erected five hundred years ago. A priest came and led us to the different parts of the edifice, which we thus inspected. The tomb of George, a former King of England, and also the tomb of an ancient sovereign of Belgium, are in this church. Builders and labourers were busy at repairs. It is a grand and lofty structure. It has some curious pulpits and altars of carved wood, very beautiful.

After a good survey, we left this place and then saw a tower, in appearance like a palace, anciently erected within the city, and so preserved ever since,—now used as a museum. There are in it the arms and implements of (all) nations,—even many of the daggers, straight and curved, and of the knives of Persia,—all arranged with great taste. Skins of celebrated horses of antiquity, ridden by such a hero, or by such a king, are made up into the very likenesses of the horses themselves, and stand there. Helmets, armour, horse-armour, weapons, complete and from head to foot, as worn of old by the champions of the Franks and others, are there (exhibited).

Leaving this at the conclusion of a general survey, we descended and drove out to the Château of Laken, the summer residence of the King and Queen. We passed along one long and very beautiful avenue, with a canal on our left hand, excavated by human labour, and by which ships ply to and from the port of Antwerp, which is one of the important fortresses of Firangistān, and belonging to the kingdom of Belgium. There is no river here that flows through the middle of the city; so they have brought from a distance with great labour potable water into the city, and distributed it to the houses.

Travelling thus a certain distance, we reached, at the outskirts of the capital, the park-gate of the Château of Laken. Its parks and its avenues are very fine. It is a private park, special to the King's use, into which no one has a right of passage. Its woods and large trees are magnificent. Here and there water has stagnated and formed, as it were, lakes. Its grass and flowers are pleasant. We went slowly along in the carriage until we reached the Château. The Queen was there and came to meet us. We conferred upon the Queen the Order of the "Sun," with its ribbon; and she herself put it on. We sat down in a domed hall, which had a capital view of the city and park. On each side of the hall there were apartments. A band was playing. The princes and others arrived. We went into the apartments. Tapestries were hung on the walls, woven of old in this very city of Brussels, and figured with portraits beautifully executed. The manufactory for the weaving of these is no longer at work. The park and lawns of the Château of Laken are very charming.

We now returned to the city and visited the Zoological Gardens; but, as I had not the time, I could not examine them properly. I saw some singular dogs in a cage, large and small, and of different colours. It had a small aquarium, into which we took a peep, and then went home.

Before driving out to Laken we paid a visit to the Hôtel-de-Ville; *i.e.*, the residence of the Governor and functionaries of the city. It is a very imposing and ancient edifice. Above it there is an exceedingly lofty tower; and it has a hall, the ceiling of which is painted in a very striking manner. There is the figure of Isrāfīl blowing the last trump, executed with so much talent that wherever one places one's self to examine it, the eyes of the figure appear directed on the observer. The works of the artist who painted this picture are marvellous, and are well known to all the world. The walls of the edifice are hung with figured tapestries. In front of it is a large square, where immense crowds had collected, and to which the fire-brigade came, performing their various exercises in a very satisfactory manner. The firemen here were not mounted, but go on foot. They have pulled down the greater portion of the streets and houses of the city, and are building them anew. They have erected the Law Courts in a very imposing pile.

In the middle of the afternoon we returned home, where we are invited to dine with the King. We all went in our state uniforms, the Diplomatic Corps, and others, being present also. We ate a good dinner, and then retired to our apartments, as we had to rise betimes in the morning and proceed to the port of Ostend on our way to England. We therefore went to bed early.

22nd (*Wednesday*, 18th *June*).—In the morning we arose earlier than usual, thoroughly worn out with a sleepless night, and hastily dressed. It was very cold. The inhabitants of the city were not yet astir. A battalion of infantry, with their band, arrived and were drawn up in front of the palace. There were also some cavalry. The King came. We took our seats in a carriage, drove through streets and avenues, and arrived at the railway station. The same train was there in readiness for us which we had used two days previously. A battalion of infantry, with band, was drawn up; others also were there. We said adieu to the King, took our seat, and left Brussels.

We traversed the Flemish provinces, where all was flat plain, populous, green, grassy, full of gardens and flowers. In these parts the people speak Flemish; *i.e.*, Dutch. We at length arrived at the sea-port town of Ostend—an important commercial town, where we found many ships. It is a flourishing place. We performed the distance from Brussels in less than three hours, as the train to-day travelled at great speed.

The Belgian officials took their leave, and the Governor, with the functionaries of Ostend had an audience. They delivered an excessive speech. We then alighted and passed from the wharf on board of the ship of Her Most Exalted Majesty the Sovereign of England, which was named the "Vigilant." Lāransūn Sāhib and the Englishmen who accompanied us led the way and performed the presentations.

The distinguished Admiral of the English ships is named M'Clintock. He has several times gone on voyages to the islands of the North Pole, and enjoys a great reputation. He had come to meet us, and was in the ship. There were also a great number of naval officers besides.

We went to the cabin specially designated for our use, and there seated ourselves. The ship is very handsome and of great speed. The Grand-Vazīr, with our personal attendants, and a few others, were in our ship; the princes, and the remainder, were in two other vessels similar to her. We waited a considerable time for the baggage to be brought, and our travelling companions dispersed themselves. On account of my drowsiness, I myself went below and took a little repose; after which I went up again. On the table I found some fine fruit,—excellent peaches, white and black grapes of exquisite aroma, some banana fruits,—which are a very nice thing. There was also a little melon,—very sweet. These fruits are all raised in hothouses, and the price of them is very high. For instance, they sell a single bunch of grapes for two thousand (Persian mites,—about twenty pence English); from whence the rest may be inferred.

From the port of Ostend to Dover,—the first place on the coast of England,—takes five hours to cross; and the sea of the British Channel is much noted for its storms and roughness. But, thanks be to God Most High,—the sea was very calm, like the palm of one's hand, so that no one was incommoded. It was like a trip on a river. Behind us followed another ship, while two large ironclad ships of war accompanied us, to show us honour, the one to our right, the other to our left. Occasionally they fired guns. When we had advanced a certain distance, there appeared another ship, with two turrets, and each turret with two guns; which turrets they can turn round in any direction they choose. This ship also is covered with iron, and, as they said, has a steam power of five thousand horses. The ship's sides were not high out of the water.

They informed me that the projectiles from her guns would smash to pieces the other ships. They fired two or three rounds from her guns, which made much noise.

Many merchant ships came and went, as well as others. At length, as we neared the English coasts, the hills on the seashore became visible, and a large number of men-of-war hove in sight, coming to meet us. They all fired guns. The surface of the sea was covered with ships, and boats, and large steamers, in which the magnates and nobles of the English had seated themselves, and were come forth to witness the spectacle. The hills at the seaside are not very high, their stones being white, like quarries of lime.

Our ship now reached the port of Dover, where they have constructed a long stone pier, so that the ships in the harbour may be safe from storms and the waves. It projects a great distance into the sea. Upon it were women and men, dames and nobles, infantry and cavalry, in great numbers. Here we stopped. The sons of Her Most Exalted Majesty the Queen of the English Dominions, with the Secretary for Foreign Affairs, Lord Granville, and the notables and authorities of London, had all arrived;—the second son of the Sovereign, the Duke of Edinburgh,—and the third son, Prince Arthur. We stood up in the ship; the Sovereign's sons, the Foreign Secretary, and the Chief Usher of the Sovereign,—a man of consideration and official in waiting, came. We went into the ship and sat down in the cabin, where we conversed until the baggage was carried out of the ship. The Queen's second son is a youth with a very pleasing countenance, and stout. He has crow's eyes (bluish grey) and a small beard; in stature he is not tall; his age must be twenty-seven or eight. The third son is shorter than he, and his complexion is darker, his body slighter. The Chief Usher (Lord Chamberlain) is named Lord Sydney. He is a robust old man.

At length we rose and went up on the jetty, where there was a wonderful assembly. We took our seat in a railway carriage,—I, the Sovereign's sons, the Grand-Vazīr, the Foreign Secretary, and the Principal Official in Waiting, being together in one compartment. They were exceeding beautiful carriages; none such had hitherto been seen. We gently went forward a few feet; and, at a building where they had prepared food, we alighted. I went into a small room. The Hakīmu-'l-Mamālik, who had been here some time, was admitted. They then told me the Governor of the town of Dover had prepared a speech which he must recite. I went into a hall and stood at the top of a high flight of steps, the whole of the English princes and notables, our princes and others, with our servants, being present, and the Governor (Mayor) recited his speech at great length, in which there was much praise and laudation of us. We replied, and Lāransūn explained in English. The people clapped (their) hands. Returning from thence, we went to breakfast, accompanied by all the princes. They served hot cooked food, fruit, and other things, of which we partook. Then arising, we returned to our train, and took our seat in a carriage with the self-same personages. We started. Everywhere we passed over the bosoms of mountains and across valleys, traversing numerous tunnels, of which two were about a quarter of a league in length, very dark and suffocating.

The country in England has no resemblance to that in other territories. It has much forest, large trees, population without interval, and cultivation enormous. The wealth of the English is famous throughout the world; there is no need to describe it (here).

We passed by the town and outlying districts of Chiselhurst, the abode of Napoleon III., and where he died. His tomb is also there. The train travelled at so furious a rate that it was impossible for one to distinguish any place. From the rapidity of our motion fire came out of the wheels, and one carriage caught fire. It wanted but little for all to be burnt. They stopped the train, got down, and extinguished the fire. All was right, and again we went on until we reached the beginning of the city of London. Again it is impossible to describe the prosperity, the populousness, the extent of the city, the numbers of lines of railway over which incessantly the trains come and go in every direction, the smoke of the manufactories, and the like. We travelled over the exteriors of the roofs of the houses; and thus we reached the station and stopped.

There was an assemblage of spectators, and a crowd, beyond all limits; there were the armour-wearing English household cavalry; there was the Nawwāb the Heir-Apparent of England, known as the Prince of Wales; and the whole of the Ministry, of the notables, and of the nobles, were present. We alighted. I, the Heir-Apparent, the Grand-Vazīr, and Lord Morley,— the Lord-in-Waiting upon us, took our seats in an open carriage, and drove off. Both sides of the road, the roofs, the upper stories of the houses, were full of women, men, and children, who exhibited much joy and pleasure by shouting hurrahs, by waving handkerchiefs, by clapping hands. It was a surprising turmoil. I saluted incessantly with head and hands. The crowd of spectators was never-ending. The population of the city is said to be over eight crores (four millions) of souls. It has most lovely women. The nobleness, the greatness, the gravity and sedateness of the women and men shine out from their countenances. One sees and comprehends that they are a great people, and that the Lord of the Universe has bestowed upon them power and might, sense and wisdom, and enlightenment. Thus it is that they have conquered a country like India, and hold important possessions in America and elsewhere in the world. Their soldiers are very strong of frame and beautifully attired; their armour-wearing household cavalry are very strong and handsome young men, exquisitely dressed, like the cavalry in Russia. Their horses are very fine and strong, but their number is few. They are but four regiments, each of four hundred men.

In this way did we reach the half of our ride, when a heavy rain set in and wet the people through and through. I was myself also a good deal moistened ; but I requested it, and the carriage was closed (in part), the

Grand-Vazīr and Lord Morley remaining exposed to the rain, so that they were wet through. We arrived at our destination—Buckingham Palace, where quarters were allotted to us, and there we alighted.

This palace is the town residence of the Sovereign. It is a very imposing and extensive structure. The Heir-Apparent and the other princes accompanied us, and led us into the palace. The whole of our suite are also accommodated in this building. There is an extensive and beautiful garden in front (*i.e.*, at the back) of this palace, with magnificent lawns and beautifully kept. They have a kind of reaping-machine like a cart and drawn by a horse. This cuts down the grass in strips a cubit (21 inches) wide, and collects it into the cart. There is a very pretty natural lake, with ships and boats to row about in. They have also erected several very elegant tents. In every corner of the garden there are some very large forest trees, and also most beautiful flowering shrubs. There were a large number of peacocks, and a crane was walking about on the lawn.

I was very tired and worn out; so I went early to bed. The Sovereign is at Windsor Castle, a distance of six leagues from town, but got over by rail in half an hour.

Upon the stairs, and within the palace, there are posted some elderly English soldiers in costumes four hundred years old, dating from the time of Elizabeth, Queen of England. An extremely singular costume.

CHAPTER IV.

ENGLAND; 18 DAYS.

23RD (*Thursday, 19th June*).—In the morning I arose, and in the course of the day paid a visit to the Nawwāb the Heir-Apparent. The road was not far to go. He has a nice house, with seven or eight sweet children. The wife of the Heir-Apparent is a daughter of the Sovereign of Denmark, and sister to the wife of the Heir-Apparent of Russia, who, with his wife, was present; having arrived a few days before on a visit, for which they will stay a month. We sat and conversed a while. Every place in the house, as far as the walls of the rooms, &c., go, were covered with figures of deer, &c., with tiger-skins, and the like.

On leaving, we went to visit Prince Alfred, whose title is the "Duke of Edinburgh." His house, too, is very fine. Heads of stags, of deer, and the head of an elephant he had shot at the Cape of Good Hope, together with many beautiful birds, striped or speckled, dried and stuffed, were collected in glass cases, and the like. There were also implements of the chase. Prince Arthur was not at home, having gone to an exercise of the troops.

Thence we proceeded to the residence of the Duke of Cambridge, cousin-german to the Sovereign[1] through her paternal uncle. He has a nice house, and is Commander-in-Chief of all the English army, besides being the Colonel of the (Royal Regiment of) Artillery and Ordnance. He is an old man, but hale and stout, rosy-cheeked and fair, with a pleasing countenance. He is a man of importance. We had a little chat, and I next went to his sister's, wife of the Duke of Teck, a prince and nobleman of Germany, a very handsome young man with scanty mustachios and a good figure. He has a good house and garden, given by the State.

As it was now the time appointed for the reception of the Diplomatic Corps and of the English Ministry, we soon rose and returned home, put on my (state) dress, and went up into a saloon of the upper story of the palace, where all our princes and officials were assembled. The Sovereign's Chief Usher had come with the whole of the Diplomatic Body, and they were waiting on foot. I addressed a few words to each, enquiring after their healths. The Russian Ambassador, Baron Brunnow, is an old man, and has been now thirty years in London as a Representative. Musurus Pasha, —the Ottoman Ambassador, is a Greek, and an elderly man. M. Beust, Austrian Ambassador, is an old, but intelligent great man, who was formerly the Austrian Premier, and is a German. The French Representative, Count d'Harcourt, is a nobleman of France. The others were also present, even the Japanese Minister. The Nawwāb Rāja Dhuleep-Singh, son of the celebrated

L

Ranjīt-Singh, came likewise. It is twenty years that he has lived in London, as the Government gives him a large allowance. He is a young man, with pleasing eyes and eyebrows. He speaks English. He had decorated himself with some beautiful jewels and pearls. He is an Indian prince.

When these were all gone, the present English Ministry, of the Whig party, Lord Granville—Foreign Secretary, Lord Gladstone—the Premier, the Duke of Argyll—Indian Secretary, together with the other Ministers and people of importance, were received in audience. We had a lengthened conversation with Lord Gladstone and the English Foreign Secretary. They also went away, and we were left to ourselves.

We made a tour of the upper apartments of the palace, which is a wonderful building. It has some very fine pictures and portraits.

For the evening we were invited to dinner with the Heir-Apparent at his house, and to an evening dancing-party at the Duke of Sutherland's, an English nobleman who has an income of a crore (500,000 tūmāns; about 200,000*l*.). We went to the Heir-Apparent's, and partook of dinner. Our princes, the Grand-Vazīr and others, the English Ministers, the Russian Heir-Apparent, and the wives of the two Heirs-Apparent, were present. After dinner we proceeded to the Duke of Sutherland's, who has for wife an intelligent, noble lady. His house is beautiful. There was a numerous company. We took our seat in a long hall. The English Princes, with their wives, the Indian Prince, and the Nawwāb Nāzim, of Bengal, with his son, were present. It is two years since he came to London about some business, and has remained here. He is a grandson of the renowned Tīpū Sāhib (*sic, read* Tīpu-Sā'ib). When the dancing was over, we returned home and went to bed.

24*th* (*Friday, 20th June*).—We have to go to Windsor Castle, the residence of Her Most Exalted Majesty Victoria, Sovereign of England, which is one hour's journey by rail. So we dressed, and then taking our seat in the carriage with the Grand-Vazīr and Lord Morley, started. Crowds beyond limit were standing at the ends and on both sides of our road. There were that number of carriages that no one could count them. Passing along the drive in Hyde Park, and through the town, we reached the station, and took our seat in the train. The carriages were most sumptuous, each side being a single sheet of plate glass. We traversed inhabited places, the open country, and green meadows; and at length Windsor Castle rose to view at a distance, appearing like a fortress with four turrets. Arriving near thereto, we alighted and got into a carriage. All our suite were of the party. At the foot of the steps of the Castle we alighted. Her Most Exalted Majesty the Sovereign advanced to meet us at the foot of the staircase. We got down, took her hand, gave our arm, went up stairs, passed through pretty rooms and corridors hung with beautiful portraits, and entering a private apartment, took our seat. The Sovereign presented her children, relations, and officers. We, too, on our part, presented our princes, the Grand-Vazīr, and the others. The Lord Chamberlain, who is the Minister of the Court of the Sovereign, brought for us the Insignia of the Order of the Garter set in diamonds; *i.e.*, the Knee-tie, which is one of the most esteemed English Orders. The Sovereign rose, and with her own hand decorated us with the Order, and cast the ribbon upon us, presenting us at the same time with a long stocking-tie. The history of this Order is as follows:—

" Two opinions are current among historians as to the (origin of the) Order that is called the ' Order of the Garter,' and which was instituted by Edward III., King of England, in A.D. 1349, at Windsor Castle.

" One opinion is that he instituted this Order in commemoration of the victory at Cressy, where the power of Philippe IV. of France was broken.

" The other is that on an occasion at a ball the stocking-tie—the garter, of the Countess of Salisbury, Edward's sweetheart, fell off, and became a source of merriment among those present. The Sovereign, out of the perfect zeal and attachment that he had for her, lifted up the stocking-tie, and pronounced the motto: ' Honi soit qui mal y pense,' which is to this day embroidered on the strap of the Order, and said: ' This stocking-tie will I raise to such a degree of estimation, that all, to obtain it, shall risk refusal.' "

Thus it was that he made it the first Order of his kingdom; and, besides the Sovereign of England, who is the Head and Governor of the Order, the English Princes, and foreign Sovereigns, this order is given to no one; also, the number of its wearers, home and foreign, can never be more than twenty-six.

I received the Order with the utmost respect, and sat down. I too presented to the English Sovereign the "Order of the Sun," set in diamonds, with its ribbon, and also the Order of my own Portrait, which she received with all honour and put them on herself.

We then rose and went to table. Three daughters of the Sovereign and one young son, who does not yet go anywhere away from her, and whose name is Leopold, were already seated. This son to-day had come to the station to meet me. He is very young-looking and very graceful. He wore the Scotch costume. The peculiarity of the Scotch costume is this: the knees are left visible up to the thighs. One of the Sovereign's daughters, sixteen years of age, is always at home with her, and has not a husband as yet. Her other two daughters have husbands. The princes, the Grand-Vazīr, Lord Granville, and others, were present. A beautiful breakfast was eaten. There were some fine fruits at the breakfast.

The Sovereign again took my hand and led me to a private apartment, she herself going away. I sat there a while. The armour-wearing household cavalry, together with a battalion of infantry, were drawn up in a small court in front of the Castle. They are very handsome cavalry and very choice infantry. The English troops are, it is true, few in number, but they are extremely well dressed, disciplined, and armed, being very stout young men. A band played beautifully.

There is a wide avenue in front of the Castle, a league

in length, and on either side of it two rows of ancient and strong forest trees, very lofty. The ground is all grass, with flowers and verdure. We descended, mounted our carriage with the Grand-Vazīr and the Lord-in-Waiting, and drove along this avenue, our suite following us in other carriages. Along the road there were numerous women and men; also beautiful women, children, and grown persons of the inhabitants of Windsor itself, were promenading in the avenues, on foot, on horseback, and in carriages. It was a pretty sight.

When we had proceeded a certain distance the concourse of people dwindled away. They have turned loose on the lawns and in the avenues about a thousand head of antelopes (fallow-deer), which were now seen in numbers, like a flock of sheep, feeding in separate batches, and not very timid of man. But no one is allowed to molest them. In reality, they are not antelopes, but of a kind between the red-deer, the antelope, and the roebuck (?), very graceful.

The avenues, the lawns, the trees were interminable. We drove two leagues, and passed along another avenue resembling paradise, both sides of the avenue being a mass of tall trees (or shrubs), all in bloom with large light-blue, red, and other coloured flowers, of the oleander family (probably rhododendrons). So charming was this, that nothing superior can be imagined.

We came to a lake of water of some extent, around which were multitudes of women and maidens. We crossed the lake to a small palace, very pretty, the property of the Sovereign. There we alighted and partook of some fruit. All our princes and suite came there also, and then went off to the station. We got into a boat and went about. On the other side of the water there was a crowd of women and men. After remaining on the water a little while, we went to a small model of a man-of-war, that has been constructed and armed with twenty-four guns about the size of swivels. We went on board, saw all over her, returned to our boat, and in her to the palace, where we again got into our carriage and drove to Windsor by a different road that was still all avenues, lawns, and numerous antelopes. There we rejoined our train and left for town. Similar crowds to those of the morning were waiting about, and mutual greetings continually took place until we reached home.

Windsor Castle is very ancient, and externally has not much ornament. It looks like an old building reared of stone, and each stone is about the size of a brick (or Roman tile). It has one large tower, with several smaller, lofty turrets. But the interior of the Castle is highly ornamented, is pretty, and full of objects, with very handsome rooms, halls, and corridors, and a museum of arms and armour. The age of the Sovereign is fifty, but she looks no more than forty. She is very cheerful and pleasant of countenance.

We are invited this evening to the house of the Lord Mayor,—the Governor of the old city of London, for an evening party and supper. At night, therefore, we mounted our carriage and drove off. From our palace to the Lord Mayor's house was quite a league. The whole of both sides of the roads and streets was crowded with so many women and men as passes all calculation. All shouted hurrahs, and we continually saluted them all. Every street is lighted with gas; and, besides this, electric lights from the roofs and windows of the houses made the streets as clear as the day. They had also arranged various designs with gaslights upon some of the hóuses, in the streets, and elsewhere. They had further dressed out the city and the streets with flags, &c. We passed along in front of imposing public buildings, magnificent shops, and open squares, and so came to the gate of the City .(Temple Bar), *i.e.*, of the old town of London, over which the Lord Mayor is Governor, though he has no authority over the other townships and parishes; *i.e.*, the remainder of the town has no Governor, but each parish has a council (vestry), and if any (grave) event happen, it is referred to the head policeman, *i.e.*, the head patrol-man, of the parish, and he refers to the Home Secretary. The police of this town is eight thousand strong, all handsome young men, in a particular dress. The citizens set great estimation on the police; whoever behaves disrespectfully to the police, is adjudged worthy of death.

Well; we arrived at the door of the Lord Mayor's house, ascended some steps, and there was a hall, where were assembled the Heirs-Apparent of England and Russia, their wives, all the Corps Diplomatique, our princes and others, the princes, the lady-princesses, ladies of distinction, the magnates, and the English

Ministers. We shook hands with each of the Heirs-Apparent, and saluted. This is a Government building, in which the Governor of London resides. It is called The Guildhall. Once a year, at the discretion and choice of the citizens, this Governor is changed. The members of the local administration wear a remarkable costume, large sable caps, gowns and robes lined with sable, &c., carrying in one hand a long thin stick, and in the other a small sword in the ancient fashion. They walked in front of us.

We remained in that room, where the Lord Mayor made a speech, and we gave a reply. After that, in a ceremonious manner, we went into an extremely spacious hall in which were chandeliers and jets of gas, having given our arm to the wife of the Heir-Apparent of England. The company of women and men was great. This evening three thousand individuals were invited. The Lord Mayor had on a robe the hinder skirt of which was very long and trailed on the ground. We went to the place of honour, where there were some steps, up which we mounted and then sat down on a chair. The wives of the two Heirs-Apparent sat on either side of us; all the rest were standing. The Lord Mayor read out a written address felicitating our arrival and enlarging on the friendship and union existing between the two States of England and Īrān (Persia). This address they had caused to be printed in the Persian language, and they gave a copy of it to each of those (present) who knew Persian. When the Lord Mayor had finished his recital, the Grand-Vazīr read out, with perfect elocution, the Persian (version) thereof. We delivered an answer, which Lāransūn Sāhib interpreted in the English tongue. The ceremonious session was now at an end.

They then gave into the hand of each person a gilt pen, having its ink in it, together with a slip of paper on which they had written a name; so that each one might write thereon the name of whomsoever he might wish to dance with. They also offered the gift of a gilt casket. Now the dancing began, which we surveyed sitting in that self-same place. Both the Heirs-Apparent, together with the ladies and others, all danced.

When the dancing was over, we again gave our arm to the wife of the English Heir-Apparent, and went to supper—a dinner after midnight. We passed through large halls and many staircases and corridors, all full of men and graceful women, and in the rooms and staircases of which they had arranged all sorts of flowers and shrubs grown in vases. Thus we reached a large hall, where they set out the supper-table. About four hundred persons were seated around this table. An individual, one of the citizens, who was the Lord Mayor's deputy, stood behind me, and every now and then made proclamation with a loud voice to the persons of the company, that they were to prepare themselves for a toast; with this signification: "The Lord Mayor drinks wine to the health of the great; all must stand up and drink." First of all the Lord Mayor drank to our health; then the Heir-Apparent of England gave a toast, and again the Lord Mayor gave one. Each time, that individual gave notice to the company beforehand.

Supper finished, we rose, returned to our home, and went to bed. Throughout our return drive, too, when it was midnight, there was the same dense crowd. This evening the Chief Usher and the Grand-Vazīr rode with me in my carriage.

The Sovereign of England keeps a book, in which each person who goes to Windsor Castle to see her inscribes his name; I, too, wrote mine to-day.

26th (Saturday, 21st June).—To-day we went to see the workshops at Woolwich, which is the arsenal, the cannon factory, and the iron-works of the English Government. From our quarters to that place is a two hours' drive in a carriage, the whole being through the town and inhabited suburbs. Woolwich, a town of itself, is really a parish of London, and inhabited quarters join the two.

In the morning we mounted our carriage and drove thither, the princes and others, with our personal attendants, accompanying us. We passed through populous quarters of the town, and over the river Thames by a bridge, then through the outskirts where butchers mostly do congregate, with labourers and pliers for hire, the faces of the whole being black with the smoke of coal, and so reached the town and city of Woolwich, a place of great importance, where are all the barracks of the entire cavalry and infantry of the realm of England. It is seated on the banks of the river Thames.

The Duke of Cambridge, Prince Alfred, Prince Arthur,

General Wood, Commander of the Artillery, and Military Governor of Woolwich, together with other commanders of artillery, infantry, &c., all came forth to meet us, and formed a procession in front of us. We, in our carriage, drove to see the factories. We traversed a considerable distance through streets and public places, where crowds were assembled on both sides of our path, shouting hurrahs, and whom I saluted in turn, until we reached the workshops. We alighted and entered these.

It is now the system no longer to cast cannons in moulds. They make, with implements they use, sheets of iron into pipes, of the size they wish the cannons to be. These they convey to another shop, place them under steam-hammers, and squeeze them, and weld them, so that they become cannons. They told me this system is held in greater consideration.

One by one we visited the workshops. In one place they draw rifled cannons (as they draw wire), in another they cut, in another they bore, in another they hammer. Quantities of useless cannon of old pattern were lying in front of the workshops; and numbers of shot, with large supplies of material, were collected; this place being the arsenal of all England.

After all these visits and venturing near to the furnaces of fire,—which were pretty warm, we mounted our carriage and drove to the edifice, by the flank of which we had, before passed. There a breakfast was laid out. It is a hall where the officers of the land and naval forces, as well as those of the artillery, eat breakfast. It was a nice place. We took breakfast; after which we mounted our charger "Blaze," and, with the sons of the Sovereign, the Duke of Cambridge, and the rest of the officers, went on to a plain (Woolwich Common) of grass-land to see the artillery exercise. It was not over spacious. More than twenty thousand individual women and men were standing around the plain and grass-land to witness the spectacle. There were seventy pieces of cannon, large and small. According to what they said, these cannons had newly arrived from India, and were to return thither. The gunners and officers were beautifully dressed. The English cannon are after the old pattern, being loaded from the muzzle by ramming, and are not breech-loaders like those of Krupp.

The horse and foot artillery marched past in our presence; the second time they came at a trot, then at a canter, and lastly at a gallop. After the exercises they fired a salute; they also made me a present of one of the nine-pounder guns.

We now mounted our carriage anew, and by the road we had come we returned home.

Having to go to the theatre in the evening, we dressed; and having taken our seat in a carriage with the Sovereign's Master of the Horse,—who is an intelligent man, and the Lord Chamberlain, we drove there. There were great crowds by the way, all of whom we saluted. We arrived at the theatre. The Heirs-Apparent of England and Russia, the wives of both, the princesses, the princes, and the magnates, were all present. It is a very large and beautiful theatre, with six tiers of seats. They acted some beautiful scenes, the number (of actors) being also large. They had sent expressly to Paris and had called from thence Patti, who is one of the renowned songstresses of Firangistān. She sang most exquisitely. She is an exceedingly graceful woman. She accepted a fabulous sum of money, and came to London. There was another also, Albani by name, from Canada in America, who sang extremely well and performed some wonderful feats. At last we rose and went home.

26th (*Sunday, 22nd June*).—This day, after breakfast, we went to the Garden of Wild Beasts (Zoological Gardens), the Husāmu-'s-Saltana and the Nusratu-'d-Dawla being seated with me in the carriage; the officers of our household, and others, going with us.

As it was Sunday, the streets were empty, all the people being in the fields and lanes taking walks. So soon, however, as they saw our carriages, they ran from all quarters and came towards us, shouting hurrahs.

The journey was long. We passed through streets, squares, and the like, and so reached the gate of the Garden of Wild Beasts, where we alighted. There were many carriages at the gate of the Garden and in the road, which made it evident that, by reason of its being Sunday, a large company had come to the Garden of Wild Beasts.

The Director of the Garden, an old man hard of hearing, came forward, and as he knew a little French, we conversed with him. There were great numbers of women and men, and we passed along a narrow way between these men and women, who unceasingly shouted hurrahs. In justice,—they do entertain a love towards us, and they conduct themselves with boundless respect and good manners.

Well; the wild beasts here are separated from one another in special cages. There were here several interesting animals, which had not been seen (by us) elsewhere. First, the hippopotamus, *i.e.*, the marine horse, which is a curious thing. There were three of them; one pair, male and female, with one young cub born in this very place, and already of considerable age. This was standing out of the water, the full-grown ones being in the water. People threw food into its mouth, which it opened like a gateway. It had very rugged teeth, and was of an enormous size. From what I could make out, this is the marine rhinoceros. Secondly, there was a monkey of great size and very repulsive in appearance; it was exactly like a human being, and more especially had it the hands and feet of a man. Its keeper made it dance; he stamped with his foot, it stood up; he spoke (to it), it understood English; it then walked forwards towards us, but it continually evinced the desire that they should hold it by the hand and lead it. They then sent it into the cage of the monkeys, where it leapt and sprang about in a wonderful manner, and played like a rope-dancer. Thirdly, the sea-lion and the sea-fox, which were in a basin of water, around which was a railing. An individual spoke to them in French; they showed great intelligence. The lion was of a considerable size, its body being covered with a fine down, and its feet resembling the fins of a fish and the wings of a bat, but it ran along with them at a good pace. At the side and in the middle of the basin there was a bench, on which a chair had been placed. It got up on the chair, and sat down. The fox (seal) was like the lion, but smaller. They dived beneath the water; the keeper gave a sound; immediately on which, they came out of the water and kissed their keeper, who had seated himself on the bench. He said: "One kiss;" "Two kisses." As many as he asked for, kisses they gave him. It was a strange sight. Fourthly, there were some very small monkeys, no bigger than the rat of Sultāniyya (perhaps the marmot, arctomys marmotta), — very curious. There were elephants, rhinoceroses, maned-lions, black panthers, tigers, and other beasts; also birds, and parrots of all colours. Besides these there were many other places to visit; but I was tired and could not go about. The crowds, too, were very great; so we returned home.

27th (Monday, 23rd June).—This day we have to proceed to the town and harbour of Portsmouth, to witness a review of the men-of-war; Portsmouth being one of the principal military harbours of England. In the morning I therefore arose early, though languid from sleeplessness, dressed, took my seat in a carriage, and with the Grand-Vazīr, princes, and others, drove to the station of the Portsmouth railway. A great crowd had collected. We took our places in the train, and waited until the Heir-Apparent of England, the Heir-Apparent of Russia, with their wives, and others, arrived. They occupied another carriage in the same train with ourselves, and we started. The whole of the road was populous, green and smiling, with larch forests. We travelled about three hours or less before arriving at Portsmouth. This is a town of importance and a great military harbour, with strong forts and batteries. At the wharf we alighted. The Governor, with his subordinates, came and made a speech, formal presentations being also gone through. They fired many guns on shore and on the water. We entered the ship named the "Victoria and Albert,"—a ship special to the Sovereign, very fast, large, and beautiful, together with the two Heirs-Apparent, the princes, the naval commanders, and others. The captain of this ship is named Prince-Linoge (*sic, for*: His Serene Highness Ernest Leopold V.A.J.E., Prince of Leiningen, G.C.B.). They had laid out a breakfast. We and the others went into the cabin and sat down to breakfast. Afterwards, the Heir-Apparent of England said: "Arise, and let us go up in the ship; the ships are going to salute." We arose and went up. All came. Two little sons of the Heir-Apparent of England had also come, dressed in the costume of sailors. We stood up. The men-of-war, about fifty tillers in number, were stationed at anchor in a double line, like a street on the sea. They fired a volley. The sailors had gone up into the yards, raised their voices, and shouted hurrahs. Other spectators, also, that had come from London, the seaports, and elsewhere, were in steamers and boats, large and small, innumerable. The surface of the sea was blackened with spectators, who all shouted hurrahs. They had hoisted flags with the Īrānī device on board every ship. It was a commotion!

We went on approaching near to the Isle of Wight,

which is in the English Channel, and is a very pretty island. A town was visible on the island, nestled in the bosom of a hill and named Ryde, which had its handsome houses arranged in successive tiers. On this island the Sovereign has a castle, built by her and her husband, and called Osborne, which was sighted at a distance. It appeared, from its external aspect, to be a nice palace built on a hill, with woods and lawns around it.

Still proceeding, we passed through the street of men-of-war, all of which fired guns and gave a salute. When we had finished the promenade, we got into a boat for the purpose of examining two ships. We went first to the ship "Azincourt" (*sic, French for* Agincourt), which is the largest ship of war of the English Government. The captain of this ship is named Fibs Hurubi (*sic, for* Admiral G. T. Phipps Hornby; *her* captain *being* R. O. B. Fitzroy), who was present with many naval officers. The length of the ship is more than 150 feet (*sic; she is* 400 feet between perpendiculars), with a steam-power of 15,000 horses * (*sic; her* indicated power *is* 6867 *horses*); her guns are very large, some of them being on the upper deck, but the greater number on the lower deck. We went below and saw all over her, even

---

* The "Agincourt" is really 400 feet long between the perpendiculars; probably the mistake has been made of saying "feet" instead of "ells," though the latter, 150 ells = 520 feet, would have been in excess. The indicated power of her engines is 6807 horses.

The Russian ship "Kremlin," mentioned in p. 57, is said to be armed with eighteen guns, six smooth-bore 60-pounders, of 97 cwts., ten breech-loading and rifled 180-pounders of about nine tons, and two 90-pounders of about four tons each.—J. W. R.

the kitchen, the sailors' mess-tier, and other places. They sounded a fife, for them to prepare for action. In one instant all the sailors came down from the upper deck, and with extreme celerity went through their fighting exercise. With the apparatus furnished they turned those guns about, notwithstanding their enormous size; which had much to surprise one. There were about thirty of these colossal guns (really twenty-eight). The ship is also armour-clad.

From her we went by boat to the other ship, named the "Sultan," which is also a very large ship, armour-clad on both sides. The name of her nākhudā (captain) is Vansittart; her guns are less (in number, being but twelve in all), but much larger. When we had inspected her, we descended, seated ourselves in our boat, and returned to our own ship. In our boat the Heirs-Apparent of Russia and England, their wives, the Mu'tamadu-'l-Mulk, the Duke of Cambridge, and others were seated, and we were taken in tow by a small steamer. As it arrived at the foot of the accommodation-ladder of our ship, it shot past that spot and went under the steam-paddle-wheel of the ship, at the very moment when the steam-paddle-wheel was set in motion. It wanted but little for the paddles of the wheel to strike our boat. If,—which God avert,—only one of the paddles had struck our boat, we should all have been drowned. Thanks to God Most High, the wheel stopped, we escaped uninjured, ascended into our ship, and returned to the seaport-town of Portsmouth. There again they had set out breakfast in a room; of which we partook.

Then, mounting a carriage, we went to see the workshops where they make the various objects used in steamers and for maritime purposes. We went through them; it was an interesting sight.

We now took our path up a ladder, and mounted to where they were building a very large ship of war, into which we went. The artificers were at work upon her. They had given her the name of "Nāsiru-'d-Dīn Shāh" (*the* "Shah," 26 *guns*, 5696 *horse-power*). We again descended (went to the station), took our seats in the train, and started for town, where we arrived at sunset.

This evening there is to be a concert, *i.e.*, a meeting with vocal and instrumental music, at the Albert Hall, to which we are to go. After our evening meal, therefore, we again got into our carriage and went, with the Grand-Vazīr and others, through Hyde Park, and entered that edifice, where the Heirs-Apparent of England and Russia, together with all the English officials, and others, were present.

We first were shown into a corridor more than six or seven ells wide (21 ft. to 24 ft. 6 in.), and covered over with glass. It was said to be of iron. On either side of this corridor were ranged various factory machines, *i.e.*, small machines like models, but beautifully made, and very pretty,—that were put in motion by steam power. We noticed many industrial processes, — sweetmeat-making, cigar and tobacco-making, the cutting of the flour threads, called *macaroni* by the Franks, lemonade-making, soda-water-making, where the bottles are filled and securely corked in an instant, Tunbridge-ware-making, silk-winding, cloth-weaving, newspaper-printing, and many various branches of art and industry that we cannot enumerate. They were performed with ease by these machines. It was in great detail.

The management of this exhibition is in the hands of the magnates of England,—of the Foreign Secretary Lord Granville, and others. They walked on before us, the Heirs-Apparent of England and Russia being present, with others.

Having inspected these for a considerable time, we mounted a great many stairs, and arrived at numerous halls hung with portraits, panoramic views, and other paintings. There were very choice portraits painted in oil, such that we had not yet seen so beautiful in any other place. The President of this collection of pictures is Prince Alfred, son of the Sovereign of England, who is the chief of the navy; and the paintings have all been done by naval officers and navy officials each out of his own imagination, and then sent here.

Leaving these, we entered into a series of corridors where were collected, for the purpose of sale, the articles produced by the machines we had inspected below. There were beautiful women and maidens, some employed at work with those machines in the manufactory below, and others occupied in the business of selling them here above.

Passing through these we came to a place the very picture of paradise. All these corridors, apartments, and manufactories were lighted up in various wonderful manners by jets of gas.

The very concert itself was in an exceedingly spacious enclosure with a roof in shape of a dome; very vast and very lofty. Around this dome were seven tiers of seats, all occupied by people, all filled with beauteous women magnificently apparelled, a great assembly, and all nobles and magnates. The pit, too, was full of women and men. Multitudes of gaslights were burning. We, likewise, went below, where, in the midst of all that assembly, they had arranged chairs. Together with the Heirs-Apparent of England and Russia, with the grandees of Persia, and with the ministers and magnates of England, we took our seats in due order. In front of us was a very large organ of the size of a palace, with iron columns, and with tubes from whence issue the sounds of musical instruments. Outspreading like a plane-tree, it was fixed to one side of the wall of the building. Right and left of the organ eight hundred individuals, beautiful women and maidens, were seated in tiers, four hundred on the one side, four hundred on the other, all dressed in white, but four hundred wearing blue ribbons, four hundred red. Above these women there were boys in handsome dresses, also to the number of eight hundred. These all sang in extremely sweet accord to the tunes of the orchestra and organ. This latter was played by one person, and its sound reached to a great distance. He played well; 'but wind was supplied to it by steam. Otherwise, how could one individual, with his feet, or with his hands, blow the needful blast? On the lower benches there were also a great many musicians. From no one did there arise a sound all quietly lent ear and looked on. It lasted more than an hour. When all was come to an end, we returned home and went to bed.

28*th* (*Tuesday*, 24*th June*).—To-day, at 2 o'clock in the afternoon, we have to go to Windsor Castle, to witness a review of some troops by the Sovereign. I arose in the morning, and the English Secretary of State for India, the Secretary of State for Foreign Affairs, and the Prime Minister, came to an audience. A great deal of conversation took place, which lasted an hour and a half. The Grand-Vazīr was also present. The meeting passed off pleasantly. We then went to breakfast.

The Grand-Vazīr now came and represented that the Indian Secretary was waiting and wished to present his subordinates, and that the inhabitants of the cities of England had brought an address, *i.e.*, a petition of felicitations on our arrival, which they wished to recite. We went into a hall; deputations were come from the great cities of England, and presented the felicitations of arrival. The members of the Persian Mission (in London) were then presented. The Jews of London, the Magians (Parsees), the Armenians of Manchester, and others, had addresses or speeches which they delivered.

Afterwards, the Indian Secretary presented his subordinates, who were in great numbers; among them being Gold-Ismīt (Col. F. J. Goldsmid, K.C.S.I.),—who had gone to the frontiers of Sīstān and Balūchistān, Ismīt (Major Smith), the telegraph-men of Tehrān, and others.

We now mounted our carriage and drove to the station. The Heirs-Apparent of England and Russia, with their wives, and others, as also the greater part of our suite, were there. We started and arrived at Windsor.

Windor Castle is, in truth, a strong fortress, built of stone in times of old on the summit of a hill. We alighted at the foot of the steps. The Sovereign had again come to the foot of the staircase to receive us. We took each other's hands, and went upstairs. All came. We stopped (there) a little, when I, with the two Heirs-Apparent, and the others, descended and mounted on horseback. I rode the charger of the Yamīnu-'d-Dawla. Some English Generals and Officers, with a squadron of cavalry, all rode in front of us, and we went down the long avenue that fronts the Castle, at the end of which was an open space, the parade ground. The road was exactly a league in length. On both sides of our path women and men stood in such crowds, that it was (almost) impossible to get along; and they shouted hurrahs in such a fashion, that, at the sound thereof, the horses of our cortége took fright and began to act as though mad. My horse, however, by reason of its long journeys, and of the shakings it had sustained at sea and on the railways, showed no signs whatever of taking fright, but remained quiet.

In this way we proceeded until we arrived at the end of the avenue, near to the parade ground. There we halted until the Sovereign should come up, with the wives of the two Heirs-Apparent, who were seated with her in the same carriage. So soon as they approached, we pushed on, and the Sovereign followed behind us. We went on to the parade ground,—a spacious greensward, around which were trees and forests. On one side, in form of a semicircle, women and men, spectators, were standing in such numbers that no computation of them was feasible. There were also erected, in a row, about ten or fifteen timber huts, like tents, in which the grandees and nobles, men and women, were seated, tier upon tier. They had hoisted flags of the "Lion and Sun," and the English flag, everywhere in front of this semicircle; while two large standards, one with the device of Persia, the other with that of England, were hoisted in the centre of the circle, where we were to take up our positions.

Well; we arrived under the standards, and there stopped. The Sovereign also came, and stopped, in her carriage. Mutual salutations took place. Then, we, with the Heirs-Apparent and the Duke of Cambridge, &c., started, passed down the ranks of the troops, returned, and took up our positions by the side of the Sovereign's carriage. The weather to-day was cloudy and inclined to rain. We offered thanks to the Lord that rain did not fall. There were seven or eight battalions; three or four battalions of Guards, who had splendid uniforms, with enormous fur caps of bear-skin, &c. These caps are very awe-inspiring. The battalions were very beautiful. There were two battalions in Scotch costume, and another battalion named after the Heir-Apparent of England, and called " Archers " (Rifle-Brigade; Col. in Chief, H.R.H. the Prince of Wales, K.G.). The artillery, the armour-wearing household cavalry, the hussar cavalry, were all very beautiful. Altogether there were seven or eight thousand men present, who went through their manœuvres beautifully. Several times they marched round the parade-ground; and then, retiring to a distance, they practised firing. I gave with my own hand a jewelled sabre to the Duke of Cambridge, Commander-in-Chief of the English (Forces). Much conversation took place with the Sovereign.

When the exercises were finished,—which was about the time of sunset, I, with the two Heirs-Apparent, the Duke of Cambridge, and others, gallopped through the crowd to Windsor Castle, a distance of a league; and on arriving there, dismounted and went upstairs, retired to a private room, and took our repose. In half an hour's time we returned to the Sovereign's presence, took leave, and went to the station.

We were invited for this evening to a dinner and ball at the residence of the Foreign Secretary Lord Granville. As the Heir-Apparent of England and his wife were fatigued, they telegraphed from Windsor to ask for the entertainment to be put off. On account of this telegram we dined at home. But, since we had given our promise, we went to the evening party and ball at the residence of the Foreign Secretary. But the ball was at the Foreign Office, *i.e.*, at the Government Office of the Ministry for Foreign Affairs. The Heirs-Apparent, and others, were present. We went there. It is an imposing and beautiful building. The wife of the Foreign Secretary came forward. We gave her our hand and went upstairs. They had collected numerous flowers and shrubs on the stairs and in the passages. The whole of the nobility of England, women and men, the Diplomatic Corps, with their wives, were invited. We went into a room and took a seat, where there was a table with chairs round it. We then arose, took the hand of the Foreign Secretary's wife, and walked round the whole of the rooms and staircases; after which, performing mutual salutations with all, we returned home and went to bed.

29th (*Wednesday*, 25th *June*).—To-day we have to go to Greenwich. It is not connected with the town, nor outside of it. It is on the bank of the river Thames; and, in reality, is accounted a suburban parish of the town.

In the morning we arose early. The Grand-Vazīr was not present. We took our seat in a carriage with the Mu'tamadu-'l-Mulk and the Lord-in-Waiting, and so started. We passed through the streets of the town and entered the city—the old town of London. We passed down the well-known street named Regent Street—full of beautiful shops, where the whole of the business of buying and selling is carried on, and which is very famous. There was such a concourse of people, and such a throng of carriages, that one became bewildered and stupefied. Again, we passed through other streets, and so entered the old Tower of London. The Governor of the Tower, who is a General, came out with all the notables and Aldermen of the City. The walls and turrets of the fortress are all of stone. The jewels, arms, &c., of the ancient monarchs are all kept there. We had wished to see them to-day, but there was no opportunity. We came out on the bank of the river Thames, where a battalion of infantry, with the band, was drawn out. The crowd, too, was such that one marvelled. They had carpeted the riverbank and hoisted flags. All the officers and grandees of England were present. They had prepared for us a large and handsome steamer. The English Heir-Apparent, the Russian Heir-Apparent, with their wives, and others, had all arrived before us, and had taken their places in another steamer. As soon as we arrived with our suite, —all our princes and followers, with the exception of the 'Imādu-'d-Dawla, being present, we went on board. The weather was very cold, and a nasty wind was blowing. The smoke of ships and manufactories invaded our vessel. This river has an ebb and flow. In the morning, up to noon-time, the water rises; and from the middle of the afternoon it diminishes, so as to make a difference of one or two ells (3 ft. 6 in. to 7 ft.). Of the English, Dīksūn, Tāmsūn, Lāransūn, and others, were present.

Our ship took the lead, that of the Heirs-Apparent followed, and we steamed off. There were such numbers of spectators on steam and sailing vessels, that they could not be counted, while there were multitudes of large and small boats; the whole coming along with us. We passed through the middle of London. Both banks of the river were covered with public buildings, manufactories, and lofty edifices. We entered a Dock. A "dock" is a number of basins constructed for ships,—in which merchantmen and others are repaired,—in which, having entered, they take in their cargoes of merchandize, or discharge the same. There are warehouses, too, built on the quays of the docks, which are furnished with mechanical appliances of large size, by which they lift the cargoes of merchandize from the ships to the shore, or from the shore to the ships, with great facility. These docks have a gate of iron arranged to the river, which is opened and shut with ease at the time of ships' passing in or out. The width thereof is small, so that large vessels pass with difficulty. So many ships, and so many spectators were seen as to set one wondering where they could all have been; and all were well-dressed, the women all good-looking.

We left the dock again and returned to the river. The same crowds in ships,—some accompanying us on our course, others fast to the shores of the stream, and all gazing at us. They fired cannons everywhere.

After continuing a certain distance, we arrived at Greenwich, where is the Naval College of England, and which possesses an imposing palace. Landing from our ship, we went to the palace of the Minister of Marine,— a very large and ancient palace, built two hundred years ago. The Heirs-Apparent, with their wives, and others, were of the party. In this hall there are some portraits of ancient commanders, and some paintings of naval engagements. It had a daïs, ascended by some steps, up which we went. Here they had prepared breakfast for us, and we sat down to it with the princes and others. The table where the remainder breakfasted was very long, and there a large party of men and women sat down to the repast.

The collation over, they showed me the blood-stained garments of Lord Nelson, which are preserved in a case. A bullet struck his epaulette and passed down by his shoulder-blade. We examined his white waistcoat, which bore the marks of blood. The action is known as the Battle of Trafalgar, in which the English Fleet engaged those of France and Spain, and, notwithstanding that Lord Nelson was killed, the English gained the victory.

We now descended, and the Heirs-Apparent, with their wives, took leave and departed, as I wished to go to the Observatory.

I proceeded to the open ground of the Naval College, in the middle of which there was a large ship of war fully rigged, for the exercises of the naval boys, who there practise their manual drills. About five hundred naval pupils, too, were drawn up in line. We stopped a while to see them exercise; and then, mounting a carriage, drove off to the Observatory.

The tower of the Observatory is built on a high hill, and is ascended by stone steps. Large telescopes are mounted in a species of turrets, which are made to revolve by machinery, so that the telescopes point in any required direction. It has a celebrated Chief Astronomer, who has so often ascended into the air in a balloon. Its view over the city of London and the environs of the river Thames is magnificent. We descended, drove to the landing-place, and again mounting the same ship (that had brought us), proceeded on our return. The water of the river towards the afternoon, acted upon by the influence of the tides, becomes low. This time, as we passed the docks by, and went straight on our course up the river, we passed under several large bridges of iron and of stone,—on which great crowds were standing, and arrived opposite to the Houses of Parliament. These are a majestic pile of building, surprisingly lofty, and with a very high tower. They told me that twelve crores (6,000,000*l.*) have been spent in its erection. The Houses of Parliament are on the right of the river (as you ascend the stream), and opposite to them, on the left bank, stands St. Thomas's Hospital, which is also an imposing structure.

We left the ship, mounted our carriage, and drove home. This evening there is to be a ball in the upper rooms of this very palace of ours. In the evening, therefore, we went upstairs. Everybody was there. We took the hand of the wife of the Heir-Apparent, walked off, and sat down. Everybody danced the ordinary ball dance; after which a man of Scotland came attired in the Scotch garb and played the bagpipes, which make a noise like the trumpet of Īrān. Prince Alfred, Prince Arthur, and others, danced a Scotch dance. Well; after this dance the company broke up, and we went to another room to supper. They had placed food and fruit, &c., on the table; of which all ate. The Indian prince was also there. We then descended and went to bed.

To-morrow we have to go to the cities of Liverpool and Manchester; also to the castle of Trentham, which is the property of the Duke of Sutherland.

Thursday, 30th (26th June).—We arose from sleep early in the morning, mounted our carriage, and started. The Mu'tamadu-'l-Mulk and Lord Morley rode with me;

the Grand-Vazīr, the princes, and the greater portion of our retinue remained behind in London.

Well; we passed through Regent Street, which has many beautiful shops, full of goods of every kind in the world. We also noticed in that same street a most magnificent hotel, where Americans chiefly resort, and therefore called The American Hotel. We continued our course, arrived at the station, took our seat in a train, and started.

From London to Liverpool is a five hours' journey, and a distance of fifty leagues. To-day the train passed through very many "holes in mountains," the ground being extremely hilly and intersected with valleys. Everywhere we found woods, green fields, cultivation, and populousness. We passed by towns, large and small. The town of Stoke, which possesses a very celebrated manufactory of porcelain, was on our way. It is here they make the English china-ware. In contiguity with the town of Liverpool we passed through a very long "hole," that occupied five minutes to clear it. Immediately on quitting it, the Liverpool terminus was visible. An immense crowd was there collected. To-day, in the course of our journey we passed over an enormous bridge, very lofty, built across the river Mersey, which flows through this very town of Liverpool, and falls into the sea. It is not a long river, but it is broad and grand.

Well; coming out from the terminus, we mounted a carriage. The Governor, with other officials and magnates of the city, was in front of the terminus. The

Governor mounted a carriage and preceded. We followed him, the Mu'tamadu-'l-Mulk, with the Lord (Morley), being in front of us again. The city of Liverpool is one of the great cities, ports, and commercial marts of England, and does business chiefly with America, from whence it principally draws wheat and cotton. The wheat crop of England is not sufficient for the food of its inhabitants. Emigrants in large numbers embark at this port for America, coming from England, Germany, and elsewhere. According to what was learnt, more than two hundred thousand emigrants annually leave this port for the New World, not one of whom ever returns. The region of Firangistān has an important company for the expedition of emigrants. There were two large ships, with emigrants, anchored in front of the city in the river, that were, according to arrangement, to have left this morning, but put off their departure merely to witness my arrival, and will start this evening. The name of one of them was the "Océanie"; she was a very large ship, and had a thousand emigrants on board.

Well; the crowds along our road, on each side, were innumerable; and the streets having been made narrow, there was no getting along with the carriages. From the windows, roofs, and roadsides such vociferations of hurrahs were there, that one's ears were deafened. Not one old woman or child was left in the town, that did not come to see the sight. It is a city of commerce and manufactures; it has therefore many working people. In proportion to the inhabitants of London, many more poor people were noticed in these parts, on whose countenances were visibly stamped the signs that they obtained a living with difficulty.

We arrived at an open space, alighted, and entered a public building named St. George (St. George's Hall), where there were a large hall and upper chamber, and on a platform in the hall of which they had arranged a throne, on which we took our seat. In the hall were crowds of women and men. The Governor read an address and commented on the friendship and concord of the two States of England and Persia. To this we made a reply, which Lāransūn interpreted. Tāmsūn and Dīksūn were both present.

We now rose, returned to the carriage, and drove to the residence of the Governor,—a nice building, where we waited a while in a room, as a light rain was falling. Thence we went into a large hall, where a breakfast was laid out on tables. We took a seat and ate some fruit, &c. The Governor drank my health as a toast, after which the breakfast came to an end. An immense crowd had collected in the square and courtyard of the edifice. We went in front of a window and saluted them for a while, returning thence to a private room, where we remained a certain interval, and then descending, remounted the carriage, and drove to the riverside.

Here we went on board a ship, together with our whole party, proceeded to the mouth of the sea and back again. The river is very broad and has a town on both shores. The air of the town was cold. We now retraced our course through the crowds and reached the station, got into our train, and by the same railway that we had come travelled back, after an interval of three hours, to Trentham Castle, the seat of the Duke of Sutherland.

Our train stopped before the gate of the park, where the Duke, with his following, was waiting. We got into a carriage and drove in. There were lawns, avenues, flowers; and deer of the same kind that we had seen at Windsor were grazing on the lawns. The Duke has erected here and there detached houses for his gardeners, his keepers, and others. He has also built a hotel, and has a small chapel. We arrived and alighted at the door of the Castle, entered the apartments, and went to a private conservatory that was within the house. We there saw varieties of flowers, palm-trees, and the like, which are found in but few places. In the centre was a small round basin of water, with a fountain, over which was the figure, in marble, of a naked woman seated. Beneath this water flowed, extremely clear and pellucid. The perfume of the flowers clung about the place; especially the odour of a species of large white and variegated lily, of seed from Japan, that was beautiful and fragrant beyond conception.

We sat there awhile and smoked a *galayān* (Persian huqqa, hookah, hubble-bubble, water-pipe), and then went in front of the façade of the building, where is a large garden, but of which the trees are small shrubs of cypress, larch, and others like orange-trees, grown in pots, placed out in the flower-beds, and clipped round into globular heads. The flower-beds were very extensive and beautiful, full of bloom, and with all sorts of evergreens permanently planted out. There were avenues, lawns like velvet, numerous fountains playing; and beyond these beds and gardens a natural lake, long, crooked, and tortuous, in which were several small islands full of copses, flower-beds, and walks, to which access was had by boats. Around this lake, again, is a rising ridge covered with green and smiling verdure; and beyond all are avenues covered in with trees, flowers, and grapevines, for which they have set up trellises of iron wire; and external to these trellises and avenues are the Duke's hothouses; which are extremely neat and handsome, being stocked with all sorts of flowers, and plants of variegated foliage, from the New World and elsewhere.

The banana was seen there, which is a pretty-looking edible thing, like a small, long, fresh pumpkin; it has a yellow skin, and when ripe has the flavour of a muskmelon, is soft, and in like manner can be taken with the fingers and eaten, though it is somewhat nauseating; it is called mūz in Persian or in Hindūstānī, and is produced largely in that part of Balūchistān which is held by Persia, and in Makrān. There were also nectarines, peaches, white and black grapes, figs, plums, strawberries, cucumbers, and other things. The whole of these fruits are found in these hothouses in the various stages of unripeness, half-ripeness, and maturity. With the assistance of apparatus and screws which they have applied, the gardener has only to turn these, and he can open the windows and rooflights, or close them, as required.

Well; we returned to the apartments. The edifice

possesses grand rooms, full of objects, cheerful, and adorned with beautiful paintings. The English Consul-General in Egypt, Ostantene (*sic, for* Colonel, now Major-General E. Stanton, C.B.), was there; he has recently arrived here. Lord Choseby (*sic, for* the Earl of Shrewsbury), who is a nobleman, and has a palace in the neighbourhood, with a garden laid out in the Swiss fashion, was also present. An Englishman who, before the war with the English and French, had been a prisoner in the hands of the Chinese, whose name was Cok (*sic, for* H. B. Loch, Esq., C.B.), and who had a long, thick beard, was there too. I asked him the particulars of his captivity, and he told me that the Chinese in his captivity had tortured him exceedingly. Some English noblemen were present, who for years have been the companions and associates of the Duke. A brother, a brother's son, and a son of the Duke, were there likewise. The Duke's son is entitled the Marquis of Stafford; his eldest brother is Lord Albert Gower, and his younger brother is Lord Ronald.

Well; in the evening we partook of an excellent dinner, and a beautiful illumination was carried out. We took a stroll. There was a place arranged for the game of bowls. In the middle was a long plank, hollow down the centre, and in two stages; within these they had passed many bowls, large and small. On either side of this a line on the ground is laid down with planks, ridgeways; and on both sides of this is a channel. One must throw the bowl with force, so that it may go and strike certain objects collected together at the (other) end. Every bowl that strikes an object they take away; and each one that does not strike, falls into those channels. The players form two sides; one party plays on this side of the wooden line, the other party on the other side. Several people stand also at the further end. When the bowls are cast into the wooden line, they come along of themselves to the players; and the objects which have been struck and have fallen down, are again set up.

We went to that place; and at that conjuncture, the Duke and the rest came also. I asked him whether he himself played. In one instant the Duke and the other Englishmen stripped, took off their hats, and played. It was a beautiful game, well worth seeing.

The intendent of the Duke's household, who, a few days before, had been wounded in the leg (or foot) by the charge of a gun that went off in the hands of one of his men, limped. His name was Raïte (*sic, for* H. Wright, Esq.,—the Duke's private secretary).

Friday, 1st of Jumādà-'l-'ūlà (*First Jumādà,* 27*th June*).—Having breakfasted in our quarters, we took our seat in a train, and started to go into the city of Manchester. The train went at a very rapid pace. The greater number of our household, &c., remained behind at home. To-day also we passed through some dark "holes." Leaving behind us various towns and "populous places," we went in the first instance to the works at Crew. Alighting from the main line of railway, we mounted a very diminutive steam-carriage that went through the works. It was a very pretty and novel thing. But soon alighting, we went on foot to see the workshops. In that place they manufacture the various parts and appliances of engines, locomotives, and railway carriages; and they saw with great facility very large and thick masses of iron, while they are red-hot. Conveying them under rollers, they soften them, form them into plates and sheets that excite surprise. And furthermore, the masses of iron which, being destined to be made into chains (*probably, for* rails), are rendered long and thin, were like so many red snakes running about on the ground. Again, in order to unite the plates of iron, to forge them, and to weld them, they had machines like two rams butting one another. They place the iron between these; they butt.

Well; after surveying all, we came away, and proceeded to another shop where finer work is done. This, too, we witnessed. Then, rejoining our train, we journeyed to Manchester. It is two hours and a half's journey from Trentham Castle to Manchester. We arrived at the station, where there was a greater assemblage and more sightseers than at Liverpool.

The city of Manchester, by reason of its exceeding number of manufactories, has its houses, doors and walls, black as coal. So much so, that the complexions, visages, and dresses of the people are all black. The whole of the ladies of that place at most times wear black clothing, because, no sooner do they put on white or coloured dresses, than lo! they are suddenly black.

The Governor, magnates, and nobles of the city, with the magistrates of the environs, were at the station waiting. We mounted a carriage and drove to the

Government House, where there was a large hall. On the top of a flight of steps they had placed a chair, on which we took our seat. The Governor made a speech; and we gave a detailed reply, enunciatory of our friendship with the Government of England, and of the pleasure and gratification we had experienced from the fact that, from the first of our arrival on the soil of England, the greatest regard had been shown us by the Sovereign and the nation. Lārānsūn Sāhib interpreted this in English. Every one approved.

We then went to another room, where breakfast was laid out. We ate a little; and then, mounting a carriage, we drove to see a manufactory of cotton yarn. We drove down a very long street, both sides of which were densely crowded with people. They so shouted their hurrahs that one's ears were nearly deafened. They showed a very great desire to see us.

We arrived at the manufactory, which was of five stories, in each of which one kind of work was carried on. For the most part, women were employed at the work, and made the yarns and other things. On the ground-floor they wove cotton cloths, which, when taken to another place, were coloured as chintzes, and are carried to all parts of the world. The lower workroom was exceedingly interesting, and was as spacious as a large public square. Certainly there were about two thousand looms there for weaving, and at each loom four women were occupied. I walked past the whole. Suddenly the manufactory was (as it were) overthrown by voices. Maidens, matrons, and men sang a pretty song. After the singing was over we went forth, mounted our carriage, and drove to the station, whence we started on our return to Trentham.

The Castle was reached an hour and a half before sunset. The Duke and others were present. We went on foot to look at the deer in the park, and then mounted a boat, the Duke himself accepting the fatigue of rowing. We landed on the islands and walked about. All passed off pleasantly. In the evening, after dinner, they played again at bowls; all were there; the Duke's son played better than any one else.

Saturday, 2nd (28th June).—We have to go to London, as we are to be the guest, in the afternoon, of the Heir-Apparent of England at Chiswick for a stroll, conversation, and refection.

In the morning we rose, mounted a carriage, exchanged adieux with the Duke, and started. It was more than a three hours' journey. We passed some towns and through numerous tunnels. Two of the "holes" were long, each occupying five minutes in the transit. We also passed along two narrow and protracted gullies (cuttings); the height of the (escarpments of these) gullies is not very great, but they were (sheer) like walls, one being all of stone, the other of stone and earth mixed together. It became apparent what expenses are incurred in the construction of these "iron-roads."

Well; we arrived at the London terminus,—where there were crowds, and from thence reached home. One hour later we left for Chiswick.

This mansion and garden are the property of the Duke

of Devonshire,—one of the wealthy men of England, and a relation of the Duke of Sutherland. He has given it, as a trust, to the Heir-Apparent to serve as a summer residence for him. Crowds innumerable were in the streets, at the windows, and on the roofs. The Grand-Vazīr and Lord Morley were in the carriage with us. The distance took about an hour. Numerous carriages were journeying to Chiswick, and bearing thither the invited. Entering the avenue that leads to the garden, we drove along until we reached the gate of the private garden. Here we alighted and entered the garden. The princes and others were of the party. They had set up some tents on the lawns and about the garden, which has a poor (*or*, small) mansion. In a tent were the Heirs-Apparent of Russia and England, their wives, with many ladies, the foreign Representatives, the English Ministers, and others. We stopped (there) a while; the Sovereign also came. We went into her presence; we sat in a tent a little while and conversed; after which I went for a stroll with the English Heir-Apparent. There was a pretty flower-garden, which also had its hothouse. The whole of the men and women walked about. In a large tent food had been set out in profusion. The people stood on foot, and all ate something. After this they made ready in the garden a cedar-tree and a spade, that I might plant the tree in memory of myself. I planted it. This custom in Firangistān is a high honour in respect of great personages. We then went to the tent of the Sovereign, exchanged adieux, and she left for Windsor. We waited a little, and then returned by the same road we came.

Arrived at home, as we had no engagement for the evening, we retired to rest.

The brother of the wives of the Heirs-Apparent of Russia and England,—a son of the Sovereign of Denmark, had to-day newly arrived. He is a youth fourteen years of age, and has a rank in the naval service. His name is Valdemir. We made acquaintance with him also. He has come to see his sisters, and leaves again in two days.

Sunday, 3rd (29th June).—To-day the weather is very cloudy and foggy; heavy rain is also falling. After breakfast we mounted a carriage with the Mu'tamadu-'l-. Mulk and (Lord) Morley, and took a little drive in Hyde Park. Although it was Sunday, and there was no one in the roads; and notwithstanding that the rain was violent, —still we saw a goodly number of men and women.

We now turned into the road to Chiswick, which we had gone over yesterday, and took our way to Richmond, passing by the side of the Botanical Garden (at Kew). There great numbers of people were walking about. It is a very large garden, but we did not go inside. It has a tall and slender tower within it, built after the Chinese fashion, and of many stories. It is a very pretty place; but we saw it from afar.

Well; we went to Richmond, which stands on an eminence. Richmond is not a separate place; in reality, it is one of the suburbs of London. It has some pleasant avenues, and a beautiful view over the surrounding country,—especially over the river Thames. On the lawns here, also, there were many deer of the kind we saw at Windsor.

As rain was still falling, and it was impossible to go about, it was proposed to proceed to the house of Lord Russell,—one of the olden English Ministers of celebrity, which was near at hand. I experienced a desire to go. We went, alighted, and entered. He and his wife came to meet us. He is an old man, nearly eighty years of age. He is short of stature. In spite of his years, he is in possession of a fine intellect and understanding. He is of the Whig party.

It is here necessary to detail what the Whigs are. All the Ministers of the realm of England are in two parties. The party now in office are of the Whigs, the chiefs of whom are Lord Gladstone, the present Prime Minister, and Lord Granville, the Secretary of State for Foreign Affairs, together with the other Ministers. The other party, who oppose the policy of this group, are named Tories, the chiefs of whom are Disraeli, Lord Derby, and others. Whenever the first-named set may go out of office, the whole of the Ministers and others must be changed, and replaced by others from the latter party.

Well; we sat a while. De Beust,—the Austrian Ambassador, and other diplomatists were there. After a few minutes we mounted again, and drove to the hotel of Richmond, which is a very beautiful establishment. A few years ago it caught fire, and they have rebuilt it. The view was very fine, but the haze and clouds prevented its being seen properly. The rain fell unceasingly; so we sat there a little, took some tea and fruit, and then drove home.

Monday, 4*th* (30*th June*).—When we arose in the morning, the whole of the Tory Administration came to an audience. The Nāzim of Bengal, with his son, was also present. Lord Russell, too, came, to whose house we went yesterday. Seymour (the Right Honourable Sir George Hamilton Seymour, G.C.B., G.C.H.), who, in the time of the late Emperor Nicholas of Russia, before the Sebastopol war has caused a cessation of relations with Russia, was (Envoy Extraordinary and) Minister Plenipotentiary at (St.) Peter(sburg), was also (admitted and) seen. In like manner, Lord Derby, Lord Malmesbury, who had each formerly been Secretaries of State for Foreign Affairs, and are of the celebrities of the Tory Administration, had audiences.

Next, some Indian merchants came, who had a singular costume and appearance. Chiefs of the Armenians, of the Jews, and of the Christians, and afterwards some other men—inhabitants of the Panj-Āb (the Five Rivers; vulgarly, Punjab) in India, with others, came (also). Among these was Iskandar Ahmad, son of the late Sultan Ahmad Khān, the Afgān; and who had been a certain time with his father in Tehrān. He is a smart youth, and a capital horseman. He said he had been several years in Russia, and he has been some time in England. He had changed his Afgān costume and turban for an English dress, and he came without his hat (on). His colour and complexion were sallow and pale.

Well; next came Lord Radcliffe (the Right Honourable Lord Viscount Stratford de Redcliffe, K.G., K.C.B.), so well known, and had an audience. He sat down, and we conversed much. This personage is one of the great diplomatists of Europe. He was for more than twenty years the English (Ambassador Extraordinary and) Minister Plenipotentiary at Constantinople, where he exercised great influence. In the Sebastopol war he upheld the policy of England and opposed the Russians. In the days of the first Napoleon even, when Qārdān Khān (General Gardanne),—the French Envoy, left Persia, and the late Khāqān, Fath-'Ali Shāh, of pious memory, received the English, he had entered the service, though not in Persia. According to one's recollections of those times, he must be nearly eighty-five years old; and still he conversed with the utmost wisdom and knowledge. He suffers from gout. Were he not so afflicted, I am of opinion that he still is in possession of the judgment, intellect, and stamina for the English Government to confide important missions to him.

When he left, we arose and performed our service of worship. This evening we have to go to the Crystal Palace, which is outside of the city of London, and where there are to be fireworks and hospitality.

To-day, before seeing the Ministers and others, the English Fire Brigade came, and in the garden at the back of our palace went through their exercise. They planted ladders, with the supposition that the upper floor of the palace was on fire; they mounted these ladders with perfect celerity and agility, and brought down people who were burnt, half-burnt, or unharmed, some taken up on their shoulders, and others let down by ropes made fast round their waists. They have invented a beautiful means of saving men. But, the wonder is in this, that on the one hand, they take such trouble and originate such appliances for the salvation of man from death, when, on the other hand, in the armouries, arsenals, and workshops of Woolwich, and of Krupp in Germany, they contrive fresh engines, such as cannons, muskets, projectiles, and similar things, for the quicker and more multitudinous slaughter of the human race. He whose invention destroys man more surely and expeditiously prides himself thereon, and obtains decorations of honour.

Well; among the others came some English prize-fighters, and performed boxing. To box is to strike one another with the fists, which requires great skill and dexterity. But they wore on their hands a kind of large gloves stuffed with wool and cotton. Had they not worn these gloves, they would have killed one another. It was very ludicrous and amusing.

In the afternoon we mounted our carriage and drove to the Crystal Palace, in which building the first Exhibition took place, that was held eighteen or nineteen years ago, and the building is still standing. It took an hour to arrive there; but a heavy rain came on, which threw a deep gloom over the spirits of the people. In spite of this, however, great crowds of women and men were standing along our road, and greeted us. We arrived and alighted in front of the building. The Grand-Vazīr, our princes and household officials, &c., were of the party. In front of the building a tent was .pitched. Prince Alfred, the lady-princesses, and nobles were waiting for us there; and they had prepared fruit, ices, and the like.

We tarried there a few minutes, until the Heir-Apparent of England, the Heir-Apparent of Russia, their wives, and others arrived. We then took the hand of the wife of the English Heir-Apparent, and entered the building.

A wonderful assembly came in view. On each side of our path they had arranged chairs, on which beautiful women in splendid attire, with men, were seated in rows, leaving a space through which we were to pass, so that it was necessary to traverse the whole of them.

The palace is of iron and crystal. It is so lofty and spacious that this evening forty thousand individuals came here with tickets.

Well; we went to the centre of the building, which has a lofty arcade. In the middle of the arcade there is a basin of water, made to represent natural rocks and mountains, with a beautiful fountain, from which water flowed plentifully. On the left hand side there was a gallery with steps to it, at the top of which was a balcony with many chairs arranged in it. I, the Heirs-Apparent, their wives, the lady-princesses, and the princes, all sat down there. The Duke of Cambridge was not present; they said an attack of gout had seized him.

Facing us there was a large organ, similar to the one in the Albert Hall. There were also a numerous orchestra and singers. They played; they sang; and such an assembly was there in that place, above and below, around and on all sides, seated on chairs, that one's eyes were dazzled. They brought me a double opera-glass, through which I looked.

Beyond the windows which were behind our back most charming fountains were playing. The wife of the Duke of Sutherland, with her daughter, was seated behind us. The Duke's daughter is extremely graceful.

In front of us some English gymnasts performed their feats; and wonderful tricks did they do, by way of leaping, springing, and hanging upon a rope, &c., which few could perform. They then brought out the gymnastic pillars of Persia, and performed pillar feats.

After these a company of Japanese came forward, from little children, up to full-grown men and women, dressed in the costume of their own country. They performed some wonderful *tours*, at which one's senses became bewildered. For the most part they performed their tricks with their feet. They lay down. They took a large wooden chest and caused it to spin about as they wished like a blade of grass, and threw it up into the air, whence it fell again on to the soles of their feet. One of them lay down on his back with his eyes blindfolded, and held upright, upon the soles of his feet, a very long ladder. A child of about ten years old went up to the top of this ladder, and there went through some feats. He threw some curious balls up into the air, and held in his hand a case with holes in it, so that the balls always fell into the holes of the case. Still continuing to lie similarly on his back, he took the fold of a door on his feet and spun it about in a manner that is not to be described.

There was a stout and long rope suspended from the roof of the arcade to the ground, a height of forty ells (140 feet). Two or three English gymnasts, acting just as they pleased, took hold of the rope, and with all celerity mounted to near the roof. There, standing on one foot, they leant on one side, and one of them came down head foremost. This was very surprising.

Again, they had fastened ropes to the sides of the arcade, so that these hung down, and beneath them a rope netting was secured. One Englishman performed on these ropes in a manner that up to this day I had never seen or heard of. I will simply note it down that it was not a performance with ropes,—he performed magic, —he flew. For instance, he leapt ten ells (35 feet) from this trapeze to that trapeze which was suspended in the air; and as a finish, he threw himself from his trapeze and fell into the net.

The play being now concluded, the company broke up. We went to the top of the building and dined at a table where all the magnates and notables were.

The garden of the Crystal Palace, which is the finest of all the gardens of England, was visible from this height; and there were fountains in the gardens, in great numbers, each one of which sprang to a height of more than twenty ells (70 feet). The source of these jets is a lofty tower built in front of the door of the palace (by which visitors of distinction are admitted privately).

Well; great numbers of people, with umbrellas over their heads, remained in the garden at the foot of the building, in spite of the rain, and shouted hurrahs.

After dinner there were fireworks in the garden,—very fine fireworks; and they discharged a great number of bombs, out of which there issued stars of many colours.

The fireworks over, we came downstairs. They had arranged an electric apparatus like a telegraph wire; and the instant that I put my hand to it, a large flight of rockets mounted from the garden into the air, which formed a grand spectacle.

On our return we again took the hand of the wife of the Heir-Apparent, and went home.

The beggars of Firangistān, instead of asking for alms, play musical instruments, as guitars or violins, and never beg. If some one gives them money, they take it; if not, they go on playing.

In the garden at the back of our palace a great number of cock and hen pheasants were seen in the trees.

There are multitudes of pigeons in Firangistān; and, as in Persia, pigeon-fliers send them up. Especially in Belgium did we see many of them.

They place sucklings and little children in small carriages (perambulators), and during the day-time wheel them about by hand in the avenues and on the lawns, in a very pretty manner; and the children go to sleep in the carriages.

We have received from the Duke of Sutherland four head of the deer which were feeding in his park, and which are a kind of argali, but resembling the stag. We have consigned them to Ibrāhīm Khān, that we may God willing, bring them to Tehrān, and that they may breed and multiply.

Tuesday, 5th (1st July).—To-day we have to visit the Bank, the Tower of London, the churches of St. Paul's and Westminster, as also the Houses of Parliament. In the morning, therefore, having breakfasted, we mounted our carriage, drove to the city, entered it, and went to the Tower. The Chiefs of the locality were admitted to our presence. We went up into a very old and ancient turret in which was a large glass case with an iron railing round it. Several of the crowns of ancient English kings were within this, enriched with rare jewels; more especially, in one crown there was a large ruby, exceedingly choice. There were staves (sceptres) of gold, and a few vessels of gold. A model of the diamond, the Kūh-i-nūr (mountain of light), in crystal, had been made and placed there; but the diamond itself has been cut into a brilliant in London, and the Sovereign has had it made into a brooch which she wears on her bosom. On the day when I went to Windsor to make my adieux, she wore it on her bosom. It is a very beautiful diamond.

Well; as time was scant, we did not go into the armouries which are in this Tower; but I drove to the church of St. Paul's. The head priest of that place was unwell, and was not present; his substitute was there. We walked about in the church, which is a very lofty and ancient edifice. Many women and men were there. The people of celebrity interred in this church are as follows: Lord Nelson, the Duke of Wellington. . . .

Coming out of there, we went to the Government Bank (Bank of England), passing by the Royal Exchange,—the Merchants' Mart. The merchants of renown of London, together with a crowd, were there.

We reached the gate of the Bank. The Governor of the Bank, with all the writers and members of this business, were present. We ascended some stairs. It is an imposing edifice. We saw its repository of archives, its council-chambers,—all. For the purpose of printing the receipt and assignat-papers (bank-notes, treasury-bonds, &c.), for assaying the weights of gold and silver (coins), and for cutting up the light coins, they have beautiful machines and instruments, as also steam-engines; the whole of which we saw. Next, we inscribed our own name in their book; and from thence going downstairs, we went underground, where numerous ingots of gold and silver were seen, each ingot being (of the value) of two thousand tūmāns of Persia (800*l*.). There was existent in that place (the value of) three to four crores of money (1,200,000*l*. to 1,600,000*l*.)

Well; returning thence, we went home. There were three curious things seen in that place. Firstly,—in each machine that prints the bank-notes, there were three (dials like those of) compasses, each with hands like those of a watch. For every number that was printed, these compasses, by the revolution of their hands, took and kept an account. At each movement given to the machine, one note came forth printed; and a hand moved from subdivision to subdivision (of the dial). The reason of this is that no one may be able to purloin any from the number of bank-notes (printed).

Secondly,—there were engines for trying and testing the weights of coins; so that large quantities of gold coins flowed down a place similar to a spout, on each side of which was a repository like a till, and every coin that was light of weight was made to fall, by machinery, into one of those tills, while those of full and perfect weight fell into the other.

Thirdly,—there were machines that cut in two, like shears, the coins that were light of weight, throwing them out of circulation, so that they have to be reminted.

Well; we went home, and rested a while. Then, mounting our carriage, we went to the house of Gladstone, the Prime Minister. He had an elderly wife, and they both came to meet us. We gave our hand to his wife, and went upstairs. It had nice rooms. An exceedingly small basin of water, with fountains, was in the upper room,--very pretty. It had a nice outlook towards the Houses of Parliament and over the town. The Austrian Ambassador, the Ottoman Ambassador, the German Ambassador, and, of English grandees, Lord Granville—the Foreign Secretary, the wife of the Duke of Sutherland, and others, were present. We sat down a while, and then went to the Parliament-House.

A description of this building, and an enumeration of its rooms, upper chambers, and corridors, is beyond the power of man. They say that a fabulous sum has been spent, in course of time, on this edifice. Its foundation is from eight hundred years ago; but ten years previously to the present time, they added very much to the pile.

The Regulator of the assembly of the Lords, who is an old man of the name of Clifford (Sir A. C. Clifford, Bart.) went before us, and we visited the rooms one by one.

It is a very grand, solid, and majestic structure. In point of fact, so great a palace is worthy and seemly for the Parliament of England. We passed through a large hall, called the Waterloo Hall, in which were two large pictures, most beautifully painted, and hung on the two sides. One is of the battle of Trafalgar, formerly mentioned in detail; the other, a representation of the meeting of Wellington with Marshal Blucher, Commander of the Prussian forces, and participator in the battle of Waterloo. After the rout of Napoleon on the field of Waterloo, they met one another on horseback, shook hands, and offered mutual congratulations.

Well; we went into the chamber of the House of Lords, where the Peers were assembled. The number of Peers in this congregation is about one hundred (*really*, four hundred and eighty-one, *barring recent changes*). We sat a little while, rose, passed through rooms and corridors, and so reached the hall of the House of Commons, the number of whom is three hundred and fifty (*then present, perhaps; the total number being* six hundred and fifty-eight, *barring any subsequent changes*). Lord Gladstone, Disraeli, and the other Ministers, Whig and Tory, were present. The Whigs were (seated) on one side (of the house), the Tories on the other side. We took our seat on a chair in a gallery overlooking the assembly, to which a narrow passage led. They brought forward a question, on which there was a difference of opinion. The President (Speaker) of the House adjudged according to the "majority," *i.e*, the greater number, the lesser number being called the "minority." The whole of the members went forth, to be counted outside; the (place of) assembly remained vacant, no one being left except the President. After a minute or so they came (back); the Whigs were the victorious party, who now hold office. Then Lord Gladstone—the Premier, came up to us, and we had a little conversation.

Rising, we went to the church of Westminster (Westminster Abbey), which is near to the Parliament (House). It is a very grand, beautiful, and harmonious pile. Its structure is ancient, and all of stone. It has a lofty and long-extending roof. Henry VII., King of England, built a chapel, most magnificent, and contiguous to the great church, being like a royal balcony, with numerous sculptures in its roof and on its walls. The tomb of Henry himself is in that place, in the middle, and has a large iron railing.

Of other sovereigns, of generals of celebrity, and even of poets, a great number are buried within this church. Its length is five hundred and thirty English feet; its height, two hundred and twenty-five. The names of the other monarchs buried here are: Edward the Confessor, Henry III., Henry V., Henry VII., Elizabeth, all the Sovereigns of the House of Stuart, and all those of the House of Hanover. Those of ministers are: Pitt, Fox, Robert Peel, Lord Palmerston; of generals, Outram, Lord Clyde.

There was a very ancient throne in that place, seated upon which the English monarchs must be crowned in this church. The stone of the patriarch Jacob—upon whom be peace—is set in that throne. It is a large stone, upon which the patriarch Jacob slept; and it came from Egypt to Europe; *i.e.*, passing from the hand (of one possessor) to the hand (of another possessor), it became the property of the monarchs of England.

Well; we returned and went home.

In the Houses of Parliament there is a very important library, in which are the written reports of the ancient and modern debates of Parliament, the laws of England, and other matters, in separate volumes.

Wednesday, 6th (2nd July).—We must go to Windsor to take leave of the Sovereign.

We breakfasted at home. The Heir-Apparent of Russia came, with whom we conversed; for we are going away, and he too, to-morrow, has to go to one of the English seaports; *i.e.*, he has ordered a yacht for himself, which is now ready, and which is about to be launched.

After his departure we set out for Windsor, all the princes, the Grand-Vazīr, and others, being in attendance. We arrived at Windsor; the Sovereign came to the foot of the stairs to meet us. We took each other's hands and went upstairs. She led me, and took me round all the apartments of the palace. It has very sumptuous rooms and halls; the view towards the city of London and over the country is very fine. There is a pretty flower-garden at the foot of the building, towards the country; also an extensive library. We saw some books in the Persian language and characters; in particular, a history of India, written like a diary, and very beautifully illuminated in the Indian style. There was also a magnificent armoury, in which all the ancient weapons and armour that have been obtained from India and elsewhere are preserved in glass cases; also some objects of jewellery and gold, as, for instance, the royal throne and the jewelled saddle of Tīpū Sāhib (*read* Tīpū Sā'ib), the Indian, which were set with many precious stones. In like manner there were great quantities of ancient arms and armour in the European styles, of presents from sovereigns, and of similar objects, arranged in the rooms;—a very large vase of malachite sent by Nicholas, the Emperor of Russia; the musket-ball that killed Lord Nelson in the battle of Trafalgar, and that had been extracted from his body, was preserved in a case; the mast of the very ship in which Lord Nelson was, and which a cannon-shot had pierced through, together with several of those cannon-balls, were in one of the rooms, and were surrounded with a railing; some Russian cannon-balls, also, taken in the Sebastopol war; two soldiers' muskets with flint locks, as used by the Russian troops, and serving as specimens, were placed there likewise. A bust of Nelson, carved in stone, was placed on the half-mast of a ship, pierced by a cannon-ball. Two cannons sent as presents by Ranjīt-Singh were also there. In the halls were painted the portraits of the sovereigns and ministers of celebrity in the times of the first Napoleon, who were called "The Holy Alliance."

When we had strolled about a considerable time, we went into a room and sat down at a table, I being there, and the Sovereign, her youngest daughter, and Prince Leopold, who to-day again had come to the station to meet me, and who was dressed in the Scotch garb. He is a very nice prince. After partaking of a little fruit, we arose, and the Sovereign conducted me to the door of a room assigned to me, and went away. I gave my reflexion (photograph) to the Sovereign as a souvenir; she gave me hers, and that of Prince Leopold. In truth, from my first arrival on English soil, down to this very day, the Sovereign has exercised towards us the fulness of kindness and friendship.

We now descended, took the Sovereign's hand, and went down to the door of the carriage; there saying adieu, we seated ourselves in the carriage. The Sovereign expressed her desire that her special photographer should take our likeness in the carriage; and he took several negatives of us. Then we drove off.

Proceeding a short distance along the avenue, we changed our direction and went to the house of the Princess Helena, daughter of the Sovereign and wife of Prince Christian, one of the princes of Holstein in Germany, whose territories are now held by Prussia, though he still makes a claim thereto, and may perhaps one day obtain possession of them. Well; we arrived at the Prince's house, and sat there a while. He has a beautiful house and flower-garden.

After partaking of some fruit we drove to the mausoleum of Prince Albert, the Sovereign's husband. It was a long way off. We passed by the side of the tomb of the Duchesse de Quint (Duchess of Kent), the Sovereign's mother, and at length arrived at the mausoleum of (Prince) Albert. We alighted and went to the tomb, which is very imposing and in good taste, built of stones of various colours. The sarcophagus is of stone, and a figure of Prince Albert himself lying in death, of very beautiful marble, is placed upon the sarcophagus. I laid on the tomb a nosegay which I had in my hand. I became extremely dejected and full of sadness.

Coming out from thence, we mounted and drove off. Everywhere Prince Leopold accompanied us. All these parts are occupied by the hothouses for flowers and fruits, the kitchen-garden for vegetables, the orchards, the fields for cows, and the dairies for taking the milk and butter, for the Sovereign's use. We alighted and planted a mountain cypress (*perhaps*, a cedar or wellingtonia) as a memorial of ourselves. We then drove to the station, bid adieu to Prince Leopold, returned to London, and went home.

A short repose soon enabled us to set out again and drive to Madame Tussaud's Exhibition. Madame Tussaud was a woman, and has now been dead for twenty years, having left a son and grandson. She originated a place in which are arranged the effigies in wax of monarchs, of men of celebrity, and of great poets, ancient and modern, clothed in the very garments of the persons themselves or of their periods, whether they were men or women, even to artificial jewels, such as crowns, necklaces, finger-rings, and the like. These figures are arranged in rooms and halls, in standing or sitting postures, &c., in such a manner that there is no possibility, for one to distinguish whether they are human beings or wax figures. Well; the son of Madame Tussaud was unwell, and her grandson explained.

They have made a figure of Napoleon III., dressed in his own clothes and lying on a bed in the agony of death, such that it appears exactly like a man still alive, but moribund. There were some living women sitting about among the figures; and however much I tried to distinguish which were in reality human beings, and which were wax figures, I could not, until the women rose, walked, and smiled; then alone did it become certain that they were living women. The effigy of the present Sovereign of England, those of her children, and of the ministers, were all there; also that of Louis-Philippe, and of the Heir-Apparent of France, with his mother Eugénie. They were excellent figures.

In addition to the effigies of sovereigns and great men, they have also taken, in a very striking manner, the likenesses of certain individuals, assassins or reprobates, notorious throughout the world for their diabolic acts and wickedness, such as Orsini,—who attempted to kill the third Napoleon, and Mazzini, the Italian.

They had bought in France a *gallows*, on which, by hanging, they put people to death, and placed it here to show the manner of killing men. They said that with this gallows-tree nearly twenty thousand individuals had been executed. (*Evidently the* guillotine *is meant.*— J. W. R.)

There were also, besides these, in a room, numerous mementos of bygone days. A large number of effects that had belonged to the first Napoleon were there, such as the carriages captured by the English in the battle of Waterloo; so that we saw the very carriage in which Napoleon used to ride, and also a plan of battle traced by himself, the whip used by his coachman on the day of Waterloo, his cloak, and some of his garments. There were likewise various effects that had belonged to certain sovereigns or magnates of England and elsewhere, in ancient or modern times.

We then came away. Below this exhibition there is an extensive bazaar, in which they sell every kind of wares that can be imagined. We walked about there a little, bought some articles of crystal and the like, and, returning thence home, retired to rest.

Thursday, 7th (3rd July).—To-day, after breakfasting at home, we went to the Crystal Palace. We drove to the Victoria Station, took our seat in a train, and started. The railway looked down on the roofs of the houses,—not in one place, not in two places; the train went uninterruptedly either over the housetops or through " holes " in hills. It took us twenty minutes to reach the Crystal Palace Station. There we alighted and walked upstairs, where there were innumerable women and men. We bought a few photographs and the like. The dealers in this bazaar are all women. Articles of every description are there to be had. The following is the history of this building.

Twenty years ago, when the English Government made the first Exhibition-Bazaar in Hyde Park, which is in the town of London, some members of the Committee, when it was over, brought the building here, where it is outside of the town, set it up again in the same manner, and established within it a perpetual exhibition, with refreshment-rooms, building also places of recreation for the inhabitants of London; and arranging fountains, basins, parks, gardens, and everything that can amuse people. It is now the very best of all places of pastime in London. Every day seven or eight thousand individuals go there for amusement or for taking the air, without any intermission; and they who originated the enterprize derive a profit therefrom.

Well; after making our purchases, we walked through the assembled women and men. I saw some black women, of the natives of the Jamaica islands (mulattoes from the West Indies), who were very graceful, and who had husbands as well. In spite of their black faces, with which they were seated in the midst of the fair and rosy-cheeked women of England, they still, through a certain sweetness they had, were very coquettish. Their complexions were of the colour of raw coffee-berries, and they had beautiful curls.

Well; after getting past, we arrived at a place where an African maned-lion and a tiger of India were fighting one another, and a dead stag was lying beneath them. All three of these animals, formed out of the stuffed skins of the very beasts themselves, were arranged in such a manner, and so made to stand up, that there was no way to distinguish them from a live lion, a live tiger, and a dead stag. Their claws with which they had attacked one another, and the blood that had flowed, were as though the flesh of their bodies were torn and blood were flowing. So well was this group executed, that in ten days one would not become tired of contemplating it. We now went to a department where they have arranged an imitation of the palace Al-Hamrá (the Red Palace, of which the word Alhambra is the Spanish corruption), built by the Arabs during the time of their occupation of Andalusia and Toledo in Spain. I examined it. It is very good and very pretty. They have there done some nice work in plaster and glazed tiles. This department took fire a few years ago, and was burnt. They have now restored it again as it was at first, though it was not quite finished. They have done the plaster-work, &c.; but the plaster-work of this country is not carried out by the same method as in Persia. There, the whole of a piece of plaster-work is cut out by hand with great labour; here, they have made moulds of glue which have various designs upon them; and whichever pattern they require, they place the mould thereof on the surface of a sheet of plaster, which instantly takes the design and dries; it is then fixed on the wall as though it were a tile. It is furnished with basins and pretty fountains arranged in the Arabian taste.

We now went on to the aquarium, descending by some steps to a place underground, a long hall, roofed, with a cool, pleasant atmosphere. Various kinds of marine animals and plants were in it, as in the one at Berlin; but at Berlin the species of fishes and of some other things were in greater numbers than here.

Again we ascended, passed through the people, went up the stairs we had mounted on the night of the fireworks, admired the garden and the fountains, and then again went through the garden to see two balloons that were to ascend into the air with men in them. We walked a great distance on foot, through multitudes of women, men, and policemen, arriving at length at the end of the garden, where the two balloons, of immense size, were already inflated with vapour and prepared to ascend; so that there was no power to restrain them. They are made of a cloth of silk, on which something is applied to make it like wax-cloth, and to give it strength. There is also a kind of network over the balloon, formed of several cords knitted together like a fisherman's net; and beneath the balloon a basket is arranged in which people sit, and large enough to hold two or three men.

With the first balloon to start, a man named Smithe, with another named Evenau, took their seats and went up into the air, and were lost to sight. The second balloon was also full and ready. A son of Smithe,—a young man, who said he had already been up with his father a hundred and seventy times, ascended in this one. On the following day, when intelligence was brought, it was learnt that the first balloon had descended at a distance of ten leagues from London, and the second at a distance of one league.

We then turned back on foot to the basins and fountains. The people were crowded together in such a manner as to prevent one's seeing. We did however manage, in one way or other, to see all the basins For our return to the palace they had made ready a carriage, in which we took our seat. Now, in spite of our road's being uphill, and of our driving pretty fast, still, the ladies, the damsels, and the children all kept pace with the carriage, and not one remained behind.

Once more we mounted to the top of the building, partook of some fruit, had our photograph taken, and then descending, went to the train, seated ourselves, and returned home.

After resting awhile, we drove to the Albert Hall; but the machines were not at work. We therefore went to some halls, where they had made a collection of all the tobacco-pipes, hubble-bubbles, and drinking utensils of every nation, together with all kinds of silken stuffs of China, Japan, and Europe, &c., ancient and modern. Having viewed these, we went up from that place to see the pictures which people, during the three months the exhibition remains open, bring and hang up here, some for sale, others merely on view. We examined the whole; but the greater part of the more beautiful pieces were either sold already, or were not to be sold at all. We selected about ten or fifteen fine paintings, Ismīt Sāhib (Major R. M. Smith, R.E., Acting Director of the Persian Telegraph) interpreted for me.

The picture of a donkey was seen, and I asked the price of it. The Director of the Exhibition, a fat, white-bearded man, who gave information about the prices, told me it was a hundred pounds sterling,—equivalent to two hundred and fifty tūmāns of Persia. I remarked: "The value of a live donkey is at the outside five pounds. How is it then, that this, which is but a picture of an ass, is to be paid so dearly for?" The Director said: "Because it is not a source of expense, as it eats neither straw nor barley (the eastern substitutes for hay and oats)." I replied: "True; it is not a source of outlay; but neither will it carry a load, or give one a ride." We laughed heartily. Then, as time was short, and we were extremely fatigued, we went home. The Albert Hall, too, has its own special garden, very nice.

Friday, 8th (4th July).—After breakfast this morning, I went to pay a visit to the English Heir-Apparent. The wives of the two Heirs-Apparent, Russian and English, with Prince Alfred, too, were there. We sat a while, and then we came back home. After an interval we went to St. Thomas's Hospital, which is opposite the Houses of Parliament. This hospital has been built by the nation. It was founded in the time of Edward IV., and it is now two or three years since it was completed. It possesses property held in mortmain; and from the time of its foundation till now people, of their own free will, have collected money and given it for the sustentation of the hospital; for the medicine and food of the whole of the patients is gratis. It is a very beautiful building, and there are always in it four or five hundred patients, men and women, children or adults. Dr. Tholozan, too, was present. The Director of the Sanitary Board of London, whose name is Simon (J. Simon, Esq., Medical Officer, Local Government Board), together with other London physicians and surgeons of repute, were also there. The little children had each a separate bed and bed clothes, with nice clean garments; to each one, for the purpose of amusement, playthings and pretty things, that had been collected, were given. As attendants, many women were there.

We went to other wards where the men were. In spite of their ailments, they shouted loudly their hurrahs.

On the lower floor they have appliances, by which, having placed a sick man on a bed, they lift him to the upper stories without his having to move. The first stone of the building of this hospital was laid by the Sovereign.

We next proceeded to the residence of Lord Dārgīl (the Duke of Argyll), Secretary for India. His house was at a distance. We went through Hyde Park, &c., and arrived there. The wife of the Indian Secretary, who is the sister of the Duke of Sutherland, and an elderly woman, together with a daughter of the Sovereign, who is the wife of the son of the Indian Secretary, came forward. Having shaken hands and strolled a space in the garden, we went into a room, sat down to table, and ate some fruit. The Duke of Sutherland was also of the party. We then went down into the garden, where a tent was pitched, in which we took a seat. A Scotch individual, in the Scotch garb, came and for a while played the pipe and drone (bagpipes). Another individual in the Scotch garb, danced a Scotch dance. He arranged four swords on a round board, and for a time danced about the swords.

An individual of celebrity, whose name is Viteston (Sir Charles Wheatstone, F.R.S.), has invented a kind of telegraph, such that when, for instance, you converse by its means from London to Tehrān, the sentence becomes printed upon paper, and can be read with perfect facility. They had set one up in the garden; we went and saw it in operation.

We then returned, and alighted in Hyde Park at a structure which the Sovereign has reared to the memory of her husband (Prince) Albert, which we inspected. It is all of stone and has upon it most beautiful sculptures, in which they have represented the celebrities, the poets, and the painters of the world, and others, in stone; the reason being that (Prince) Albert himself was a man of science and of art. The crowd, however, prevented us from examining it properly; so we turned away, mounted our carriage, went home, and in the evening drove to the theatre of Drulelam (Drury-Lane Theatre).

In the streets the crowds were prodigious. We reached the Theatre, where the Heir-Apparent of England had also come. He met me, and gave me his hand. We went up into a box near the stage and took our seats. Prince Alfred came also. There was an opera, and also a ballet. They sang and danced charmingly. The dancers were graceful and prettily dressed. The theatre has five tiers of seats. It is somewhat small, but very pretty. There was a young woman, a celebrated singer, of the name of Nelson (Nielson), from Sweden, whom the Heir-Apparent caused to be sent up, and with whom some conversation was had. She was very loquacious and shrewd. She goes every year to the theatres of (St.) Peter(sburg), the New World, &c., and makes a large income. She is now married to a Frenchman of the name of Gousseau.

The play over, we passed, in returning home, by St. James's Palace. The palace is an ancient building; and the Court of England is still designated as the Court of St. James. The Sovereign used formerly to sit there in state (at drawing-rooms); but since the death of her husband she has never gone there. At present, the mother of the Duke of Cambridge is held to reside there. We reached home.

Yesterday the Sanī'u-'d-Dawla left to go to Paris, in order to arrange our halting-places and the like.

Well; had we the wish to write as they deserve all the particulars of the city of London or of all England, we should have to write a voluminous History of England; but during a stay of only eighteen days in London it really has not been possible to write more than we have done. In justice (we can but say that), the demeanour of the English, and everything of theirs, is extremely well regulated and governed, and admirable. In respect to populousness, the wealth of the people, the commerce, the arts, business, and dolce far niente, they are the chief of all nations.

Saturday, 9th (5th July).—To-day we have to go to the seaport of Cherbourg, in France. In the morning early I arose from sleep. During these eighteen days of our stay in London, every day has been cloudy. Many purchases, too, have been made in London.

Well; the Heir-Apparent of England, Lord Granville, —the Foreign Secretary, Lord Sarni (Lord Sydney?),

Prince Alfred, Prince Arthur, and others came. We mounted a carriage and drove for the station. Large crowds were present, showing great regret. It was evident that the people of England were all sorry and grieved in their hearts at our departure. We arrived at the Victoria Station, where the Heir-Apparent took leave and returned. Prince Alfred, however, with Prince Arthur and the Grand-Vazīr, took seats in our car. The son of the Hakīmu-'l-Mamālik remained behind in London to study.

We started for the seaport town of Portsmouth, the journey occupying three hours, or less. But on our arrival (in England) we did not travel by this road. In (point of) proximity the (proper) port (for proceeding from London to the continent) is connected with our former route. The following are among the towns and populous places through which we passed: Mitcham, Epsom, Dorking, Horsham, Arundel, Chichester.

We reached the seaport town, where crowds were collected. They fired guns from the forts and ships. The Admiral-in-Chief resident there, Reaucham Seymur (Rear-Admiral Frederick Beauchamp Paget Seymour, C.B.), received us; after which we went on board a French ship,—a vessel named "L'Aigle," which had belonged to Napoleon III., he having ordered it to be built as a yacht for himself; but now that a republic has come about, its name has been changed, and they have called her "Rapide." She is a beautiful ship.

We breakfasted. M. Nicholas—the French Interpreter, together with the interpreter Biberstein, M.

Méliné—newly-appointed French Envoy to Tehrān, M. Bel—lately French Chargé d'Affaires in Tehrān, M. Blie—captain of the ship, and the other naval officers, were received in audience. A few minutes later the ship started on the voyage. The direct, best, and nearest route is that by the port of Dover, in England, to Calais, a French port, which is a sea voyage of only one hour and a half; whereas, by this route from Portsmouth to Cherbourg, the sea voyage is of eight hours' duration.

Well; there was another ship behind us, in which our household and the rest were embarked. Four large English ships of war, too, were on both sides of us as (a convoy of) honour. As soon as we got to sea the waves arose; the weather, too, was cloudy and hazy. Every one became so unwell that not an individual could either walk about or sit down. They all fell prostrate. I myself became so ill that I went and lay down until we arrived near to the port of Cherbourg. Eight tillers (sail) of French men-of-war came out to mid-channel to meet us. They fired many guns. The English ships, too, having fired guns, consigned us to the French and returned.

We arrived at our port by the time of sunset, the ship dropped anchor, all became quiet, and we had dinner.

French officials, as here below detailed, came on board: Vice-Admiral Penhoat,—Marine Prefect of the town of Cherbourg, Vice-Admiral Regnaud,—Naval Commander-in-Chief, General Dumoulin,—Commanding-in-Chief the forces at Cherbourg, M. Vaultier,—Prefect of the

Department of La Manche, M. Larnac,—Prefect of the town of Cherbourg; as also other officials, adjutants, &c., military and naval; who were received in audience and returned. On board the men-of-war a beautiful illumination and exhibition of fireworks took place.

[1] The Persian word "pādshāh," rendered by "Sovereign" in this work, applies to Emperors, Kings, or Queens equally. There is no exact equivalent for either in Persian.—J. W. R.

CHAPTER V.

FRANCE, GENEVA; 19 DAYS.

SUNDAY, 10th (6th July).—To-day we have to reach Paris. We rose early in the morning, went down into a boat, and pushed off for the shore. The weather was very cold. We arrived at the landing,—a very handsome flight of steps. A very pretty and choice triumphal arch had been erected also, of flowers and shrubs, bunches of flowers, chandeliers and the like, various devices with weapons—such as pistols, muskets, lance-heads, &c. In truth, they had displayed talent.

We went up the steps; a numerous assemblage of officials, military, naval, and civil, national guards, Government clerks, and the like, were drawn up in ranks; and the Prefect of La Manche presented the whole. I, too, inquired after their healths. And thus we reached the train and took our seats in a carriage, which had yet to wait a little.

The majority of the women and men in France are small made and attenuated of limb; they are not like the inhabitants of Russia, Germany, and England, but more resemble the people of the East.

The fortifications of Cherbourg are very strong. Facing

the sea, it has turrets and batteries of great power; and on the land side also, it has its works and a wide ditch always full of water. The capture of this city by force would be a very difficult matter. The town is not so very large, but it has a population of more than thirty-seven thousand souls. It is an excellent harbour. The commencements of the forts date from the days of the first Napoleon; they were completed in the time of Napoleon III., but some work is still going on.

Well; our train started. To-day we traversed the province of Normandy,—a beautiful country, abounding with produce. Extensive meadows, trees, flowers, grass, in abundance were there. Beautiful oxen, mares, sheep, are kept in great numbers, by reason of the plentiful pasturages which they possess. We saw quantities of shrubs and of tamarisk-trees, which cause it to resemble Persia. To-day I saw the greater part of the flowers and trees of Persia in these parts, such as the willow, the "tabrīzī", the tamarisk, and others. The surface of the soil hereabouts is all up-hill and down-dale, with many peaks. The apples of the province are famous for their good quality; and we saw large numbers of apple-trees.

Well; we reached the city of Caen, the capital of Normandy. We stopped there half an hour, when breakfast was taken. It is a very pretty town. After leaving it, we passed through many "holes in mountains," one of them being about a league in length. During the transit (through these), one feels a very suffocating kind of sensation about the heart. From Cherbourg to Paris the journey by rail occupies eight hours, and the distance is ninety leagues. At about an hour to sunset we arrived in the environs of Paris; we passed over the river Seine by a bridge that is outside the city, and so entered into the capital. Thence, taking the line of railway that goes all round the city within the continuous walls, we reached the quarter named Passy, where the whole of the present Government and leading men of France, together with a crowd of spectators, were awaiting us.

The Saní'u-'d-Dawla, Marshal MacMahon—the present Chief of the French Government, the Duke de Broglie—the newly appointed Minister of Foreign Affairs, other officials, ministers, &c., were at the station. We alighted; compliments passed with the Marshal and the Foreign Minister. There was an avenue that they had carpeted and greatly ornamented. We walked a certain distance on foot, and the Marshal presented the commanders, the military officers, and others, until we reached a carriage, in which we took our seat with the Grand-Vazír, the Marshal, and the Minister for Foreign Affairs. Our suite, too, were seated in other carriages. We started, and a volley of cannon was fired. From that place to the Corps Législatif, our appointed quarters, on both sides of the road were posted infantry of the line, cavalry, and gens-d'armes, all in beautiful uniforms. Behind the ranks of the troops crowds of spectators were standing. We passed through the Bois de Boulogne, which is outside of the fortifications; again entered the enceinte of the city; went along the Avenue de la Grande Armée, and arrived at the Arc de Triomphe, which is one of the grand structures of the first Napoleon, is built of stone, and on it are sculptured, within, without, and all round, the battles of that leader. It is a very imposing pile; but in the late wars with Prussia, great damage has been done to it by cannon-balls.

The interior of the Arc de Triomphe was carpeted, chairs were placed there, and much ornamentation had been achieved. Here we alighted and sat a while. The Governor of the city, a fat man and bulky, named M. Duval, came with the "Kalāntar" (mayor), and made a speech, to which we replied. Several persons charged to represent the Deputies of the city of Paris came also and made a speech, which we answered. We then rose, remounted our carriage, and entered the avenue of the Champs Élysées, which is very spacious and pleasing. On both sides of all these avenues through which we passed they have planted handsome trees, and built beautifully-grand houses. And so we reached the Place de la Concorde, where they have erected a lofty obelisk brought from Egypt. This is a charming public place, having two basins of water with fountains. The fountains do not always play; but whenever they wish, they cause them to flow. Passing by a bridge over the Seine, we entered the edifice which they have assigned to us. At the foot of the steps of this edifice M. Buffet,—the actual President of the National Assembly, together with some of the Deputies, made a speech based on congratulations for our arrival; and we replied thereto.

We went upstairs. It has rooms and halls spacious and very handsome. The bedstead which they had prepared for us, was the bedstead of the first Napoleon at the time when he espoused Marie Louise, daughter of the Sovereign of Austria.

To-day we noticed a singular frame of mind in the French. First of all, they still keep up the state of mourning that followed the German war, and they are all, young or old, sorrowful and melancholy. The dresses of the women, ladies, and men, are all dresses used for mourning; with little ornamentation, and very plain. Now and then some of the people shouted: ".Vive le Maréchal," "Vive le Schah de Perse;" from another one I heard, as I strolled about by night, a loud voice saying: "May his reign and rule be firm and enduring." From the whole of these (circumstances) it becomes evident that there are at present in France numerous parties who desire a monarchy; but they are in three sections, one desiring the son of Napoleon, another the dynasty of Louis-Philippe, and the third Henry the Fifth, who is of the Bourbon family; and although this and the family of Louis-Philippe are really one race, they have distinctions. The wishers for a republic, on the other hand, have great power; but they are not all of one mind. Some are for a Red Republic, which is a fundamental commonweal. Others are for a moderate republic, in which monarchical institutions shall be found, without a monarch's existing. Others again wish otherwise. Among all these diversities of opinion it is now a very difficult matter to govern, and the consequences of these incidents will surely eventuate in many difficulties, unless that all combine on one plan and establish either a pure monarchy or a pure republic.

Then, France is the most powerful of States, and all must take her into their calculations; whereas, with all these dissidences it is a difficult matter for her to preserve her institutions.

Well; the troops drawn up to-day in line were nearly twenty thousand in number. This edifice which is allotted to us as our residence, was formerly the Council-House, *i.e.*, the House for the meeting of the Deputies of the nation. Since the expulsion of the third Napoleon from the sovereignty, and the establishment of a republic in France, the Deputies and the Government have all gone to Versailles, and have left the city of Paris entirely void of the governmental administrations. The city of Paris is now in reality the property of the peasantry and common people, who do whatever they like, as the Government has no adequate means of repression. The palace of the Tuileries, which was the finest building in the world, is now a mass of ruins, as the men of the Commune set fire to it. Nothing remains of the palace but its walls. We were sadly grieved for this; but, thanks be to God, the palace of the Louvre, which adjoins that of the Tuileries, has been saved and is not destroyed.

The Hôtel-de-Ville, one of the fine buildings of the world, and the Palace of the Legion of Honour, were entirely burnt. The column of the Place Vendôme, which the first Napoleon cast out of the materials of the enemy's guns, and on which he set up his own statue, pourtraying all his wars around the same, has been broken up by the Commune, and carried away, so that nothing of it remains but the block that was the base of the column.

Paris is a beautiful and graceful city, with a delicious climate. It generally enjoys sunshine, thus much resembling the climate of Persia.

In the evening we mounted a carriage and drove about the city with the Mu'tamadu-'l-Mulk and General Arture. We passed through the Rue de Rivoli and the Boulevard Sébastopol, — well-known thoroughfares, through the Place Vendôme, and by the palace of the Tuileries, near to certain bazaars and the like. The lamps of the city are all illuminated with gas; so that it is a very bright, beautiful, and charming city. Numbers of people were seated in carriages and driving about; or, seated in the cafés and similar places, were enjoying themselves.

The river Seine is not like the river Thames. It has less width and less water. Large ships cannot navigate it.

Within our palace there is a pretty little garden, with a basin of water and a fountain of porphyry in three stages. A tent, too, has been erected there. From here one can go to the Ministry of Foreign Affairs, which has been assigned as quarters for our princes. It is a grand and beautiful building, where formerly the department of the Minister for Foreign Affairs was located. It has a very pretty flower-garden; and a small fountain throws up its water. The upper floor of our palace possesses a handsome bath-room, which I admired exceedingly, and which is supplied with hot and cold water, so that in whichever way one wishes to have it, there is no difficulty.

Monday, 11th (7th July).—After breakfast we mounted our carriage and set out for a drive about town. We passed along a street named Parc-Monceau—a very beautiful street, by a very pretty flower-garden, and arrived at the Arc de Triomphe, going from thence towards the Bois de Boulogne, where we first visited the Jardin d'Acclimatisation. Here we alighted and entered the garden. There were some flowers; and there was a place built up of rocks, like a natural mountain. Passing by these, we came to the park for wild animals, and for birds. They had prepared nettings of wire around rooms, and within these they had set up trees and introduced water for the use of the animals and birds. We here saw various kinds of birds and of parrots from the New World, Africa, India, and Australia. There were also monkeys and other things. There is an animal called the kangaroo, that is found in Australia,—very similar to the jerboa. It is a singular thing; it jumps swiftly, but cannot walk. Its fore-legs are short, its hind-legs long. It must jump always. It is of the size of a large jackal. The female has a pouch on the lower part of her belly, where she puts her young after they are born, and so jumps and runs about. They are very swift runners.

There were some very curious pheasants, with beautiful plumage, of all colours, that we saw also. There were likewise two elephants on which litters were arranged, and so women and children rode about on them. There was also a droshka in which a man was seated, harnessed to an ostrich, which drew it about easily, having the strength of a small horse.

After a long stroll, we went to the aquarium, which resembled those of other countries, but was very circumscribed and of no account. The Director of these gardens and plants is (M.) Drouin de l'Huys, who formerly, in the time of Napoleon, was Minister of Foreign Affairs. He was not himself present, but was represented by his substitute (M.) Geoffroy de Saint-Hilaire, who pointed out to us the plants, and other objects.

We now mounted again and went for a drive in the Bois de Boulogne, where there was an island in the midst of a piece of water. We got into a boat and went there. A military officer chanced to be present on the island, who gave us some account of the circumstances of the war, and pointed out to us where cannon-shot and musket-balls had struck the trees. The greater part of the trees bore the marks of shot; from which it was evident that severe engagements had occurred in that neighbourhood, both with the Prussians and with the Commune. At the further end of the island there was a small wooden pavilion called Pavillon de l'Impératrice, *i.e.*, the pavilion of the wife of Napoleon. It was built of wood, was very handsome, and small.

Having admired this for a while, we returned to the other side of the water, remounted our carriage, and, wandering as we went, drove home.

Again in the evening we went out, and noticed a covered bazaar, like a corridor. Here we made a few purchases and returned to our palace.

It is extremely difficult to write up our diary in Paris day by day and in detail. Our strolls about the beautiful promenades by night as well as by day leave no chance for us to carry on the diary. However, all that is needful shall be entered in a succinct manner.

One day the members of the Diplomatic Corps came all to an audience. There is here an Ambassador, or a Minister, or a Chargé d'Affaires, from every Government,—even from Japan, and from the Republic of the Island of Haïti. The Ambasosadrs were: Chigi—the Papal Nuncio, *i.e.*, the envoy of the Pope; Lord Lyons—Ambassador of England; Olozaga — Ambassador of Spain; Prince Orloff—Ambassador of Russia, whose left eye was struck by a ball at the siege of Silistria during the Crimean war, and became injured; he also received other wounds from sabre-cuts and the like; he had a black bandage tightly bound over his injured eye; Appony—Ambassador of Austria; Server Pasha—Ambassador of Turkey; M. Nigra—Envoy of Italy; Mr. Washburn—Envoy of the United States of America; Naonobon Sameshima—Envoy of Japan.

We here received also Prince Menschikoff, who attended us in Russia, and Mīrzā 'Abdu-'r-Rahīm Khān, the Sā'idu-'l-Mulk, (Persian) Envoy at (St.) Peter(sburg). Furthermore, we received M. Pichon, M. Miniac, and M. Sartiges, former French Envoys at Tehrān, as well as M. Mouny, a former French Chargé d'Affaires at that capital. They were all fatter, and all younger looking.

One day after breakfast we went to the palace and park of Versailles. The weather was very sultry. We went in state. There were great crowds on both sides of the road. We passed along the Champs Élysées, by the Arc de Triomphe, through the Bois de Boulogne, and across the river Seine. The prefect and other authorities of the department of Seine et Oise, a separate department on the other side of the river, came to an audience and delivered an address, to which we replied. We then proceeded through the town of Sèvres—famous for its manufactory of porcelain, the village of Chaville, and the village of Ville-D'Avray, so reaching Versailles. Troops of cavalry and infantry were drawn out, and stood in a line on either side of our road. Great crowds were also collected.

We went to a mansion that was the residence of M. Buffet, the President of the National Assembly, and one of the palaces built by Louis XIV.; that is to say, the whole of Versailles, palace and park, was called into existence by him. I saw some beautiful paintings and portraits in these few rooms. The whole palace is of stone, and very solidly built. It is the first building of the Franks in point of sculptures, paintings, and architecture.

M. Buffet came to meet us at the bottom of the stairs, the other Ministers of the Government being present. We went upstairs into a room, and sat down on a chair. The wife of M. Buffet came into our presence. We then rose; and by the same route through which we had arrived, we returned; until, at about half way, we came to a palace where Marshal MacMahon has his quarters. Alighting there, the Marshal, with other commanders, met us, and we went upstairs, taking a seat in a room. That place was also an imposing, handsome, and highly decorated palace, being part of the pile of Versailles. The wife of the Marshal was received in our presence. She is a very noble woman. The Marshal has one son, grown up, apparently of about seventeen or eighteen years of age; also two daughters. They came into the room. The Duc de Broglie—Minister of Foreign Affairs—was also there.

We now descended; we and the Marshal took seats in a carriage, went into the gardens of Versailles, and drove about. They have many basins and fountains of water, the source of which, like that of the fountains at the Crystal Palace of London, is derived from a steam-engine. They had opened the sources and let the water on in the fountains. There was a lake below the basins and fountains, very beautiful and spacious avenues, forest trees, the heads of which were all intertwined so as to form a kind of roof, with every here and there a circular open space of grass with trees around, having in the centre a large basin with a fountain of great altitude. It is a very charming place.

One spot was formed into a kind of artificial mountain, with a cascade falling from the mountain. Several marble statues were placed behind the cascade,—one, a group named Apollo, who was the specific deity of manly beauty, of light, and of poetry. He is adorning (himself), the others round him are holding a mirror, flowers, or implements of the toilet. It was so beautiful a piece of statuary, that one could not even imagine it. I formed the desire to go up near to these statues under the cascade. The Marshal and General Arture said it would be very difficult to go there, as the path was altogether precipitous, of rocks, and steep. I said I would go; I alighted from the carriage, and went up. It is true that the way was disagreeable; but to us, who had seen and traversed much worse paths in the hunting-grounds of Persia, it offered no difficulty. When we had arrived near the statues, General Arture came (also); but, meeting with a fall, all his clothes were bemired, and his sword was either bent or broken. The Marshal likewise came up; but with great difficulty, and with the assistance of several persons. But this manner of getting up there by a Marshal and a general of France, is in no way derogatory to their firmness and courage. Well; the statues were very beautiful, though somewhat soiled, and covered with cobwebs.

Coming down from there, we went to another place made like a circus. In the middle of it were a basin of water and a fountain, and all round it two rows of stone columns. Between these columns was a tall stone basin on a pedestal, from the middle of which a very lofty fountain spouted. There were about eighty or ninety basins of water, from each one of which a fountain sprang, the whole of the columns, fountains, and floor, &c., being of stone.

In like manner, in other parts of the garden, there are numerous fountains, marble statues, and other adornments, with many spacious and beautiful avenues, to do full justice to which, in writing their description, is an impossibility: what is requisite is that a person should see the whole for himself. Women and men, spectators, had formed a rare crush; they uttered cries, they shouted hurrahs.

We turned back and went upstairs in the palace, strolling about for a while through the apartments. Marshal Canrobert, and Palikao—who commanded the expedition to China, were received in audience, and conversed with. Palikao is now unemployed. He said that from want of something to do, he was engaged in writing a diary of (his expedition to) China. Canrobert is also out of employ, but is a very able commander, possessing judgment and firmness. In the Sebastopol war he commanded in chief, and at the siege of Metz was under the command of Marshal Bazaine. At the surrender of that fortress to the Germans he was among the captives, and was greatly mortified at being under Bazaine's command.

We next saw the sons of Louis-Philippe. In the time of Napoleon they were expelled from France and went to England, returning to the French territory after the republic (had been proclaimed). We saw two of them to-day; one, the Duc d'Aumale; the other, the Prince de Joinville. The Duc d'Aumale is a very talented man; de Joinville is also a handsome prince, but is somewhat hard of hearing. The Comte de Paris, grandson to Louis-Philippe, and heir to the royalty of the House of Orleans, was not there; *i.e.*, he had gone to a house that he possesses at a summer station near Paris. We had some conversation with the princes, who then retired. They are now deputies in the Assembly on the part of the people. As they were officers in the military (and naval) service in the time of their father, so they now also, on state occasions, wear military (or naval) uniforms. They have a claim to the sovereignty of France, up to the point which God may ordain. The names and orders of these princes are the following: the eldest son of Louis-Philippe is the Duc de Nemours; after him, de Joinville; next, the Duc d'Aumale; and then the Duc de Monpensier—who is now in Spain and has a claim to the sovereignty of that country. The Comte de Paris is a grandson of Louis-Philippe, and son of the Duc d'Orléans, who was a son of Louis-Philippe, and his heir-apparent; when he fell from his carriage and died, his son became the heir-apparent.

Well; after a while Marshal MacMahon came, and we went to the room in which is the bedstead, with the bedding, of Louis XIV. After seeing these we went to table to dinner. The table was very long; the dinner very good. The most part of those present were military commanders and officers, deputies, and the like. On our right was seated M. Buffet, the President of the Assembly; to our left, the Minister of Foreign Affairs. Opposite to us was Marshal MacMahon, with the Grand-Vazīr to his right. In like manner, the princes of Persia, with the others, were seated along the two sides. The Sanī'ü-'d-Dawla stood behind our chair and acted as interpreter. It passed off very pleasantly.

The (dining-) hall was a long apartment, very handsome, and highly decorated, with numerous chandeliers.

After dinner we came down stairs, and I, with the Marshal, took my seat in a carriage, proceeding to witness the illuminations of the palace and gardens. Armour-wearing cavalry, each man holding a flambeau in his hand, preceded us; and the crowds were very great. Afterwards we turned in another direction of the gardens, where there was a lake. The further side of this was arranged in stages, over which water flowed as in a cascade, while fountains spouted from the basins. Great numbers of commanders and grandees, the members of the Diplomatic Body, nobles, notables, deputies, and others, were present. They had placed a chair, and on it we took our seat. Then all sat down, and a very beautiful display of fireworks took place. It was moonlight; the weather, too, was extremely beautiful and pleasant.

At the conclusion of the fireworks we mounted our carriage, and went past St. Cloud—which was a noble royal palace, but took fire, and was burnt in the German war, though its avenues and park are still left,—through the Bois de Boulogne, to the city, and home. On our road we everywhere conversed with General Arture.

One day we went to the Invalides, where are seen the tomb of the first Napoleon, those of his commanders and brothers, together with others of older commanders of the days of Louis XIV., &c. At our quarters, which were formerly the Palace of the National Assembly, *i.e.*, at the Palais de Bourbon, there is a vast area fronting the Invalides, with avenues full of trees. We arrived there. The aged veteran soldiers, wounded, some without arms or legs, and some blind, were drawn up in line, and did us military honour, we returning their salute. In the court of the Invalides are some large old cannon, mortars, and the like. The Governor of the Invalides, a very aged personage, and palsied, was present, whose name was Martinprai. He came to meet us with his aides-de-camp and other officers. He was formerly a Governor in Algeria, and Chief of the Staff in the Crimean and Italian campaigns.

We entered the chapel, where was a handsome altar of stone, with gilt-work, which Louis-Philippe, the former King of the French, had set up. It is a grand structure. On the other side of the altar, under a dome, is the tomb of the first Napoleon, whose body was brought from the island of St. Helena by Louis-Philippe, and buried here. The stone that covers the tomb, of a pea-green colour, was brought from the island of Corsica; while the stone above that, a most beautiful Siberian stone, with a ruddy tint, was sent by the Russian Emperor Nicholas. The general structure of this chapel of the Invalides is of the time of Louis XIV.; but the altar and some other of its arrangements were constructed by Louis-Philippe. It was the latter who excavated the interior of the dome, in which the sarcophagus of the tomb is placed. Around it, above, is a walk to which people come to visit the tomb. The palace of the Invalides is a very noble pile, the dome of which was gilt by Napoleon.

We saw there a few veterans who had been in the battles of Waterloo, Friedland, or Iena, who were still hale and hearty, and who gave descriptions of those battles. The following are their names: Captain Duchemin, Chassy, Branche.

On the other side of the tomb was a place where, in a glass case, they had placed the hat worn in his battles by the first Napoleon. We lifted the hat and examined it long. We held in our hands the hat of a very great monarch and commander. It was evident from the hat itself that Napoleon had always worn this very hat which was a plain hat. The sword of Napoleon that was by his side on the field of Austerlitz, was also there. We took it up, and examined it. The sword was small and straight; its hilt was of gold, but the sword was rusted, and could not be drawn from the scabbard. With the utmost veneration did we replace both articles, and came away.

We now proceeded to the museum, in which they have collected and arranged specimens of ancient and modern cannon, with inventions relating thereto, ancient weapons of commanders and champions of old, quantities of armour for man and horse, all ticketed with a number and with the names of their owners. There were also other places used as armories, &c., but, as we were somewhat fatigued, we deferred to another day a visit to them, and returned home.

The present number of inmates of the Invalides, officers and men, is five hundred and ninety souls. Of these, thirty-five are from the days of the first Napoleon, the rest from later times. The palace was founded in A.D. 1670 by order of Louis XIV., Louvois being then the Minister of War, and its builder.

There are thirty-two pieces of artillery at the gates of the Invalides, which are fired when any event of importance occurs, such as a great victory or the like. On our arrival in Paris, too, these guns of the Invalides were fired.

The flags taken from the enemy in battle in the time of the first Napoleon, and since, are kept at the Invalides, as are also those taken in the days of Louis XIV., downwards. Around the tomb of Napoleon forty-six flags are disposed, taken by himself in battles; while within the chapel other two hundred and forty-five flags are seen, taken at earlier periods, or later.

The following are some of the commanders of France (Marshals), ancient and modern, buried in the Invalides, where most of those officers have their tombs: Turenne, Vauban, Lannes, Colbert,—who were marshals and ministers of Louis XIV.; Mortier, Jourdain,—generals of the first Napoleon. Around the tomb of Napoleon are those of Jerome, his brother, of Marshal Duroc, and of Marshal Bertrand.

Three days before our arrival in France, two trains came into collision on the Cherbourg Railway, when a number of people were killed or wounded.

M. Crémieux, one of the French national deputies, and a Jew, who was always in opposition to Napoleon III., and is a marvellous orator, came to an audience. He is an old man, and very short. He still speaks in the Assembly, and is in opposition to the Government.

The celebrated Rothschild, a Jew also, who is exceedingly rich, came to an audience, and we conversed with him. He greatly advocated the cause of the Jews, mentioned the Jews of Persia, and claimed tranquillity for them. I said to him : " I have heard that you, brothers, possess a thousand crores of money. I consider the best thing to do would be that you should pay fifty crores to some large or small State, and buy a territory in which you could collect all the Jews of the whole world, you becoming their chiefs, and leading them on their way in peace, so that you should no longer be thus scattered and dispersed." We laughed heartily, and he made no reply. I gave him an assurance that I do protect every alien nationality that is in Persia.

M. Lesseps, so well known, who has joined the Mediterranean to the Red Sea,—*i.e.*, a large company having been formed, has, through the exertions of this personage, opened that road, and by this means shortened for commerce the passage to India, Persia, China, &c., from Europe, by about two thousand leagues,—came to an audience, together with his son, a youth. He has now a fresh scheme in his head,—that of making a railway from the town of Orenburg in Russia to the city of Samarqand, and thence on to Peshawur in British India. But this is a notion very remote (from reason) and distant (from practicability).

Nadar, a Parisian photographer of talent, had an audience, and took our photograph. Formerly, he has several times made ascents in balloons; but has now dropped that fancy, and occupies himself with his photography. He is a pleasant man and corpulent.

M. Tardieu, Chief of the Sanitary Council of Paris,

had an audience, together with Larrey, a distinguished surgeon, and son of the Larrey who was Surgeon-in-Chief to Napoleon I., and Jules Cloquet, uncle to the Cloquet who was Principal Physician to the late Shāh (Muhammad Shāh, father of the present monarch), and also physician to ourselves, who of himself by night inadvertently at Tehrān drank some (tincture of) cantharides in lieu of wine, and died (in consequence).

M. Bouré, a former Minister Plenipotentiary at Tehrān, and subsequently Ambassador at Constantinople and elsewhere in the time of Napoleon III., was also received and conversed with at length. He is a man of ability.

Well; very many Prussian shots struck this very Palais Bourbon, so 'that the marks thereof are still patent.

One day we went to Longchamps to a review of troops. We breakfasted and mounted our carriage. All (our suite) accompanied us. We went by way of the Champs Élysées, the Arc de Triomphe, and the Bois de Boulogne. In the middle of this latter Marshal MacMahon was waiting with (a number of) generals, officers, and others, on horseback. There were also great multitudes of women and men. The Duc de Nemours,—eldest son of Louis-Philippe, whom we had not before seen, was also there, mounted, and we conversed with him. I, too, alighted from my carriage, and mounted my charger "Blaze."

General Ladmirault, the Commandant of the garrison of Paris, together with his staff, *i.e.*, his aides-de-camp, was present.

Well; in this very order did we proceed and came upon the armour-wearing cavalry—the Cuirassiers, and the light cavalry—the Hussards. They were drawn up on either side (of our road), and were a thousand strong.

After passing down between these cavalry, we went on to the plain and meadow of Longchamps—a spacious piece of grassland. To our left an artificial mountain had been constructed, down which much water poured, like a waterfall, and which is a part of the Bois de Boulogne.

The regular troops (on the ground), too, were about a hundred and twenty battalions; but each battalion had only about four or five hundred men present, not more; the remainder being on furlough at home. We went down in front of the ranks of the infantry and artillery. These troops are from the remoter environs of Paris. For instance, some of the battalions had come a distance of thirty leagues to be present at this review. There were three hundred pieces of artillery present, harnessed to their horses. The whole of the troops in military fashion, and, as a mark of respect and honour, drooped their colours. We, too, returned the salutes.

Round about the grassland, within the woods, up in the trees, everywhere were people.

After inspecting the ranks, we went to some rooms built of timber long ago on this plain for the purpose of similar reviews and horse-races. We went upstairs and took our seat; upon which the Marshal went into the grass and meadow. French commanders, together with certain military attachés—Ottoman, Austrian, Russian,

Prussian, drew up in front of the Marshal. In the upper chamber where we were, the French Minister for Foreign Affairs, the President of the Assembly—M. Buffet, Marshal Canrobert, and others, were present. As Canrobert is not now in the army, and has no appointment, he was not on horseback.

Well; the infantry and artillery came and marched past; after them, the cavalry did the same. The whole of the deputies of France,—five hundred in number, had come, and had all taken their seats. In the building to our left the Diplomatic Corps, and others, were seated. The wife of Marshal MacMahon was there. Around us were seated an assemblage of graceful women and ladies. As each battalion passed by, the national deputies clapped hands and shouted hurrahs. Marshal MacMahon, too, took off his hat to each battalion. It lasted nearly three hours before the whole of the infantry, artillery, and cavalry had marched past. All included, too, they were more than eighty thousand men. The forces went through an admirable review.

After all those defeats and ruin of the French, no idea had been entertained of such a collection and such discipline of their forces. They were beautifully dressed; the muskets of the men were the same old Chassepots, and the artillery the same guns used in the German war and anterior to that. When all was over we returned home by about sunset.

Another day we went again to Longchamps to witness the horse-racing. The Marshal came himself to our residence, where we mounted a carriage and started.

The rest (of our people) went also. We followed the same route to the Bois de Boulogne that we had taken on the day of the review. From thence, however, we went behind the cascade, but only to arrive at the same stand where we were seated to witness the march past. The Minister of Foreign Affairs, M. Buffet, the wife of the Marshal, the commanders and others, the Ottoman Ambassador, and the Austrian Ambassador, were there. Women and men in multitudes were assembled around the race-course. Four heats were run. They had given to each race the name of a Persian province; such as Ispāhān, Shīrāz, &c. In the first heat they ran half round the course, which is one horse-distance. One jockey, whose dress was green, in accordance with the Persian ribbon, won the race. In the next two heats they ran round the entire course; but, as the distance is not great, most of the horses came in together. The horse that gets ahead, say, by one head and neck, of the others, is counted to have been first in. The Persian rule for horse-racing is better, and affords a better spectacle. The Persian race-course is half a league round; six rounds, that is, three leagues, and sometimes seven rounds, are run in one heat. Whichever horse gets the start has given proof of his power. Here, where at the utmost once round is the length of a race, which is but half a league, the powers of a horse are not fully brought out in evidence.

In the last race the horses had to jump at full gallop over several barriers of wood about an ell in height

(42 inches), and garnished at top with wild brambles and furze. This was much better as a spectacle.

The races lasted rather more than an hour, after which we returned home. The Marshal went his own way, in order to be present in the evening at the fireworks and illuminations.

We came along, and having reached the Arc de Triomphe, alighted. A number of our suite were with us. We went to the top of the building. It had two hundred and eighty-five steps. It is very high; the steps are narrow and winding, so that it is exceedingly irksome to mount. I got to the top in a breath, but the others followed slowly. From the summit the whole of the city of Paris is visible, with its environs and its forts. The people that were returning from Longchamps and the races were all in sight. From the Bois de Boulogne to the end of the Champs Élysées seven rows of carriages were counted; and in like manner, in the other streets multitudes of carriages were seen. It was a grand spectacle.

After a certain stay there, we descended and remounted our carriage. On starting there was no possibility to get along, by reason of the crowd of vehicles and of pedestrians; so that we had great trouble to reach home.

In the evening the Marshal came; we mounted together, and passing through the Champs Élysées, &c. From our residence to the site of the fireworks, both sides of the road were full of people. This evening there must have been a collection of a crore (half a million) of women and men seen by us. They all shouted: " Vive le Schah de Perse," and they also spoke well of the Marshal, saying: "Vive la France."

They had prepared a beautiful illumination. In all the streets they had suspended crystal lamps like round globes; but the wind somewhat interfered with these.

We drove a long way, and at length reached a place where the river Seine occupied the middle, and the fireworks were prepared on the other side of it. On that side of the river, and opposite to us, was the parade-ground and the military College (the Champ de Mars and the École Militaire), which were all illuminated. The place where we were seated is named the Trocadero. On this side of the river, also, every avenue was illuminated. They had prepared some sumptuous apartments for us, of timber, hung with numerous chandeliers and furnished throughout with curtains newly woven of silk, velvet, and satin. But the wind and the rain somewhat disarranged the preparations. The lamps, however, being lighted with gas, were but seldom extinguished. The fireworks were magnificent. The whole of the French high officials, of the Corps Diplomatique, &c., were present. Thanks be to God, the whole passed off pleasantly, and we came home. The Marshal again rode with us in our carriage to our residence.

During the fireworks the armour-wearing cavalry—the Cuirassiers, to the number of three thousand, passed along the bank of the river, flambeaux in hand, and their band playing. It was a majestic sight.

One evening we went to the Circus, which is near our

quarters. It is a place like a theatre, but is better. They have constructed a circular edifice, around which are tiers of wooden stages, on which people sit. It has also a roof, and many chandeliers are suspended. The middle part of the edifice is like the pit of a gymnasium, strewed with earth. The place is spacious enough to hold three thousand spectators. On the night, more especially, that we went there the assembly was very numerous. They had hired seats at the prices of thirty to fifty tūmāns (12*l.* to 20*l.*). There were some extremely beautiful women. The Grand-Vazīr, the princes, and others, were all present.

The place had three doors. One of these is the door to the stables of the circus, and is near to the arena where the performances go on, as (the horses and actors) come and leave by that way. They have from fifty to sixty very handsome horses, of curious coats. I had never seen similar horses anywhere. There were some extraordinary speckled horses, which must have been worth a thousand or five hundred tūmāns (400*l.* or 200*l.*); and in such a manner had they disciplined and accustomed these horses that, at one signal, they did whatever was desired. The whole of the horses understood the language. Their teacher said: "Stop;" they all stopped; he said: "Go on quickly;" they all ran; he said: "Stand up;" and lo, suddenly they reared up on their hind feet; he said: "Run away;" and they did so. In short, whatever he told them to do, they did. Many a moral lesson could be learnt there. There was a large whip in the hand of the master of the horses, which he continually kept in action, and which made a report like that of a musket.

Beautiful women, elegantly dressed, rode upon the horses and cantered round. They jumped upon the horses' backs, they turned summersaults, forwards and backwards, and again they fell to the earth without receiving injury.

Several men, stationed round the arena, held scarves, and all put up their hands on high. One lovely woman mounted a horse and put him to a canter around the place; and when the horse was at the top of his speed, she, on arriving successively at each scarf, sprang up from the horse's back, turned a summersault backwards, passing over the scarf and coming down on her feet again upon the back of her steed. Twice she succeeded in performing this feat all right; at the third scarf she fell to the ground. She was not hurt, however; but again leaped on the horse and thrice repeated her summersault.

They then held up wooden hoops, and a young man mounted a horse, put him to a gallop, and, as he arrived near the hoops, leaped up, passed through the hoops, and alighted on his feet upon his horse.

Some hoops were prepared like tambourines by having skins stretched over them. The horses, running at a gallop, dashed violently through, tearing the skins to pieces; while a man, mounted on them, leaped over the hoop and again alighted on the horse.

Several women and children mounted and performed such feats as cannot be described or recounted. For instance, in one breath and all together they turned over five hundred (many) summersaults backwards upon the horses;—a thing beyond the power of man. Little children, of graceful forms, turned summersaults in a fashion that cannot be imagined; performed most beautifully upon ropes, so that monkeys and spiders alone could imitate them. In short, they worked wonders, and it was a delightful spectacle.

We went from thence to the palace of the Louvre, where all the philosophers and learned men of Paris were assembled. The Minister of Sciences,—a very fat and tall man, whose name is Batbie, was also present. We went to the ground-floor of the building, where the marble statues, ancient and modern, are arranged. The armour-wearing cavalry, flambeaux in hand, preceded us. The philosophers and learned marched on either side, and the Minister of Sciences walked near us. After a protracted promenade, we came back to our own home.

Some very fine statues had been viewed. There was one large statue of marble, of colossal proportions and gigantic mould, leaning against a mountain and seated with his feet extended, having in his hand a vase out of which water was pouring. This water is the water of the river Tiber, which is seen at Rome, the capital of Italy. There were also some marble statues of Venus, the specific deity of beauty, one of which has been beautifully carved, but both its arms are broke away at about the middle of the upper-arm. There were also many other statues that are rarely to be matched elsewhere.

One day we went to an establishment called the

Panorama, *i.e.*, a scene all round. This is a very wonderful piece of science and art, the inventor of which is a man from the New World. It was not far from our residence. The Grand-Vazīr and the others were all present. We came to a place where a circular edifice rose to view; having a small door. We entered, and first we reached a panorama representing a street,—one of the streets of Paris, at the time when the Prussians were besieging the city. Shot and shell were falling like hail from the sky. The time was the winter season. People were coming out of their houses, holding their wives and children by the hand, and fleeing away. The more one examined this scene with attention, the more real and substantial did it appear, so that one could not tell it was a painted picture and not an actual occurrence, an incident of the struggle. One man had fallen down, his head broken, and the blood flowing. It was impossible to discern the pigment from real blood; and so of the other features of the scene depicted.

From thence we had to ascend by some stairs to a place where was a circular enclosure, from which one could look in every direction. The city of Paris, its forts and environs, the guns and their projectiles, the turmoil of battle and siege, the flight and bursting of shot and shells in the air, all appeared before one. It was as though at that moment one were in the city of Paris, and all the incidents and confusion of the war with the Prussians were before his eyes. In short, unless one see it with his own eyes, he cannot understand how it is that a fictitious picture and a nonexistent circumstance cannot be distinguished from a real event and a current fact.

This place has always been used for the exhibition of works of the same kind, so that whenever people have felt inclined, they could come here, pay their money, and obtain entrance to view the spectacle. The keepers of the place make a good income by it. The wonderful part of the matter is that for a length of time they exhibited here a view of the conquest of Sebastopol, in which the English and French defeated the Russians. This was removed to make place, during a certain season, for a panorama representing the victories obtained over the Austrians by the French forces at Solferino, Magenta, and elsewhere. Now they have depicted and exhibit the defeat and humiliation of France.

But as the air is very much confined in this establishment, should any one remain in it more than ten minutes or so, he becomes subject to headache and other more disagreeable ailments, so we also soon withdrew.

On another occasion we went to the church of Notre Dame and to the Cité, which are on an island in the river Seine, and are within the city of Paris. We passed by the Hôtel de la Monnaie, and by the Conseil d'État— a large edifice and office of one of the Ministers, built in the time of the first Napoleon and utterly burnt by the men of the Commune; so arriving at the church. The priests came forward to meet us. The edifice of the church is very grand, and is entirely of stone. It has been built five or six hundred years. Entering, we surveyed every part of it with great attention. It possesses some pulpits and some railings (screens), of ancient carved wood, exceedingly rich. Its windows are all of coloured glass in various tints and very beautiful. We saw the treasury of the church, where were some chalices and vessels of gold, gilt, silver, and so on. I there held a conversation with the chief priest; I asked him: "What is your belief concerning His Holiness Jesus, on whom be peace; used he to drink wine or not?" All at once, the whole of the priests, as though I had asked a strange question, unanimously said: "He certainly used to drink wine. That is a small matter. He himself also made wine." I then said: "Used he to drink seldom or often?" They all said: "He used even to drink often."

We now left and went to the École des Mines—the mining academy. The name of the Director is M. Doubré. It is a surprising place. In it there are specimens of all the mineral ores of the world, beginning with gold, down to coal, and the like. The whole of them are numbered and ticketed, being kept in glass cases. There is an emerald mine in New Grenada, America, from whence emeralds are now obtained. Some crystals of emerald, of good colour and free from defects, were seen, still imbedded in the matrix. I saw also specimens of the emeralds from the mines of Siberia and elsewhere; but these were all large and of bad quality. In short, there were so many specimens of minerals that their number is unknown; and it would require the power of a person's examining them one by one through a long period and with all attention, of putting questions to the professors and hearing their answers, for him to comprehend something about them; not for us, who had to see the whole of these stones in five minutes, as well as to hear from whence each came, so that it was an utter impossibility to understand anything as to their natures and properties.

We then proceeded to the upper floor, where fossils are kept; *i.e.*, the bones of animals from before the time of Noah's flood, and since then, as well as animals (*qy.*, plants) that have become petrified. There were many strange and marvellous things, a knowledge of which is a science by itself, incompatible with the scope of this narrative. After these wanderings we returned home.

The palace of the Luxembourg is another place to which we one day rambled. This is a stately and extensive palace with its gardens, of the time of Louis XVI., its gardens being now open to the public, so that people go there every day to walk about. Its beds of flowers are very beautiful. The Hôtel de Ville or town-hall being now a ruin and burnt down, this edifice has been assigned as the place for the offices of the city.

On our arrival in the garden, M. Duval, the Prefect of Paris, together with M. Alfand, the city architect, and others, were waiting for us. The streets of Paris,—thus straight, broad, and level, together with the avenues in which trees have been planted so regularly and tastefully, were all planned and laid out on the instructions and under the supervision of M. Haussman, formerly Prefect of Paris in the days of Napoleon, and of this architect.

We sat in the gardens awhile, and then entered the palace to view the pictures and other objects. M. Vautrain, President of the Municipal Council of Paris, was received in audience. This palace of the Luxembourg is one of the finest edifices in Paris; and in it did Louis-Philippe establish the Senate, adding to it a very sumptuous structure in which that body should hold its meetings. The Senate continued to sit here until the end of the reign of Napoleon, but was abolished when republicanism made its appearance, and we saw in that very chamber of the Senate one or two professors who were examining pupils from the colleges. Each pupil who passes this examination, has the right to enter gratis into the other superior places of instruction.

The Senate consisted of one hundred members, more or less, of the magnates, notabilities, and aged commanders of the State, in order that they should not be without something to do. To each of them was assigned a salary of three thousand tūmāns (120*l*.), with a seat in this Council, for the purpose of reconsidering every enactment that came from the Chamber of Deputies; since, until it had received the ratification of this Council, it was not put in force. Now it is altogether abandoned.

Well; the palace had some very magnificent halls and rooms; but alas, a thousand pities,—the whole of these apartments were cut up and partitioned off with wainscotings, and in each subdivision an office, or a committee of the municipal administration, was installed, each with a number of members, and with registers, ledgers, books, and writing materials thrown about, such as paper, pens, ink, and the like. In short, they have deposed the palace from all its majesty. Still, whenever they may desire it, they can remove these boards, and restore the place to its pristine condition. It possessed many beautiful portraits, ancient and modern, which we examined in great detail.

There is in Paris a very large and lofty church, which I had noticed from the top of the Arc de Triomphe, and which is named the Pantheon. Louis XV. built it. First of all it was a church; then a cemetery for men of eminence; and now again, latterly, it is a church and place of worship. There were numerous scaffoldings all around it to carry out repairs, as the Communists, in the days of anarchy, had done much damage to it.

Another church also is in Paris, ranking next after that of Notre Dame, and named St. Sulpice, which is very handsome; and again the Madeleine, built by the first Napoleon, and also extremely grand. Many other churches were likewise seen, of which it is not here necessary to give any account.

The Palais Royal we visited one evening. This is a very extensive place. In the middle of its court there is a garden and a basin of water, around it a colonnade with a walk covered in overhead, and on each side of this walk rows of shops to the number of four or five hundred, where everything is sold—most beautiful jewels, real and supposititious, cutlery, glass, porcelain, and the like. I strolled into every shop, and I laid out sums of money. There were crowds of spectators.

The Mint formed another day's visit. It is called the Hôtel de la Monnaie; its Director is named M. Marcott, and he came to receive us, together with numerous other persons.

We first went to the upper floor, where there is an extensive collection of the coins of different nations, ancient and modern, arranged in glass cases—coins of the ancient monarchs of Persia and Tartary, China, India, and the various countries of Europe; coins of every description, and medals of all kinds.

Next we visited a chamber called the Chamber of Napoleon, in which were collected everything pertaining to that sovereign, such as obverse and reverse dies of his coins, as well as those of the medals struck in his days in commemoration of the battles won or provinces conquered, of decorations for his troops, and the like. A model of the column of (the Place) Vendôme was also there, which column the men of the Commune destroyed altogether. This was about two ells high (7 feet), and made of cast metal. It is the fac-simile of the column itself; but the height of the real column was forty-six ells (161 feet), with a diameter of two ells (7 feet); whereas that of the model is only one span. There were also in that place several figures of Napoleon. A shot from the Communists had come in there, had perforated the glass over the obverse dies, and then penetrated into the wall. They have preserved these things exactly in that condition, and have not changed that glass, saying they so keep it as a memorial. To this I remarked: "It is a sad memorial."

Well; we came down stairs and viewed the coining machinery. It is worked by steam. The coins they were striking were of silver, each of five francs, a very large coin. They said that gold, owing to the sums paid to Prussia, was very scarce. Silver, however, was plentiful, and all the money was silver.

Three large medals, one of gold, another of silver, and the third of copper, were struck, then and there, in our presence, in commemoration of our visit to the Mint, with Persian inscriptions, and offered to us as a present.

We now went forth, and mounting a small steamer, went up the river against the stream, passed beyond the fortifications of the city, and arrived at the spot where the river Marne enters the Seine. From thence we returned. The banks of the river had no beauty. The water of the Seine was scant, and its depth about two ells (7 feet). At a short distance after leaving the city, both sides of the river are occupied by the poor tenements of peasants, principally washerwomen or bathing establishments. These are all built of wood in the stream of the river, as we saw. The baths are in this wise:—a large wooden room with a roof is constructed in the river, through the middle of which the water flows. Every one who wishes to bathe must go into that room and there wash himself. Clothes-washing-houses, again, are on the same principle. They sit in them, and they wash the clothes in them. The clothes-washers are all women. There are also baths heated by steam, where a man may really wash and cleanse his body. After all this, we went home.

The establishment of the Gobelins was the object of another day's excursion, and far enough off it was. It is a very ancient manufactory where they weave carpets, rugs, and similar things, which they sell and buy for fabulous prices. The manufactory belongs to the State. The heads of the manufactory, as also the workmen, are salaried and paid by the Government. These rugs and tapestries are to such a degree beautiful and choice, that they are hung in the halls and apartments of monarchs in lieu of paintings, simply as ornaments. In Prussia, in Belgium, in England, and in France itself, I saw that they are kept in mansions with the utmost consideration. A tapestry was in progress of manufacture, being woven for a hall in the palace of Fontainebleau, a town of the towns of France. But they told me that over each tapestry of that size they had to work eight years. Very long are they in completing such. And then again, a defect they have is that the sun causes the dyes of the tissues to fade; whereas the dyes of Persian carpets are not easily deteriorated by the sun.

They weave these tapestries according to any portrait or painting of celebrity that may be desired. They place the copy of that painting before them: if the copy be small, they enlarge it; if it be too large, they reduce it in weaving the tapestry. In short, just as they please, they manage it. It is also a very perfection of art, that by merely looking at the copy, they weave its fac-simile.

There were several beautiful pieces of tapestry half woven for the great theatre, that Napoleon III. had ordered, and are still in hand; but I know not when that theatre and those tapestries will be finished. It is an extensive establishment, and the workmen are numerous. The Director's name is M. Darsela.

From the Gobelins we went to the National Printing-Office, where they print books and the like. Some by hand, some by steam, in whatever way they wish, they can print with celerity and despatch.

Turning our steps from thence, we went to the palace of the Louvre, and on our road viewed several places burnt and ruined by the men of the Commune. More especially, one great storehouse, the Halle au Blé, a very large and imposing structure where the Government stores of wheat were kept, and which was utterly destroyed. They likewise ruined several bridges.

We also passed through the Place de la Bastille, where there is a column known as the Colonne de Juillet,—one of the structures of Louis-Philippe, and very lofty, with the statue of an angel in gilt brass upon it. The column itself, too, is of cast metal.

Well; we reached the Louvre, which is a noble edifice, and, as to sculptures, paintings, and the like, has no equal. There was a long hall, of very pleasing arrangement, and named the Galerie d'Apollon, *i.e.*, of the specific deity of beauty, poetry, and singing. Here were large numbers of vases in jasper, and jewelled, in rock-crystal, and the like, of ancient goldsmiths' and silversmiths' work, of articles of gold and silver dug up out of the earth, and of curiosities and gems of art of the whole world,—the whole in cases or under glass. There is also, in a case, an arm-bone of Charlemagne, who was

Emperor of the whole of Firangistān. A gold casket, antique, in most exquisite goldsmiths' work, was the property of Anne of Austria, mother of Louis XIV. This hall is itself one of the buildings of the last-named monarch. They have made a copy of the Crown of Louis XV., with false jewels, and have placed it there. The sword and sceptre of Charlemagne are there also.

We then visited the whole of the halls where the paintings are hung. These are all works of artists of celebrity, and one would have to sit under each of them all day to understand the subtleties of the master's art; whereas I, being hurried in my survey, have necessarily not been able to seize those niceties. There were some works by Raphael, a renowned painter, though I myself gave a preference over all others to the productions of the pencil of Albani, who was a master of great taste. Murillo, too, was very good. There were also many pictures by other artists; for instance, there was one valued at more than thirty thousand tūmāns (12,000*l.*).

Having completed this survey, we went into the gardens of the Tuileries, and had a thorough view of the burnt ruins of the palace. It was an edifice without an equal in the world, and is now an utter wreck. To rebuild it as it was would be difficult, as the expense would be enormous. They burnt this palace, with all it contained; thereby causing damage to the extent of at least a hundred crores of tūmāns (20,000,000*l.*). I was grieved beyond measure. The garden of the Tuileries, too, by reason of the ruin of the palace and a lack of constant care, has fallen from its beauty. A band plays there of afternoons. We walked down to the very end of the gardens, thereby greatly fatiguing ourself; and thence, mounting the carriage, drove home.

Napoleon III. built a theatre better and more magnificent than all the other theatres of Firangistān, spending upon it five crores, although it is not yet completed. To finish it will require two crores more. It remains as he left it. I did not go to see it, but I heard much about it.

Again another day we went to Versailles, taking the Porcelain Manufactory of Sèvres on our way. This is an ancient and very famous manufactory, and is situated on an eminence. There was a very extensive collection in the rooms of ancient and modern porcelains, among which some eminently beautiful articles were observed. There were some that were painted from works by the great artists of antiquity, such as Raphael and others, and the estimation in which each of these works is held is equal to that of the finest and grandest pictures. I should have wished to buy the whole for any price they might have named; but these specimens are never parted with, are sold to no one, and never leave the works. The establishment belongs to the State; and any order thence given, is executed. In the same manner as at the manufactory of tapestry, the workmen receive wages, and the chiefs are salaried. They told me that a new manufactory has been prepared, that the present site will be abandoned, and the works transferred to the new establishment.

We went about for a long time from one department to another, until we arrived at a place where they were manufacturing, painting, and baking the porcelain, which we went and inspected also. From thence we returned through all the places we had seen, and they presented to us, as a souvenir of our visit, two large and most magnificent vases,* together with two cases, each containing a very choice service of tea things.

Proceeding from thence, we reached Versailles. At his residence, M. Buffet, President (of the Assembly), met us, and we went into the Chamber of the (National) Council of Deputies. We passed through a gallery where were arranged most beautiful statues in marble of ancient kings, ministers, magnates, commanders, and the like, all carved by the old masters; and so reached the Assembly itself; taking our seat in a chamber. Seven hundred deputies were present at that sitting, and on the upper tiers of benches a great company of women and men were looking on. This hall in which the Assembly now sits was formerly the theatre of (the palace of) Versailles, and was built by Louis XIV.

As the President, M. Buffet, had been away at his own house for the purpose of our reception, his substitute was acting as President in his stead. The two sons of Louis-Philippe, d'Aumale and Joinville, were also present. The

* Of the two vases, each in the Etruscan style and of the value of about two hundred guineas, one was ornamented with a view of the Château of Pierrefonds, the other with one of the Château of Pau, both by Jules André. Of the tea-services, one for four persons, with its tray, painted by F. Rolard and representing a hunt and view of Fontainebleau, was of the value of about six hundred, and the other, for six persons, also with its tray, painted by Devilly, and representing the ceramic art, of about three hundred and fifty pounds.

deputies of the Left and of the Right were all in their places. Those of the Left are in opposition to the present administration. Several generals and others spoke, among them being General Noisel. His voice was very slender and weak; no one could hear what he said. Incessantly did the deputies of the Left call out for him to speak louder. It was a strange wrangle. The President-substitute continually rang a bell to induce silence. It is a difficult matter for any one to speak in this Assembly. It was very interesting to witness, and we sat there an hour.

Rising at length, we returned by the same way we came. Marshal MacMahon had then arrived. We now went over all the rooms, halls, and galleries of (the palace of) Versailles with the Marshal, M. Buffet, and others. These apartments are extremely handsome. There were so many pictures, statues of marble, and other objects, that one forgets them. There were some grand pictures, the works of Horace Vernet the painter, very beautifully drawn, pictures of battles with the Arabs of Algeria in the days of Louis-Philippe, &c., of the battles of Napoleon III. in Italy with the Austrians, &c., of those of Napoleon I., &c., and also many of older masters. So that, should one wish to survey them all carefully, he would not finish them in a year. The greater part of these rooms are now converted into offices for the deputies, ministers, and others. By reason of the great traffic of feet, and the scattering of papers, the heaping of registers, the placing of chairs and tables for the ministers, their secretaries and clerks, the halls are degraded from their majesty.

I was much fatigued. I came down and drove about the gardens for a while in a carriage. They had opened the source of the fountains of a part of the garden. These were therefore playing, and produced a very agreeable effect.

We now returned home, passing by the village of Ville d'Avray, St. Cloud, Boulogne, the Bois de Boulogne, and so to our quarters. At St. Cloud several battalions of troops were encamped in tents, and at Boulogne there was a good market where all kinds of commodities were collected.

To-day at Versailles, among the statues I saw one of Joan of Arc that the princess Marie, daughter of Louis-Philippe, had executed, and was extremely beautiful. The princess died young, unmarried.

I one day went to see the Zoological and Botanical Gardens (the Jardin des Plantes), which was a long distance from our residence. The Director of the establishment, named M. Blanchard, of whose days seventy and five years had passed away, came to meet us, with his assistant and others. A large company was present, from the quarters in the outskirts of Paris, generally peasants and artizans, who had come with their wives to see the sight.

These gardens are of great extent. In the botanical section, most beautiful flowers were planted out in great taste. Every flower and plant in this part is numbered and ticketed, and all plants and medicinal herbs that are employed in the curative art are here raised and propagated. Professors of botany and zoology are constantly at work there investigating and teaching the qualities and properties of each vegetable product.

We first visited the hothouses, where they raise, grow, and multiply tropical plants, and thence proceeded to view the animals. Here they keep, shut up in cages, all kinds of animals, whether birds, or carnivorous or herbivorous beasts. Birds great and small, of all colours, and beautiful, beasts of prey and others, of every sort were seen. The establishment is of greater extent than the zoological gardens of other countries; but every animal that I saw here, I had seen elsewhere, with the exception of a few I had not yet observed:

One of these was a large and strongly built bird, called the Cassowary, that is brought from Australia. It is a very singular creature, about the size of an ostrich, which it also somewhat resembles; but it is of a different species. Another was a quadruped, called the Tapir, from South America, very much resembling the rhinoceros, but smaller, being an animal half way between a rhinoceros, a pig, and a calf. There were some savage, ferocious tigers, and some curious leopards; also a species of brute between a tiger and a leopard, called the Jaguar; but more approaching the leopard. It is a very ferocious, bloodthirsty creature. The leopards had given birth to two young cubs, very graceful. There were some African maned-lions, together with lions of other kinds, and one elephant. In one large cage there were about fifty monkeys; and there were also various kinds of antelopes, &c.

A source of the greatest interest was a collection of

dead animals, kept in the museum of the establishment, which I had not seen in any of the countries hitherto visited. We here saw animals of every class, fishes from all seas, and other creatures, such as snakes, crabs, crocodiles, tortoises, and all kinds of birds, which afforded much pleasure and gratification. For instance, the fishes, small or large, up to the crocodile, are arranged in such fashion that one cannot say whether they are alive or dead. Every bird, again, small or large, that is on earth, from the little humming-birds of the New World, up to the ostrich, all are there. The humming-bird (*lit.* fly-bird, bee-bird) is a bird of the most beautifully-coloured plumage, and small—no larger than large bees (wasps, or hornets); but all its parts are those of a bird. There is no bird in the world prettier than these, and they are found nowhere else, but in the New World only.

The whole of these dead birds have been procured in pairs, male and female, with their eggs, and with the very nests they had constructed for themselves; and are arranged in glass cases. They are placed in the postures they assume when they sit on their eggs in their nests, and in such a manner that they cannot be distinguished from live birds. Beginning with the eggs of the humming-birds, than which no others are smaller, being less in size than a pistachio-nut, up to the egg of the rukh and the ostrich, the largest of all eggs, have they collected in one room. But I there saw four bird's-eggs, each of which was of the size of a large melon, and they informed me that the kind of bird to which they belonged is no longer in existence in the world. These four eggs have been found and ultimately brought from Africa and the New World after great research and much travel in every region of the earth. They lifted these eggs; they were very heavy. According to analogy, the chick that would come out of one of those eggs would be of the size of a very large domestic cock. The birds called Sīmurg and Rukh, that we read of in books, must have been the produce of eggs such as these. At present, they would not sell one of those eggs for a thousand tūmāns (400*l*.).

Strange and marvellous fishes were seen, which, in respect of immensity of bulk and singularity of form, admit of no description. Monkeys, too, of curious or uncouth forms, were there of various classes; one kind being of the bulk of a horse, another no larger than a rat. According to their varying sizes, these were also arranged in like manner, as though alive. Among them was one species called the Gorilla, that is found in Africa, bigger and taller than a tiger, with its bulk and size, its strength and muscular limbs, its claws, feet, and teeth. Its stature was twice that of a man, or even more. There were a pair of them, male and female; the latter being the smaller.

Another of the monkey tribe, a native of the islands of Borneo, Sumatra, and Timor, is the Orang-outang, smaller than the gorilla, but still well worthy of remark. It is very large and fierce.

They had placed a tortoise upon a table, which was of the size of a donkey,—extremely large. That, too, was a wondrous thing, that required to be seen in order to be imagined.

· There were some enormous snakes, which, in reality, are the dragons of which one hears. They had arranged an artificial tree, and around it had coiled the folds of one of those large snakes, in a manner to be mistaken for a live reptile. It was wonderful to look at. Not that they have increased or diminished by one hair's breadth the size of these creatures with a view to deceive people by artifice; but, whether large or small, every thing in that museum is a real animal, such as the Lord of the universe created it; and the Franks have really, with great trouble and at a fabulous expense, brought them together from the uttermost parts of the earth, for the advancement of knowledge, the increase of observation, and the display to the people of God's power in His wondrous works of creation; the same unceasing care being bestowed upon their safe-keeping. Truly have they incurred great trouble therein. Were a man actually to sit for five months in the contemplation of these dead animals, bones, and birds, he might then come to understand something about them; but what can I learn in a quarter of an hour?

We came down; and although I had no time to spare for the view, I went to the cages of the live animals, looked at them all, and then returned home.

The Director, whose age was seventy-five or perhaps eighty, went about everywhere with me, and walked a good league. As often as I requested him to turn back, so often did he come again. He said that in his life he had never taken intoxicating liquors, and had always cautioned others against their use. There is in Firangistān a special society, with many members, who are continually engaged in furthering the cause of a total abandonment of drink; but this is a very difficult undertaking, and especially in Firangistān.

The megatherium is (the name of) an animal that lived on the earth before Noah's flood, of the same family as the elephant, but larger, and without a trunk. They have discovered its bones, and have placed them in (the museum of) the zoological gardens.

Paris has many theatres. One evening we, too, went to a large theatre. The whole of the Diplomatic Body, with their wives, Marshal MacMahon, M. Buffet, the whole of the officials, and others, as well as those of our suite, were present. It was a very large theatre of great estimation, with five tiers of seats, and many chandeliers. The audience was very numerous. Dancers danced, and singers sang, beautifully; more especially in a scene laid beneath the sea, when the sea-nymphs danced.

We one night visited the Élysée for an evening party. All the ladies of celebrity of the capital, the Foreign Representatives and their wives, the officials of France, and the Persians, were invited. They gave a magnificent exhibition of fireworks and an illumination in the grounds of the palace, which are laid out as a very beautiful garden, with basins of water, fountains, lawns, and trees. The middle of the garden was lighted up like moonlight by means of electric lamps worked from the roof of the palace, which threw their light on to the ground. The men and women who walked about in this artificial light, wore an aspect and acquired a charm that were very peculiar.

We went up to the first floor and took a turn through the apartments. It is a magnificent place, and has some handsome Gobelins tapestries. It was built by the Comte d'Évreux a hundred and fifty years ago. After his death the mistress of Louis XV., Pompadour, bought it and greatly extended it. When she died, it reverted to the King. Subsequently it was purchased by Murat, the brother-in-law of Napoleon I. Well; after a stroll, we returned home.

On another evening De Broglie—the Foreign Minister, gave an evening-party and *buffet* at the Ministry of Foreign Affairs, which is near to the Corps Législatif, our residence. In the evening, although the distance from our quarters to the Ministry was very short, we were conducted with all honours in a carriage escorted by cavalry, &c., and taken round the circuit of the palace to the Minister's reception. Feasts and receptions had always been accustomed to be given at the Ministry; but, since the Prussian war, and the emigration of the Government to Versailles, up to this evening, the edifice had been closed. Marshal MacMahon, M. Buffet, the whole of the officials, generals, and Foreign Representatives, besides others of the nobility and magnates, women and men, were present. As the bride of the Minister of Foreign Affairs was the mistress of the house, we gave her our hand, and strolled about the garden and apartments. In the garden there were beautiful fireworks and an illumination. All went off pleasantly. After an interval we returned home.

On one occasion we went for a turn to Vincennes,

which is outside of Paris, to the south. It is a plain with meadows and woods. Napoleon III. caused avenues, lakes, and pleasant places to be arranged there. We passed through the Boulevard Prince Eugène, the Place du Châtelet, and the Place de la Bastille, and then through one of the gates of the city. These city-gates of Paris do not resemble the gates of Persian towns, which really have doors. Here the gates (barrières) are merely iron railings.

Well; we alighted from our carriage and went to view the fortifications and ditch of Paris. The parapet of the fortification, which is really the scarp of the ditch of the city, has an elevation of nine ells (31 feet 6 inches), besides one ell (42 inches) of earthwork upon the wall, making ten ells altogether (35 feet). Nine ells are of hewn stone, of the size of (Roman) tiles; one ell of earth, and on that a coping of large hewn stones. At the angles of the wall, also, they have used large hewn stones. But the counterscarp of the ditch—the bank next the country, has not so great a height, and is so greatly sloped that one can walk down it into the ditch. The width of the ditch is also ten ells (35 feet). The whole city of Paris is surrounded in this fashion, and these works were constructed in the time of Louis-Philippe about thirty years ago.

Returning, we again mounted, and arrived at a lake on the border of a river (the Marne) with very excellent water. This was a charming spot, with abundance of flowers and verdure. We crossed a bridge and went on to an island in a lake, where they had constructed a small pavilion with stone columns, &c., upon a pavement of flags; and beneath this they had dug a cavern, where stones (stalactites) were pendent as though in a cavern of snow. From above, a hole was opened with a small tube inserted, from which a thread of water trickled on to the stones and fell in drops as though it had been a natural phenomenon. It was a very pleasant sight. We sat there awhile. There were several Franks there and some women, with whom we conversed. We then walked on.

On this island there was an hotel, where they had built a pretty pavilion from which a band should play. They brought us two boats, into which we got, and, pulling about awhile, we went to a place where our carriages were waiting. We came up out of the boats, mounted our carriages, and proceeding to another gate (of the city), we drove along the Boulevard Dumesnil towards our quarters.

In a street near to a public building we observed a large concourse of people standing and waiting for us. It became evident that General Pajol had given notice to the Sisters of Charity. We alighted and entered their school. One of the priests spoke Persian well. He had been for some time a teacher of the local Romanist children in the school at Khusraw-ābād, near Urūmiyya in Āzarbāyjān. A considerable number of women who have renounced the world and who dress in black, with white bonnets of a curious shape, like the ears of elephants, were there, and give themselves up, in a meritorious way, to the instruction of their pupils. Their scholars are in six classes; the school, too, has six stories, each being appropriated to one class of the pupils. Beginning with children of three and four years old, up to girls and boys of twenty study there, there being a thousand of them maintained. The most part have been brought there as orphans; they (the sisters) act as servants and give them instruction in every science,—in mathematics, in geography, languages, sewing, flower-making, &c. The girls make very pretty flowers, and gave us a beautiful bouquet of them as a souvenir. About two hundred children of four years old were ranged very nicely and orderly on the stages of the gallery in the class-room, who had been taught by an aged religious woman, their preceptress, a song or hymn in French verse commemorative of our arrival, which they had learnt by heart, and which they now sang in a strain of perfect melody. Grown up girls, too, on the upper stages sang songs and poetry very sweetly. The manners, the way in which the children and pupils were there attended to, gave me great pleasure.

We then returned, and in the evening went to the circus. We there saw such feats of horsemanship and the like, as surpassed imagination. For instance, one horse sat down at table and ate food, while another horse went, took with his mouth a napkin, a basket, some wine, &c., and brought them, performing the office of a servant. Another horse turned (or spun) a large jar with his fore-foot. The trainer said: "Be lame," and instantly the horse limped; he said: "Be dead," and the horse lay down (as though) dead. And thus of other feats.

A sculptor, who makes marble statues, came each day

to our quarters to make our statue of clay. He exercised wonderful patience, working from early morn till dusk, and produced an excellent likeness of us in clay, which he will reproduce in marble. The first is made of a kind of clay special to this artistic work, and with which they prepare the likeness correctly of the subject in hand; next they prepare it in plaster; and after that cut it out of the marble. According to what he said, he will, God willing, send our statue to Tehrān in four months' time.

In Paris there are numerous coffee-shops; but, according to what was told me, there are two coffee-shops more especially held in very high repute, where there are music, dancing, and singing, and which are called "Cafés Chantants." They are places like theatres, within the city, and near to one another. There are there many trees and beautiful avenues; every evening they are lighted up with many lamps, and they begin, as soon as the sun goes down, to play music. Numerous chairs are placed; and opposite to where the public sit, is the edifice of the coffee-shop. Mimics, singers, dancers, rope-dancers, acrobats, and others, play and perform or sing within the building in the presence of the public.

The acrobat's performance is a curious sight. He is a young man, a gymnast; he wears a dress of the colour of the skin, tight and close-fitting, so that he appears to be naked. He takes a child of four or five years of age,— the ugliest little urchin imaginable, and also a lad of twelve or thirteen, whom he plays upon his hands or feet, or throws up into the air, in a manner similar to what one might do with a little mouse. In whatsoever way he may throw them up, they alight on the ground on their feet; and in an instant, placing the child, or the lad, on the top of his head, or the tip of a finger, he spins him round, tosses him up, catches him again; and they, too, on their part also, while on his head, or hand, or foot, turn summersaults in a way impossible to describe. When he tosses the child up, he certainly sends him five or six ells high (17½ to 21 feet), the child turns a summersault in the air, and alights on the ground on his feet.

True, I did not myself go to these coffee-shops; but such is what I heard, and such is what I witnessed at the circus.

This circus is open in the summer-time; but there is a winter circus also, at a considerable distance from our palace.

There are many handsome hotels in Paris. The "Grand Hôtel," which is the largest and best of all, being like a magnificent royal palace, contains all the articles of splendour one can desire, while every kind of food and drink are always ready.

A garden exists in Paris, called the "Jardin Mabille," which is a very fine garden and is open every evening. It has a strong iron gate, where, from each individual who enters they take five shillings Persian (4s. English). Every evening about two thousand visitors come there. The garden is lighted up with lamps innumerable; there are beautiful avenues, basins of water, places like natural hills with cascades or waterfalls; and in the middle of the garden a pavilion where an orchestra performs. It also has coffee-shops and handsome apartments well lighted with lamps. Beautiful women of every description frequent this place, which is a curiosity in its way. There is a garden like it in London also; but neither of them came under our observation.

It is said that the population of Paris is about four crores (two millions).

While at Paris, intelligence came from Tehrān that the Fakhru-'d-Dawla, our aunt, daughter of the (former) Prince Regent (the Shāh's grandfather, 'Abbās Mīrzā, son of Fath-'Ali Shāh), and a most venerable woman, had passed to another world. It was a source of grief, sorrow, and sadness.

In Paris, England, and Germany, there are some wonderful horses, of strong frame, with legs, feet, and hoofs like those of elephants, that draw very heavy loads. I saw many of them, harnessed to carts and waggons.

A custom prevails in Firangistān for each family to be dressed all in clothes of the same colour. For instance, four sisters must be all attired alike. It is a pretty fashion.

Saturday, 23rd (19th July).—Left Paris for the town of Dijon, one of the cities of France.

We rose early, and found Marshal MacMahon, the Minister of Foreign Affairs, the Austrian Ambassador, the President of the Assembly—M. Buffet, together with other French magnates, generals, and civilians, in attendance. We mounted a carriage and drove off, the Marshal, the Minister, and the Grand-Vazīr being seated with us. We passed along the Boulevards des Italiens, the Boulevard Montmartre, the Boulevard du Château-d'Eau, the Place de la Bastille, &c., where great crowds were collected, the weather, too, being sultry, and so arrived at the Gare du Midi.

We alighted and sat awhile in one of the rooms of the station, where great numbers of women and men of importance, and others, had assembled. The Marshal presented M. Vitry, who, in the time of the third Napoleon had been in the ministry and President of the Conseil d'État, being now the chairman of the southern railroad to Lyons and Dijon. The Prefêt of Dijon accompanies us.

Well; after a quarter of an hour's stay, we entered the train,—the same, to all appearance, that had brought us from Cherbourg. We started, and Paris faded from our sight, as we travelled towards Dijon. The condition and appearance of the country were like those in other parts, everywhere cultivation, green fields, meadows, trees, population, in uninterrupted succession; rivers, large and small, with valleys and hills, also, were seen now and then. The following are the names of the towns and stations passed on the road from Paris to Dijon; viz.: Montereau, Laroche, Tonnerre, Arcy, Dijon.

Well; we travelled over the distance in six hours and a half to seven hours, the train going at its utmost speed—ten leagues per hour. We reached Dijon at sunset. The governor of the town, who is the prefect of the Côte-d'Or, is named Léon de Nassan. He and his deputy, with the magnates of the town, and others, were at the station, waiting. This magistrate was appointed to his post about a month ago by Marshal MacMahon.

The whole of these parts of the country is named Burgundy, and one section of Burgundy is the Côte-d'Or, of which Dijon is the chief town. The crop of grapes is beyond all computation hereabouts, and the wines are celebrated, being carried to all parts of the world. Whoever beholds the vineyards of these plains and hills becomes puzzled to know how they can all be consumed.

We reached the town, and passed through some narrow streets. In the late war this place was twice occupied by the troops of Prussia, and they exercised various kinds of molestation towards its inhabitants. They extracted a large ransom, and took heavy contributions in kind. We saw several women whom they wounded, the poor creatures having thence become cripples.

A large building was observed, erected in days of yore; *i.e.*, it was reared by the Lords—the Dukes of Burgundy. It has, further, a high tower, like those of the public edifices in Persia. As this country was in ancient days a separate State, with an independent sovereign, they had made the structures of the city of great strength. Afterwards France incorporated it with her own dominions, of which it now forms an integral part.

We noticed several very ancient churches—imposing old structures. One had become dilapidated, and was in course of repair. There was one theatre, closed at that season.

We went to the residence of the governor,—a handsome house, recently constructed and renovated, with a small garden in front. Well; we retired to rest early. They manufacture a good mustard in this city.

Sunday, 24th (20th *July*).—This day proceeded from Dijon to Geneva. In the morning the magnates of the town came to an audience, after which we drove to the station, the Grand-Vazīr and the Prefect being seated opposite to us in the carriage, and crowds collected everywhere. The population of this town is forty thousand souls.

To-day's journey to Geneva is of seven hours' duration, the towns along the road being as follows: Chagny, Mâcon, Bourg, Ambrieux, Culoz, Bellegarde—the last place in France on our road. As far as Ambrieux the whole distance was across plains or small hills and vales; but from that station onwards we met with high mountains and deep valleys, the river Rhone flowing on our right in a valley, after issuing from the Lake of Geneva. It goes on to Lyons and other places, and flows into the Mediterranean near to Marseilles. Its source is in Mount Saint-Gothard, in the Alps. The same quantity of water that flows into the lake (of Geneva) leaves it again, being then called the Rhone.

Well; we breakfasted in the train, which travelled at a very rapid rate. When we had passed the station at Ambrieux, the whole country became hill and dale, huge mountains on both sides of the road, villages, and many beautifully-pleasant streams of water. By degrees, as we proceeded, we successively passed through several "holes," one being of great length, and occupying five minutes in the transit. When we had traversed these mountains and valleys, a small quantity of level country came in sight, and then again all was mountainous in general. These mountains have snow on them, the Alps, Mont Blanc, and peaks of the mountains of Savoy and Italy coming now into view.

We arrived at Geneva at sunset. The President of the Canton of Geneva is named M. Ceresol, the President of the Council of Geneva is M. Eugène Bopel. These, with the Swiss Envoy who was in Paris, the magnates of the town, and General Dufour—a man ninety years of age, who served in the armies of the first Napoleon, who is greatly esteemed in Switzerland, and is celebrated as a geographical cartographer, were awaiting us. There, the territory of France being at an end, the French officials in attendance upon us took leave and returned. Their names were as follows: General Pajol, General Arture, Colonel Chevron, M. Biberstein.

We stopped in a room at the station; the President made a speech, and we gave a reply. We then mounted an open carriage with the Grand-Vazīr and the two Presidents, and drove off. Our quarters are in the Hôtel de Berg. This hotel was at no great distance; but there was no possibility to get through the streets, by reason of the dense crowds. Although several policemen were on duty, they could not repress and drive back the people. Women, men, old and young, as also children, were all mixed up together indiscriminately; and the horses exerted themselves in such a manner that it wanted but little for an accident to happen to the carriage. The horses and the people were so jammed together, that the latter were near being drawn under the wheels. Children wept; girls and boys shrieked from the great pressure.

At length, after a thousand perils, we reached our quarters, a very imposing edifice. Above and below it contains numerous apartments, and resembles a kingly palace. The greater part of the larger buildings seen in Europe, and especially in this city, are hotels. The Rhone flows by the front of the hotel; its water is very light of digestion and very sweet. Owing to its clearness it assumes an azure colour. In the middle of the river opposite to the hotel there is a small island with trees, and around it a railing. It communicates with the shores by several bridges; but there are two long wooden bridges on stout piers that are very important, and that lead to the hotel.

The city is on both sides of the river, and it possesses many very great buildings, excellent colleges, and spacious streets beautifully paved with stone. The whole of its buildings are of five and six stories; but, in spite of this height, the city is handsome and captivating. It has a hospitable population, and the manufactories of watches and musical boxes of this city are well known. All musical instruments in boxes, all singing nightingales and crowing cocks, that act by mechanism, are made here and exported to other countries.

The whole of our suite is lodged in this same hotel. The method of government in the Swiss Confederation is a thing unique in its species, and their customs are different. They have no house or place specially appointed for government; and for this reason our quarters were at an hotel. Other sovereigns and people of importance that come to this city can have no other quarters than at an hotel.

The Alp mountains and Mont Blanc* are seen from the outlook of the hotel. They are much covered with snow; but the Persian mountain of Damāwand is considerably more lofty than these, and more picturesque.

Dr. Tholozan, who had gone to the town of St. Étienne, in France, has not yet rejoined us.

Monday, 25th (21*st July*).—Remained at Geneva. To-day we went on board a Swiss steamship, and proceeded on a jaunt round the Lake of Geneva. The whole of our suite, two of the head men of Switzerland, the Swiss and the Italian Envoys to France, M. Dubeski—Austrian Envoy to Tehrān, and recently arrived from Austria, with others of the Franks, were present.

The right-hand shore of the lake was at first, for a short distance, Swiss territory; after that it belongs to the province of Savoy, dependent on France. After the

---

* Black's Atlas of 1856, gives the height of Mont Blanc as 15,781 feet; that of "Demawand" at 15,000 feet; of Kazbek, 15,345 feet; and of Elburz, 17,796 feet—both these latter being in the Caucasus. Mr. Grove's letter in *The Times* of 26th August, 1874, gives an altitude of 18,500 feet to Elburz. Mr. Grove, however, places the Caucasus in Europe, and dethrones Mont Blanc from its supremacy as the highest in our quarter of the globe, raising Elburz to its vacated pre-eminence. General Monteith, in the map to his "Kars and Erzeroum," published in 1856, gives the same height to Elburz, 18,514 feet, but assigns to Kazbek an altitude of 16,518 feet.—J. W. R.

war that Napoleon III. waged against Austria, in which he defeated her and took from her the province of Lombardy,—a part of Italy that the Austrians had occupied for several years, restoring the same to the Italians, Italy, in acknowledgment of the toil of France, ceded the two provinces of Nice and Savoy to the French Government, the territory of Savoy reaching to the shore of the Lake of Geneva, and actually held by France. Again, on the other hand, the river Rhone, after passing the city of Geneva by a very few feet, enters the territory of France.

Well; when we first moved away from the port of Geneva, the width of the lake was inconsiderable, widening out by degrees, so that the greatest breadth of the lake is more than two leagues, while its depth is from fifty to a hundred ells (175 to 350 feet). They said that everywhere in it the largest steamers can navigate, while there is not one large rock or island in the middle or along the shore of the lake. At whatsoever time a storm may arise, great waves are thrown up. The length of the lake is twelve leagues, and we compassed it with our steamer in six hours. The ship ran three leagues an hour. The circuit of the lake by land, however, must be thirty leagues. There are three or four steamboats belonging to a Swiss company, under Swiss colours, that perform voyages every day, carrying passengers and goods; and there are also two or three steamers under French colours. Many sailing vessels also are in use. The population of the shores belonging to France is less than that on the Swiss parts. All round the lake are lofty mountains, with the Alps visible in the distance, snowy and picturesque.

We partook of a frugal breakfast on board the steamer, and then started. We passed the further end of the French shore, the valley by which the Rhone falls into the lake, and arrived before the town of Vevay. This is a very pretty town on the shore of the lake, with a western aspect. On the shores of the lake and on the skirts of the mountains detached residences were seen. The whole of the produce hereabouts is grapes. In whatever direction we looked, from the foot to the very summit of the peaks of the mountains, wherever it was practicable, and the soil was capable of being worked, there were grapevines. In the middle of the town there were many fountains, the sources of which were in the higher parts of the mountains; so that, these being at great elevations, the fountains threw their jets to considerable heights, and produced a very good effect. There were some very grand hotels.

M. Ceresol, the President, whose native place was Vevay, had invited us to a breakfast, and had caused the repast to be prepared at an hotel named "Les Trois Couronnes;" *i.e.*, the Three Crowns. We went ashore from the vessel and mounted a carriage. We noticed some most beautiful women. Great numbers of Americans, English, and others, come to travel in these parts. Citizens of the town and foreigners crowded the streets in great numbers. We entered the hotel, which is a magnificent edifice. The King of Holland, William or Wilhelm, who has been some time travelling here, was standing in a hall of the hotel, waiting for us. On arriving we shook hands with him, and entered into conversation, after which we went to table and sat down. There was a most elaborate breakfast, at which musicians played. The whole of our suite were at table, and the King of Holland sat opposite to us, so that we conversed at great length.

Breakfast finished, we rose and went for a stroll in a garden in front of the hotel on the shore of the lake. Great numbers of women and maidens, as also of all classes of men, were there. As we were yet strolling about, the King of Holland came and said: "I wish to take leave." We shook hands.

Going now to a shop, we purchased some very beautiful panoramic views of the Alps and other places; thence, mounting a carriage, we returned by the way we had come, went on board our ship, and again got under way. We passed several towns and cities of note on the Swiss shore of the lake; among these were Lausanne, Nyon, Rolle, Morges, and Cully, arriving at Geneva after dark, where they had arranged a beautiful illumination and exhibition of fireworks, both on the shore and on board the vessels. After these we went home.

From the shores of the lake they have laid down two lines of railway on the Swiss territory to the valley and town of Sion. On the right-hand side of the lake is the mountain chain of the Alps; on the left, that of the Jura.

Tuesday, 26th (22nd July).—In the morning after breakfasting, we mounted a carriage, crossed the Rhone, and went for a drive in the direction of the mountains of Savoy, which are French territory. On our route the Sanī'u-'d-Dawla received his congé to proceed to the city of Turin and make arrangements for quartering our suite.

This day, also, the 'I'tizādu-'s-Saltana, the 'Imādu-'d-Dawla, the 'Ala'u-'d-Dawla, Mīrzā Malkam Khān, the Hakīmu-'l-Mamālik, and M. Richard also set out for the city of Vienna.

Well; we drove on and passed beyond the environs of Geneva. Our carriage-road was all uphill, tortuous, and lop-sided. The weather, too, was excessively sultry. As one passes beyond the city of Geneva, one comes on to the territory of Savoy and France, the territories of France and Switzerland being intermixed. There were some small and picturesque villages along the road, perched on eminences and at the foot of hills. We crossed a considerable stream that comes down from the mountains and valleys of Savoy and ultimately flows into the Rhone. We drove up an ascending road which terminates at a handsome hotel; but before reaching the hotel I mounted the horse of the Yamīnu-'d-Dawla, and Ibrāhīm Khān mounted that of the Husāmu-'d-Dawla. Other horses were also procured from the Franks, on which the rest of our suite mounted. The Mu'tamadu-'l-Mulk went on in the carriage to the hotel.

We now pushed on for the summit of a hill that overhung the hotel, the others following us. One Frank, proprietor of the horses, who was a man of a certain position and kept good steeds, was also of the party; but he could not climb up with us to the mountain-top on horseback. He followed us everywhere on foot. The road was bad, and lay through a tangled thicket, so as not to be at all distinguishable. We made our way, however, somehow or other, through the bushes and trees, arriving ultimately at the hill-top. Here the Lake of Geneva, the whole of the snow-clad peaks of the Alps of Savoy, with Mont Blanc and others burst into view. After admiring this spectacle for a time, we retreated from the intense heat to the shade of a wood, and there sat down. Again mounting, we descended by a very bad path and went to the hotel. Great numbers of women and men, travellers and others, were seen on our road and in the hotel, where we found no other refreshment than iced water. We sat down a while in the small garden of the hotel, and washed our hands and face. At this juncture, with all our fatigue, and in spite of the heat, the Mu'tamadu-'l-Mulk came to say that the priest, with the local substitute of the district, a portion of France, desired to have an audience. I gave permission, and they came. The substitute made a speech as though I had arrived in the city of Paris, and to it we gave an answer. After that, we returned home by the same road followed in our ascent. As the carriage had to go gently downhill, we got home late, *i.e.*, it was dark before we reached our quarters.

Wednesday, 27th (23rd July).—To-day we are invited to breakfast at the Hôtel de la Paix by the Swiss Confederation, of which the Presidents are come.

We mounted our carriage and went. The distance

was very little. Alighting, we went upstairs. We remained a short time in a room, and the Italian Envoy to Switzerland, the Swiss Envoy to Paris, whose name is Dr. Kerk, the Prussian Envoy to Switzerland—a son of Prince Gortchakoff, the Prime Minister of Russia, who had come here from Berne, were received in audience, together with the others.

After an interval we went to table and took our seats. The princes, Grand-Vazīr, and the rest, were all present. A beautiful gold box, enamelled, including a watch and a singing bird, and also a musket, as used by the troops of Switzerland, with a thousand balls, were presented on the part of the citizens of Geneva.

The breakfast was very protracted. There was a band playing. Crowds of women and men were in the streets, on the stairs, and in the rooms. Breakfast over, we returned home.

Two hours later the President and others came again. We mounted a carriage and went to see some localities. The whole of those who sat down to the breakfast were present, excepting our princes.

We first went to a building where are collected sets of philosophical apparatus and some other things, such as a museum, dead animals and the bones of these, just like those seen in Paris; only that the collection here, in comparison with those of Paris and elsewhere, were very much less in number, and contemptible. The professor of physics made a room dark and showed us some experiments and interesting sights produced by the power of electricity in coloured glass vessels; but as, during this exhibition, the curtains were let down and the windows closed, the room was very dark and hot. We then walked through some other rooms, and from hence proceeded to another building.

This was an Exhibition of paintings by Swiss and other artists, of which I purchased six or seven very beautiful. In one room there was also a plan of the whole Swiss territory, which General Dufour has prepared with the labour of many years. To say the truth, so beautiful a plan had never been seen before. Village by village, valley by valley, the mountains and the rivers are all laid down in relief.

After admiring this plan for a time we descended, got into our carriage, and went for a drive. We were also engaged to a party in the afternoon at the gardens and summer-residence of M. Favre, one of the wealthy nobles of Switzerland.

Those gardens were outside the town on the shore of the Lake of Geneva, in the direction of the territories of Switzerland, and a good distance away. We passed near to the mansion and summer-residence of the famous Rothschild, and so reached the house of M. Favre, which is very handsome. Many beautiful ladies, of the nobility and otherwise, were there present. We sat a little, strolled about a little, and conversed. The lawns and the view over the lake and its surroundings were superb. We returned at sunset; but the President and the others remained.

We came home; but we passed a most uncomfortable night from the noise of the carriages, the roar of thunder, the plashing of rain, the striking of clocks, and the jangling of bells in the various hotels.

The State of the Swiss Confederation is a republic, and they have very strange customs of administration. It has altogether a population of five crores ($2\frac{1}{2}$ millions), and is subdivided into twenty-two cantons. Each canton has a President, a Government, and an exchequer apart. There is a Supreme Council of seven members, which has its President, and he is superior to the others; but one by one these can give no orders concerning public affairs of importance or otherwise. The twenty-two (Cantonal Presidents) report to this (Council of) seven, and these, acting in concert, and each appending his signature, issue the necessary decrees. In reality, they have no President-General or Absolute Ruler in any one of the cantons or towns; but, whenever the whole agree together as to any matter, it is put in force; otherwise, not. This is a state of affairs the exposition and elucidation of which is extremely difficult, and our Diary is not sufficiently voluminous to embrace a commentary on the laws of the government and details of the regulations of the Swiss State. More than we have given is unnecessary also. They have no standing army at all. Whenever a war breaks out, they arm and drill the peasantry, and lead them to battle. In time of war they can assemble an army of a hundred thousand men. The seven regents of the State reside in the City of Berne.

There are four rivers which have their fountain head in the mountain of St. Gothard, one of the Alps, and belonging to Switzerland. Two of these are very large;

one, the Rhine, falls into the Lake of Constance; the other, the Rhone, flows into the Lake of Geneva. Both issue again from those lakes.

Thursday, 28th (24th July).—We proceeded this day from Geneva to Turin, the ancient capital of the kingdom of Sardinia and Piedmont, which now, after wars with Austria, the conquest of the provinces of Lombardy and Venetia, the four strong fortresses of the Quadrilateral, the annexation of Naples with the island of Sicily, and the occupation of the city of Rome, has become one united kingdom of importance, the kingdom of Italy, the capital of which is the city of Rome, the ancient capital of the Cæsars, as afterwards of the Popes,—the chiefs of the (Roman) Catholic sect, who seized upon sovereign power, which has been totally taken away from them in the days of the present king, and the capital restored to the united kingdom.

Well; we rose early in the morning and took our seat in a carriage together with the President and the Grand-Vazīr. We entered a train and went as far as Bellegarde, the first French station, by the road passed over in coming. Thence we diverged to the road that leads to Turin and Italy. We passed over the valleys and the territories of Savoy, where all around were extensive vales filled with streams and trees, most charming. On both sides of our road were huge lofty mountains covered with snow, from which waterfalls innumerable leaped. In these localities they have constructed the iron way most scientifically, with immense labour, and at enormous cost. Everywhere is rock and mountain, acclivity or declivity; and across the rivers enormous bridges of iron have been thrown.

The country was picturesque and populous until we reached the city of Chambery. Before arriving there, however, we passed the districts of Aix les Bains, which are a part of Savoy, and where there was a clear and beautiful lake, long, deep, and narrow. At Chambery, the chief town of Savoy, the train stopped. The whole of the military officers and generals of the forces in garrison, the magistrates and civil functionaries, with a regiment of infantry, another of cavalry, and their bands, were in readiness to receive us. We alighted, passed down in front of the troops, rejoined our train, and proceeded.

All was now stupendous mountains, covered with forests or with snow. Waterfalls gushed from the heights incessantly on both sides; and so we reached Modane, the last station in France. Here the Italian officials and generals sent to meet us were admitted to an audience. But the frontier between France and Italy is in the middle of the "hole" through Mont Cenis, the half of this belonging to Italy, and the other half to France.

Leaving Modane, we reached the "hole," and twenty-eight minutes elapsed ere we again issued therefrom, two leagues and a half, or thereabouts, being the length of this "hole." It is as though a hole were pierced from Manzariyya in the Alburz Mountains, coming out again at Shahristānak. It is a most wonderful work.

At first I closed all the windows of the carriage, in order to prevent the entry of the smoke. After a few minutes we experienced a difficulty of breathing, and I let down several windows, when a slight air came in. At times strange sounds arose as though a dragon were passing swiftly by and roaring; at other times, in the midst of the darkness another train would pass us, making a wonderful noise. On either side of the road now and then a lamp and a roadsman were seen, and we could not imagine how they could live in these places. At length, towards the end of the tunnel, as the height and diameter of the mountain begin gradually to decrease, some windows have been opened and light admitted into the "hole," those on the left hand being larger and those to the right smaller. Before we came to these windows, there was another long hole opened up on the left-hand side from the tunnel to the mountain side, for the purpose of ventilating the (principal) "hole;" and through it light and air are both admitted. But the whole of this tunnel, of two and a half leagues in length, is very dark and terrific. For nearly twenty years the ablest engineers of Europe worked at opening out this tunnel at an enormous expense; and before the hole was pierced, the road from France to Italy lay over the surface of the mountain, and was travelled in carriages, on horseback, or on mules.

At length we emerged from the "hole" and entered the territory of Piedmont, of which the city of Turin is the capital. Again were lofty mountains, covered with snows and forests, and waterfalls without number, seen on both sides of the road; and again did the train pass through two very long "holes," and after a space, through several others; so that altogether we must have passed to-day through at least eighty "holes."

On the Italian territory the railway passes by strange and perilous places, such as mountain-slopes, precipices, deep gullies, large streams, and torrents, over which bridges have been made. In the construction of these roads many a marvellous piece of work has been carried out, that squares not with one's (previous) conceptions; and so strongly have they built the roads and the bridges, that for a thousand years they will show no defect.

The river that flows from these mountains in the direction of Italy is the Po;—a mighty stream, but its water is black and unsavoury. It passes by the side of the city of Turin; and lower down, by that of Venice, flowing ultimately into the Adriatic Sea.

As we went on, the valley became more spacious, opening out at length into a broad and level plain, a vast expanse covered with trees. But, before we reached the station at Turin, the sun had set and the atmosphere had darkened.

On alighting from the train, His Most Exalted Majesty Victor Emmanuel II.,—the Sovereign of Italy, the Nawwāb Prince Humbert—the Heir-Apparent, Prince Amadeo—second son of the Sovereign, who for two years exercised sovereignty in Spain, and then abdicated, M. Minghetti—the Prime Minister, M. Visconti-Venosta—the Minister of Foreign Affairs, the Prince of Carignano—son of the Sovereign's paternal uncle and a man held in great estimation for nobleness of character, Commander-in-Chief of the Italian Army, and also holding a post in the Navy, who, whenever the Sovereign goes forth on a campaign and the Heir-Apparent is also absent, is always appointed Regent, the Saní'u-'d-Dawla —who had come on beforehand, together with other officials, governors, and notables of the city, were at the station ready to meet us.

We shook hands with the Sovereign and the princes, with mutual salutations; after which, we and the Sovereign took our seats in an open carriage and drove off. It was night, and they had prepared a beautiful illumination. Great crowds of women and men were in the streets and at the windows. The town has spacious streets and lofty buildings of five and six stories. The street through which we passed is called the Street of Rome.

The first open space we came to was St. Charles's Square, in the middle of which was an equestrian statue in bronze of one of the Sovereign's ancestors. After that we reached the square in which is the royal palace. This is a spacious arena, in the middle of which there is a marble statue of a soldier with a flag, which the people of Lombardy, after their emancipation from the hands of Austria, presented to the city of Turin.

We arrived at the palace, alighted, and, with the Sovereign, went up stairs. The steps, walls, and corridors were all of marble; the ceilings were lofty and highly ornamented with figures and gildings. On the balustrades were placed vases of marble, out of each of which sprang gas-fittings with several branches of great beauty. We passed through many rooms, all intercommunicating, all ornamented with ancient gildings, some with decorative mirrors, and all full of objects of great splendour, such as magnificent oil-paintings, sofas, tables, chairs, and the like.

After the Sovereign had thus pointed out the whole of the apartments of our quarters, he took leave and went away. We waited a few minutes, and then went to the apartments of the Sovereign, which were in the same palace, and returned his visit. We remained there a short time, returned, took off our state costume, and made ourselves at home.

The air of this city is extremely sultry. The Sovereign was out in tents at hunting-grounds high on the mountains, and came into town merely on account of our arrival; otherwise, he has no liking ever to remain in town; winter and summer he is always out in hunting-places. He told me that he held the town and palace in detestation, that he always wished to be in the hunting-grounds on the mountains.*

The age of the Sovereign is near upon sixty years; but he is very hale and robust, so that he does not appear aged. The Heir-Apparent is thirty years of age; Prince Amadeo, twenty-eight. Of his two daughters, one, the wife of the Sovereign of Portugal, is named Marie; the other, the wife of Prince Napoleon, is named the Princess Clotilde. The wife of the Duke of Aosta—that same Prince Amadeo, has been extremely unwell

---

* " It is whispered that the King of Italy prefers shooting in Piedmont to all the pleasures of a palace." *Leader in* "Times," 27th August, 1874. The paragraph in the text was first read by me on that day—a singular coincidence.—J. W. R.

these last few days; and his apartments also are in the lower story of the palace in which we are quartered. He has three sons; one, an infant at the breast, the other two being three or four years old, whom their nurses bring out every day into the garden in front of the palace, and give them a turn about.

In one of the squares of the city is a very large and lofty fountain, the water of which springs up with great force.

The river Po comes from the uttermost right-hand outskirts of the city, and on the further side of the river all is mountain and forest, with beautiful isolated houses here and there in the valleys. The river and the mountain are contiguous to the city. On the summit of one of the peaks, the highest of the whole, a beautiful church is built, named the Superga, where are the tombs of the Sovereign's ancestors. To the left of the city, as far as the range of the Alps, is a level plain.

A synagogue is being constructed by the Jews in this city—a very stately edifice; that is to say, the wealthy Jews of Italy have united together and are building it in common. It is not as yet completed.

CHAPTER VI.

ITALY; AUSTRIA; 19 DAYS.

FRIDAY, 29th (25th July).—Remained at home. After breakfast the Sovereign came and we went together to the armoury that is in the palace. There were large numbers of weapons, ancient and modern, such as Persian swords on which were inscribed verses of Persian poetry in letters of gold; of which we saw several, and also Persian coats of mail and helmets. There were also some dead horses, made to stand up as though alive, and men, clothed in ancient Frankish armour, made to ride upon them. There were some arms of the ancestors and forefathers of this very Sovereign, such as swords and the like. A sword that the first Napoleon, on the occasion of his adieu at Fontainebleau, gave to an Italian general who was in his service, was there and was examined. There was a sword, long and pointed, like a spear. We went up and down for a long time, saw the whole of the arms, and then returned to our own apartments.

In the afternoon there was a dinner-party in this same

palace. The Sovereign came. We went. In a most magnificent hall a large table was spread. There were one hundred persons around it. We sat down. A most splendid dinner was served, and music also was played. The Sovereign himself partook of no food. I asked the reason. He replied: "My custom is to dine at midnight and immediately to go to sleep." In like manner, the Sovereign's cousin paternally, by reason of this same habit, took no food, and also said that he had never drunk wine, preferring iced water.

The beard of the Sovereign's cousin is long and white; his face is ruddy and fair, his age appears to be about sixty-five; but he is very robust.

The whole of our suite, excepting those who had gone to Vienna, were of the party.

To-day the Sovereign had sent some most beautiful and costly objects as souvenirs to be presented to us; such as portraits in mosaic, the work of Italy, each one being of fabulous value. This art is special to Italy, and has no connexion with the inlaid work made in Persia. That of Persia is made of bone; here it is done with mineral stones of various colours, is most beautiful, and is very rare. A very large table in mosaic, very handsome fowling-pieces, a painted oil portrait of the Sovereign himself and strikingly like him, besides being well executed, some models of buildings executed in marble, some figures of bronze, and a casket in mosaic. In short, many beautiful objects. To the Grand-Vazīr and to the princes, as well as the others, also, had he given decorations.*

In the evening, in company with the Sovereign, we went to the theatre which is in this very palace, but at a great distance. We passed through sundry apartments and that selfsame armoury, arrived at a beautiful and far extending corridor, lighted up as in an illumination, and so reached the theatre. We sat in the first box. It was a very pretty theatre, not very large, and not too small, with five tiers of seats, and many gaslamps. The audience was numerous. They sang; they danced; the curtain went up. As the weather was very sultry, we did not sit out more than two acts, that is, two scenes. There was a singer, Urbin by name, who was very beautiful and young, with a good voice, from the New World.

* The following is a list of these presents :—
    1. Roman Mosaics.
A large view of the Colosseum.
A large view of a Lion Hunt.
Four smaller views in Rome.
    2. Florentine Mosaic.
One casket of gilt bronze.
    3. Bronze Figures.
Antinous.
Cæsar Augustus.
An Athlete.
The Faunus of Praxiteles.
    4. Marbles.
Three *giallo antico* models of monuments in the Forum of Rome.
One goblet of *rosso antico*.
    5. Painting.
One large portrait of His Majesty the King.
    6. Arms.
Five rifles.

They said she had a husband, and in two days' time was to go to (St.) Peter(sburg) as a vocalist. Rising, we came home.

The city of Turin has a population of two hundred thousand. The uniforms of the officers, and the horses of the regular cavalry were beautiful.

Saturday, 30th (26th July).—On rising in the morning the weather was very sultry. We breakfasted, and then went for a tour through the apartments of the palace, viewing the very beautiful pictures, and then the library of the Sovereign, which is in the lower story of the building. There were many books. The arrangement of the library was that of a long corridor.

We then went upstairs and strolled in the palace garden, passing thence to the animals that belong to the Sovereign, which we viewed in this garden in their cages. There were many lions, one black leopard, wolves, foxes, jackals, hyænas, a pair of elephants, a pair of giraffes, tigers, leopards, black bears of Tibet—which are strange beasts. In one cage were many monkeys. There were various kinds of antelopes, a zebra, and other things. Two curious animals were seen there, that were not in any other of the zoological gardens. One was the "lion-yūz," (puma, felis concolor). I had seen a "leopard-yūz" (the Youze, Chetah, Hunting-Cat, gueparda jubata); but had never even heard of a "lion-yūz." It resembles a lion, though it is like a leopard, and very engaging. The other was a monkey of very perverse disposition and savage, that was kept by itself. Man could not pass in front of it. Its teeth were like those of a tiger, and its head enormously large. It had a yellow beard, a nose all red, blue cheeks marked with streaks. It is called the Mandrill, and was brought from Africa.

We returned home; that is to say, that, since it is only with much trouble that a great number of stairs can be mounted, they have arranged a curious apparatus, with a chair resembling a carriage, and in this we seated ourselves; they worked it by winding, and we were slowly lifted, with the greatest comfort, to the upper story of the palace where our quarters were.

After a few moments they announced the arrival of the Sovereign, who was waiting in one of the chambers. We went together in a carriage for a drive through all parts of the city, which was beautifully illuminated. The women and men were very numerous. It possesses very beautiful women. At length we went to the parade-ground, around which are large oak-trees and beautiful avenues. These we traversed, as well as some streets. There was one long street, exceedingly handsome, which they had illuminated, and which extends to the river Po. On the other side of the river, on the tops of the mountains and hills, they exhibited some fine fireworks, which produced a very pleasing effect. These ended, we returned home. I was in the carriage with the Sovereign, the Grand-Vazīr, and M. Bertoleniani (il Cavaliere Ettore Bertolè Viale, Major-General), the Sovereign's Grand Huntsman, aide-de-camp, and companion; we thus reached our quarters.

It is some time since the death of the Sovereign's royal consort that he once had, and he has not again married a royally contracted state wife, having taken a privately-wedded consort, in like way with myself. His wife was not here, having gone to the coast for the purpose of sea-bathing. I sent her a courteous message of attentions, and received a corresponding answer, through the medium of M. Aghemo, private secretary to the Sovereign, who is the son of the paternal uncle (*i.e.*, a cousin) of this consort. The Sovereign said: "My present wife has been with me in my campaigns, and is with me in my hunting excursions. She has even shot two deer herself." By this wife (the Contessa di Mirafiori) he has a son, who is an officer of the cavalry; also a daughter, who was married to a colonel in the army (the Marquis Spinola); but he having died, she is now a widow.

Sunday, 1st *Jumādà-'l-Ukhrà* (*Latter Jumādà*; 27th *July*).—We have to go from Turin to the city of Milan. By rail this is a distance of four hours. Rising in the morning and dressing, we received the Sovereign, who came to visit us, sat down, and had some conversation. Prince Amadeo, the Sovereign's second son, also came. His wife was still unwell, as before. The Heir-Apparent set out yesterday for a summer residence (*sic*; probably a typographical error for Milan) in order to our reception. The Sovereign told me he had shot a deer, which was in the corridor, as he wished me to see it, and to say whether that species exists in Persia or not. I rose and went. They had placed the dead deer in the hall. I saw it. It was of the same species as those deer which

I had seen in the parks in England. It is a kind of stag, but is smaller.

We descended and mounted a carriage, the Sovereign being also present, and we drove to the station. From this place we made use of an Austrian train of cars, which were very beautiful. They have put the whole party, with the luggage, &c., into this one train; and the whole of the carriages communicate with one another, like those of the train we used in Russia.

The Sovereign, with all the magnates and notables of the State, were standing on the platform at the station until the train was put in motion. Saluting each other, we passed on.

The right hand side of the city is all hills. They have built here and there on the hills and in the valleys, which are clothed with forest, very pretty summer-residences. After the train had proceeded a certain distance, the hills on the right hand side receded to a distance, and all became a level open plain, teeming with man and his works. A large proportion of the crops was Indian corn, and this was newly ripe. A difference in the Indian corn of these parts from that of Persia is, in the first place, that the stems of it here are very tall, and secondly, that while the (ears of the) middle of the stems are the same as in Persia, being edible, the tops of the stems are of another sort, bearing ears like wheat, and pendulous, which they also make into flour and eat;* two kinds of Indian corn being thus produced on one stem.

* Probably a mistaken idea of *corn-flour*.—J. W. R.

The wheat and barley were harvested. Many mulberry trees for silkworms were noticed in the neighbourhood of Milan. The silk of Italy is renowned for its good quality; but for several years past, it has not succeeded well. The whole plain was full of trees and crops.

We passed several rivers, large and small. The name of one of the large rivers is the Dona (Dora Ripaira, or, Dora Baltea?), another is the Stura, and the Sicia (Sesia), and the Gicino (Ticino). Well; we pursued our journey, and stopped awhile at Santhia, which is a small town. At every town where the train stopped, the inhabitants, such as soldiers, military officers, civilians, the governor, and the like, came to meet us. We then reached Novara, which is on the skirts of a mountain, the greater part of the houses being on the hills and up in valleys, so that it is very picturesque and striking. From Turin to this place the whole road has been through a plain; here mountains again make their appearance; that is, on the left, where the town is, there are mountains, but on the right, a plain. On these mountains, again, verdure and forest are scarce; but everywhere they have built for themselves isolated houses and mansions for summer residences and other purposes, in very good taste.

When we had left Novara a few leagues behind us, we arrived at the village of Magenta, celebrated ever since the battle fought there and on its fields against the Austrians in the time of the third Napoleon, when the Austrian forces were utterly routed and put to flight in these fields by the French and Italians. A tall column was noticed that has been erected by Napoleon in commemoration, and as a tombstone for those killed in that battle who were French.

We arrived at Milan while it yet wanted two hours and a half to sunset. It has a magnificent and very large terminus, constructed by the Austrian Government at the time when they possessed this city. We had seen but few stations with such beautiful and extensive accommodations.

We alighted from the train; the Heir-Apparent of Italy, who had come here yesterday, who is also himself the special Governor of the place, where he always resides, was awaiting us, with the magistrates, military officers, and civilians. After mutual salutations with the Heir-Apparent, we mounted a carriage. Immense crowds were in the streets and at the windows. The atmosphere was intensely hot; hotter than at Tehrān. We passed through beautiful streets. It is a very handsome city, and possesses very lovely women. We drove a long way, and at length reached the square of the Government Palace, and of the famous church (the Duomo), renowned in all the earth, which they have there erected. Such a church and such an edifice is in no other spot in the world.

Well; we reached the palace. It is a very imposing structure, and full of effects, such as tables, chairs, bedsteads, looking-glasses, and the like. The whole of the rooms, halls, and doors, are ornamented with gildings and paintings; in each of them beautiful stuffs and oil paintings of merit are hung against the walls, numerous chandeliers being suspended from the ceilings. This palace was built in days of old. When the first Napoleon conquered Italy and this city, he thoroughly restored and redecorated the palace, and it remained long in his possession; for Prince Eugene for eight years ruled in this city as viceroy of Napoleon. After that, the country and the palace fell into the hands of Austria, and for years she reigned over them. Prince Maximilian, brother of the present Emperor of Austria, who afterwards became Emperor of Mexico in the New World, where they put him to death, was viceroy for the Emperor of Austria over this city and province. Since the defeat of the Austrians, they have formed a part of the kingdom of Italy.

Well; after a short rest, we felt an inclination to go to the top of the church that is opposite the palace. We rose, and in the first place went into the church. Being Sunday, we found there a great concourse of men and women. We walked about a while. From the interior of the church there is a way, up steps, that ascends to the top. With the Heir-Apparent we went up. There are five hundred and seventy steps to the very summit, and by degrees we mounted. For the first two hundred steps, the way was narrow, dark, and winding; after that, there are spacious terraces and roofs, from whence upwards the steps are easy.

From the summit, the ranges of the Alps and of Mount St. Bernard were visible; over which the first Napoleon led the French forces into Italy. The railway trains, emitting their smoke, and either entering the city from every quarter, or departing therefrom, were very interesting as seen from that elevation. Two triumphal arches erected outside the city by Napoleon on his first conquest of Italy, and a canal, a very large stream, that he caused to be constructed to convey water to the city of Pavia, were also in sight. From the great height of the building, the people below appeared like pismires.

The whole of the church is of white marble, and it has four thousand marble statues in various forms, the utmost of the sculptor's art having been expended in their production. The greater part of these statues are outside the building, standing, sitting, and carved back and front. Some spring out from the walls or building (in alto-relievo), and others are attached to the walls (in basso-relievo). Above, below, the outside and the inside of the church is nothing but marble. The edifice has been built by degrees as time has rolled on, and they are even now still at work upon it, executing sculptures. From five hundred years ago, until now, every day have they laboured in edifying, repairing, or adding to it new works, and they say it will not be completed for another hundred years. The interior of the church contains some wondrously large columns of marble; the roof is also of marble so carved as to make one marvel. And so high is the roof that when one stands up there, he cannot bear to look straight down. It has beautiful altars, pulpits, and figures of all kinds. If a talented sculptor were to work at all hours the whole of his life, exerting the whole of his art in the production of one small casket in marble, still he would not equal the feats of sculpture that are in this church. It is so great a production of genius that if a person were to come, say, from the New World, and after specially inspecting this church, were to return, he would be independent of seeing any other work of art.

Upon the surfaces of the roofs, in the passages, and on the steps, ten thousand persons and more could walk about or sit down without feeling a want of space. The outer surfaces of the roofs are all in large slabs of marble. There are many sculptured spires of marble, each with the marble statue of a man on its summit, and one large central spire, taller than all the others, which has a brass statue upon it, with a flag in its hand. From the top of this statue to the ground or floor of the church is a distance of one hundred and fourteen ells (399 feet); and there are steps up to the front of this statue.

We now descended, passed through the interior of the church, and went to a market, resembling an (eastern) bazaar, and covered in with glass, having been newly constructed. It is not very long or broad; but it is a very pretty bazaar, and we strolled about there a while. Great crowds were there; so we returned home.

In the evening dinner was taken in a very sumptuous hall at an enormous table, where we were the guest of the Heir-Apparent. All the Persian and Frankish grandees were of the party. They gave an excellent dinner, that was spread out over a great space of time. The Governor of the city of Milan, a very fat man, was also present.

Dinner being concluded, we went to a window that faced the church and the square. At least twenty thousand individuals were congregated in this space. They had illuminated the whole church with Bengal lights, which produce different colours. At one moment the entire building from summit to foot was red; at another moment, green, yellow, or some other colour. The white pigeons that have their nests in the upper parts of the towers took fright and flew about. In the darkness of the night they flashed like lightnings in the air from the glare of the lights, and produced a very pleasing effect.

Monday, 2nd (28th July).—We must go to Saltzburg, a place in the dominions of Austria. In the morning we early mounted a carriage, the Heir-Apparent, his officers, and the authorities of the city being present. We drove along the street by which we had arrived the day before, reached the station, took our seat in the train, and started. We passed by numerous cities, in the following order; first, Treviglio; secondly, Bergamo; thirdly, Brescia; fourthly, Desenzano; fifthly, Verona, which is a fortress of importance. As far as Bergamo the country was flat, and everywhere sown with Indian corn or planted with mulberry-trees for silk. We also crossed several rivers, the largest of them all being the Adige, which passes by Verona. Its waters were turbid. When we had passed Bergamo, mountains again appeared on our left hand, the town itself being on the skirts of a hill. Detached houses are here and there built on the hillside, which are very handsome. The hill was verdant, and had a small show of forest.

In every city where our train stopped, the inhabitants in crowds, together with troops, infantry and cavalry, magistrates, and officers, came to meet us. To our left the mountains continued in the same manner, while to our right, as far as the eye could see, all was plain, full of trees, full of produce. The mountains on our left gradually became loftier; but in the greater part of them, up to the very peaks, the people had built for themselves beautiful summer-residences.

And so we went on till we came to a lake, very large and picturesque, inclosed on three sides by lofty mountains, and the water of which was pellucid and extremely pleasant to see. It is smaller than the Lake of Geneva, but still of good size, and had a very charming island in its midst. Many edifices are constructed on that island, which had a bridge-like communication with the mainland. It is called the Lake of Garda. All around it is Italian territory, excepting a small portion of the upper end, which belongs to Austria. The fortress of Peschiera, one of the strongholds of Italy, is on the shore of this lake, and its ditch is always full of water from the lake. There is always a garrison with artillery stationed there by the Government. They fired a salute of cannon from the fortress.

Leaving Peschiera, we reached the city and fortress of Verona. This city is in the midst between the plains and the mountains. All round the city is a fortification, with a ditch, and with powerful batteries, in which are many cannon. Around the mountains, also, they have constructed towers and batteries. The great river Adige, which flows in front of the fortress, has added to its strength. They fired many salutes.

We arrived at a station somewhat above the fortress, and there we stopped. The Governor of the town, and the Commander of the troops of the fortress, with infantry, cavalry, and people of the city, were there waiting. Afterwards the train, returning by the road over which we had come, and passing by the fortress and town of Verona, turned into the road to Saltzburg and Innsbruck. We entered a narrow valley, through which a mighty stream flowed. On both sides were high mountains and a few forests. The name of the river was Aisache (German for the Adige). Our road led continuously through the banks of the river, valleys, and high mountains. The valley was sometimes spacious, sometimes constricted. The mountains became gradually more lofty, more precipitous, and more clothed with forests. Sometimes the mother stream was lost, and secondary waters were met with, coming from other valleys. Numerous are the bridges which they have built over these streams. The beginnings of the valley were little inhabited or cultivated; but, the farther we went, the more of these were seen. Numerous vineyards were planted.

After having traversed this valley for a certain distance, we came to a place named Ala, which is a frontier between the territories of Italy and Austria. At the station of this place the train stopped, and the Austrian officials who were to be in attendance upon us were received in audience. The chiefs of these were a personage of note and Principal Chamberlain of the Emperor. He was also a military officer, his name being the Count de Grenneville, and M. Barb, an Assistant

Master of Ceremonies, who spoke Persian fluently. We had some conversation with these; after which the Italian officials in waiting, the chief of whom was Count Pianelli, received their *congé*. One half of this station belongs to Italy, the other half being the property of Austria, and garrisons from both States are quartered there.

Well; after a delay of ten minutes we resumed our journey, and travelled at a rapid rate. On all sides were lofty mountains, valleys, and immense rivers. The higher we ascended the valley, the more lofty were the mountains, the denser the forests. In the valley itself all was one vineyard, vines supported by trellises, beneath which was a very grateful shade. Along the skirts of the mountains were pretty picturesque villages and works of man.

At the entrance, in the jaws of this valley, the Austrian Government has constructed two strong forts, so that it is impossible for the troops of an enemy to penetrate through this pass. They have placed many a cannon on the summit of the forts and batteries, and always are there officers of trust and garrisons in these two forts. The name of the fortress is Franzansvest. Here it was made known that it is a great distance to Saltzburg, our destination, so that, if we travel continuously, we shall reach there to-morrow afternoon.

At sunset we arrived at a station where the train was stopped for an hour, and where a dinner was prepared in a room for our attendants. I, too, alighted, and inspected the troops that were drawn out. The generals and officers in the place were presented. M. Gersich, a professor of the science of artillery, who was formerly a professor in the College of Science at Tehrān, and of whom Muhammad-Hasan Khān, son of the Commander-in-Chief, with Muhammad-Sādiq Khān Qājār, are two of the best pupils, was there received. His beard had become somewhat grizzled, but his frame was in first-rate condition.

We again took our seat in the train. I had not yet dined; but our suite returned from dinner, and we continued our journey. Although it was dark, still we were aware that there were many rivers, and that we crossed over bridges. On either side were lofty mountains, covered with forest, and narrow valleys; the road, too, was all uphill. A violent storm of thunder and lightning occurred, accompanied by heavy rain. We dined and lay down.

Once we were awakened and heard numerous voices and sounds, from which we gathered that the train had arrived and stopped at Innsbruck. The inhabitants of the town, women and men, the governor and officers, were all in attendance, creating a marvellous hubbub. When we were again left alone, we slept, and on awaking in the morning, again was there discussion and controversy. The train went on, and anew did sleep obtain the mastery. Two hours later, we arose and dressed. We were now in the German territory of the kingdom of Bavaria. I looked out upon the open country, which was like a paradise—huge mountains full of forests, trees of fir and yews of the forest in great numbers, lands all verdant, meadows, numerous flowers of every colour;

and although it was the middle of the hot season, the plain and the mountains [were as in opening spring. There were numbers of rivers, branches of the Danube, flowing into the Danube, and everywhere crops, which here were not yet reaped. The air was cool as in a hill-station.

And thus we reached the town of Rosenheim, one of the cities of Bavaria. From hence to the Bavarian capital, Munich, or to Saltzburg, our destination, is an equal distance, about one hour and a half's journey. The train stopped here a short time, and then we again set off with our faces towards Saltzburg.

We everywhere passed through charming sites and forests of larch, and by a pretty little lake, arriving thus at the station of the city of Trauenstein, where there was a great concourse. We held a long chat with one of these inhabitants of Germany who knew French; and one of the people of the town who had made a pipe out of the stem of a tree, in an artistic manner, presented it to us as a souvenir of the place, and we accepted it. The population of this city is about four or five thousand.

Well; we arrived at the river Saltza, which is the boundary between the states of Austria and Bavaria, and flows past Saltzburg. We crossed a bridge and reached the station, where the inhabitants of the town, and the troops were waiting.

It is a handsome city, with a pleasant climate, and situated by the side of a wooded mountain, having a population of fourteen thousand souls. This is the place where the third Napoleon had a meeting with the present Emperor of Austria. It has a famous salt-mine.

We mounted a carriage and drove to the palace. It is a handsome palace, very ancient, with a small square in front, a stone basin of water, with a large fountain, the water pouring from the mouths of two horses and men of stone also. Around the square are a church and a hotel.

The greater part of our journey to-day and yesterday was through the Tyrol, Austrian territory. The mountains thereof are styled the Tyrolean Alps. From Milan to Saltzburg the distance is more than two hundred and fifty leagues, which we traversed in twenty-three hours.

This city and province were formerly in the hands of the priests, who exercised sovereignty here; and this very palace in which are our quarters, is one of their buildings. A hill, covered with forest and verdure is in the middle of the town, on the summit of which the priests, in the days of their rule, constructed the palace and a strong castle for the defence of the place. They led a wall along the middle of the hill; *i.e.*, there is a great vein of rock, upon which they built the wall. There are some handsome hotels in the town, especially one called the Hôtel d'Europe.

To-day, on the frontier of Bavaria and Austria, we saw a castle, from whence they fired guns, and named Hofstein, to which they send political prisoners.

Tuesday, 3rd (29th July).—God willing, we have to go to the city of Vienna, the capital of Austria.

We rose in the morning. In the neighbourhood of the town there is a place known by the name of Schönbrunn, at the distance of half an hour's drive, constructed in the days of the sovereignty of the priests. The word "Schönbrunn" in the German tongue has the meaning of "clear spring" (*read:* "beautiful spring"). We mounted a carriage and drove out, the princes and others following us. The weather was a little warm. Leaving the city, there was an avenue that afforded a shade. Everywhere the carriage drove along avenues, until we reached a park and a palace. In this place, and in a few others, I saw many plane-trees, differing somewhat, however, from those of Persia, as the trunks and branches of those seen here are darker, blacker than those in Persia; but the leaves show no difference.

Well; we reached the park, which was laid out with flower-beds and grass. There were numbers of women and men, travellers or spectators. This park, together with certain other establishments, and buildings with basins of water, of old construction, is situated at the foot of a hill covered with forest and verdure. Numerous springs of clear water issue forth from the skirts of the hills, and over each of these springs they have erected a pavilion or a place like a basin or like a waterfall, into which the water flows from the spring, and passes thence by broad channels. The water was cool and pleasant to drink; and there were a great many trout, the "red-spotted trout" of Persia, seen in the water there. Going down along the bank of the stream for a stroll, we came to some very pretty places, where again many springs and basins of water were seen; also some places where establishments for basins of water, as it were, were constructed of rock. Others were made to resemble cabinets, the summits being upreared, and six or seven cocks, called in French "robinet" (and in Persian "lion"), were visible. Upon turning any one of these cocks, water springs forth from some fountain, or from the earth, or from the roof of a chamber. For instance, there was seen one place with a basin of water, in the middle of which was a small fountain, with a crown of brass over the fountain. Upon gently opening a cock, the water filled the under part of the crown, and gradually lifted the crown until it touched the roof of the chamber, which was then gradually made to descend again. This is at the discretion of a man; should he wish it, the crown could be raised to a height of twenty ells (70 feet) and again made to descend. Another thing in which there was much to laugh at, and which was a novelty, was this: As people or spectators were unconcernedly amusing themselves by walking about in the gravelled avenues and environs of the corridors, without knowing that the earth beneath their feet among the gravel of the avenues was full of fountains and small holes, so as not to be noticeable, they suddenly opened the cock that shut off the source from these fountains, upon which the water spouted forth from all sides, from the soil, from the avenues, from above, and from below, wetting all the people, who thereupon took to flight. This was rare fun; and in justice it may be said that herein great cleverness has been displayed, the whole having been so well kept from the days of yore till now.

The air here was cool and resembling that of a hill-station.

Another sight was this: They have made a town of pasteboard or of wood, replete with all manner of objects, and placed it on the other side of the stream opposite to the spring. Every one of the people of this town is busy at some kind of occupation, one dancing, another making a bear dance, one riding in a carriage, another drinking water beneath a spring and a tree; and so on, in many other ways. This piece of mechanism is also set in motion by the water power of the springs. It has a screw, or a cock, or a small apparatus, the which, on being handled, sets the people of the town in motion, who then perform strange and marvellous things. It was very amusing.

Again; there was a water-channel, and on either side of this a tortoise was set, with their mouths so exactly opposite to one another that the water which spouted with great force from the one, poured into the other, and one could not distinguish whether it was water or a tube of crystal passed from the mouth of the one tortoise into that of the other; but on interposing the hand, and so interrupting the communication, one ascertained that it was water; and when the hand was removed, the crystal rod was re-established. This was a very curious contrivance.

Furthermore; within the channels of water they had arranged, as a specimen, a spectacle, and an amusement, a manufactory of earthenware, a cotton-carding engine, a knife-grinding wheel, and other similar things,—the workmen being all small, the wheels and machines all toys, but so arranged that there was no dissimilarity from real workshops and real workmen.

The whole of these things were made and arranged a hundred and twenty years ago, merely for the display of ingenuity.

Well; we strolled about a long time; but, as it was necessary to be in the train by a certain given hour, in order to proceed to Vienna, we could not spend more time in sight-seeing. We therefore returned to the city, driving straight to the station; we there waited a space in one of the rooms, and then took our seat in the train.

By railway it is a distance of seven hours from here to Vienna. The Grand-Vazīr sent a message to say that the Governor of Saltzburg wished to take leave and return. We arose, stood by the side of the railway carriages, and exchanged salutes with the Governor; upon which he took his departure, and we at length started.

This line has no high mountains; but on both sides of the way we saw pretty little hills,—green and cheerful, and forests—full of firs and yews. Some cultivated places were newly reaped, showing the yellow colour of the crops in the midst of the green meadows and grand forests. But, on our right hand, at a great distance off, the high mountains were reached; while on both sides of the line all was gentle hill and dale, populous, teeming with crops, and abounding with woods, most beauteous. It was a charming journey. The weather, too, was moderate; at times, even cloudy, with a cool breeze. At every station where we made a stop, there were people to receive us, with troops of the line and bands.

At the city of Lintz, where the train stopped, multitudes of women and men were collected in front of the station. We alighted, and inspected the troops. We then retreated to a room assigned to our use, where they had prepared a breakfast. This place possessed some most beautiful women. Austria, in point of beauty and engagingness, is the queen of all lands.

Well; when our party had breakfasted, we returned to our train and again proceeded. The appearance of the country was still the same with that above described; perhaps more beautiful even. We then arrived at a small town called Hammelbach, and shortly after passing it, we saw the mighty river Danube on our left hand. Our road lay for a short distance along its bank, and then swerved to a distance. Next we reached the town of St. Polten, where, on the summit of a hill in the middle of the town, we noticed a palace, a church, and a college, of very imposing structure, and belonging to the priests. That must be a very charming place, with a beautiful view. As we approached more and more towards the city of Vienna, the more did we see beautiful towns, populous places, sumptuous summer-residences in the valleys and at the foot of the hills covered with forests, together with most charming sites. The houses were of a most pleasing aspect, and lovely streams of water occurred on our road.

At about sunset we arrived at the station of Penzing, where the train stopped, His Most Exalted Majesty the Emperor of Austria being on the platform awaiting us, with the Nawwāb the Heir-Apparent and the Princes, who had come out two (probably ten) leagues from town to meet us. Alighting, I gave my hand. The Emperor's name is Francis-Joseph, who is of the House of Habsburg, and his father is still alive, bearing the name of Francis-Charles and being of the age of sixty-five. Of the persons who were with the Emperor were the Count de Bellegarde and Baron Schlechta, the Persian interpreter, who spoke extremely well; besides many other officers and officials, high and low, with others also.

After salutation we entered the railway carriage, where I was with the Emperor, the Grand-Vazīr, Mīrzā Malkam Khān, Baron Schlechta, Count Dubeski—the Austrian Envoy to Tehrān, and Count Grenneville—in attendance upon us. We proceeded.

Our quarters are in the Château of Laxenburg, built by Maria-Theresa, a former Queen of Austria, at a distance of five leagues from the city of Vienna. The Emperor's quarters were at Schönbrunn, which is nearer to town. As the air of the city was sultry, we did not make it our residence.

Well; we arrived at the Château of Laxenburg. There were a few households in the environs, which gave it the appearance of a town. The Château itself is a square building of two stories, with a court in the middle, and a small square. All the rooms communicate with one another. The princes, the 'Alā'u-'d-Dawla, and Hasan Ali Khān—Minister of Public Works, are quartered in a mansion at some little distance from here. In front of our palace there is a very extensive park, with beautiful avenues, a lake, and a small river.

Well; we reached the palace with the Emperor and others. The Emperor presented his grand functionaries of state, his princes, and others. First, the Heir-Apparent of the Empire, who is fourteen years of age, and who is the only son. He is a very polished, courteous, engaging, handsome youth, and his name is Rudolf; also Charles-Louis and Louis-Victor, both of them princes, Count Andrassi—the Prime Minister of Austria, and the other Ministers, military and civil. After which, we also presented the Grand-Vazīr, the princes, and the others. The Emperor then withdrew, and we received the princes and others who had preceded us to Vienna. In the evening we dined and retired to rest.

Wednesday, 4th (30th July).—This day we went to the palace of Schönbrunn, to return the Emperor's visit. By rail it is at a distance of half an hour. After sitting and conversing for a short time, we returned to our own quarters.

Thursday, 5th (31st July).—Rose in the morning and breakfasted. The weather was sultry to such a degree that it was impossible to go out of doors. Dr. Polack, who was formerly Professor of Medicine at Tehrān, and for several years was also our own Chief Physician, was received in audience. I was extremely gratified at seeing the Doctor. He is a nice man, has grown somewhat aged, has taken a wife, had been for a time in Egypt, and is now in Vienna.

In the afternoon we mounted a carriage and went for a drive about the park of the palace. We noticed a large canal, like a river, that passes through the park, and it has some handsome bridges over it. There was a pond with multitudes of fish in it. They scattered some crumbs of bread, when some good large fishes made their appearance. They informed me that these fishes have been here in the pond these two hundred years. The park and its avenues are of great extent; and there was a large lake in it, with trees and lawns surrounding it, and with some pretty islands in it. We noticed many wild geese in one of the islands, and there were multitudes of women and men on the shores of the lake, who had come out sightseeing. Here we alighted from the carriage and took our seat in a boat for a promenade on the water.

There is an old edifice on the shore of this lake, built in times gone by, that has a threatening keep of great strength, and is called the "Knight's Castle." It has some columns, and upon the summits of these are the figures of men, cocks, and the like, in cast metal. Its gates are of iron and very strong. This palace and castle are exactly like the palaces of the demons, magicians, wizards, and genii, of which one has read in story-books and legendary tales. We passed through several doors, and arrived at strange-looking apartments and passages. Each room and each corridor has also its iron door. There was one dark place, very frightful, in which they have placed a dead wolf upon a platform, arranged with its skin and its hair to look like life. A dreadful-looking man, made of pasteboard, was set up, and chained with chains as prisoners are secured. Beneath this room are secret appliances, the which, being put in motion, cause the hands and feet of that captive to move about. Should any one uninformed and alone happen to enter that dark place and witness those movements of the imprisoned man, he would doubtless feel alarmed.

There was also another place seen, circular in form and roofed over, in which they have set up large marble statues of the ancestors of this (present) Emperor, and of the Sovereigns of the province of Austria, which are finely sculptured.

After that, all that was viewed of the apartments, small or large, above or below, was altogether frightful, harrowing, and suffocating; which is as much as to say that a castle of knights must be in this manner. There was, however, one other room in which were pasteboard figures of olden knights clothed in their iron armour, while other ancient weapons were suspended to the roofs and walls. There were many awe-inspiring apartments communicating with one another. It was like the talisman of Zangūla; and we also saw there the drum and Pandean pipe of the wizards spoken of in tales.

After this stroll we returned home. The Grand-Vazīr and others who had been into town to visit the Exhibition gave a description of the heat and unwholesomeness of the atmosphere.

We also went to-day to the quarters of the Heir-Apparent, sitting and conversing there a certain time. The Heir-Apparent, although young in years, is well instructed and an attractive youth. In the empire of Austria he is (fitted to become) an excellent souvenir of the Emperor.

Friday, 6th (*1st August*).—To-day, after breakfast, some German princes came to visit us. Their names are as follows : the son of the ex-King of Hanover, who now resides with his father in Austria, Prussia having taken possession of his kingdom, is named Ernest-Augustus; one of the Bavarian princes, named Arnulf; one of the princes of Wurtemburg, named Maximilian ; a prince of Saxe-Weimar, named Hermann.

After these, the Prime Minister of Austria, Count Andrassy, came to an audience, and a long conversation ensued. Then, the Ambassador of England, named Buchanan (the Right Hon. Sir Andrew Buchanan, G.C.B.) ; and next the Ambassador of the Ottoman State, Qabūli Pasha, came also.

We now left and proceeded by train to the palace of Schönbrunn, where we were to be the guest at the table of the Emperor at dinner. We arrived at the station, mounted a great number of steps, found a carriage waiting, took our seats therein, and drove (to the palace).

Schönbrunn is a town, the houses of which are in continuation with those of the suburbs of the city of Vienna, so that it is not very distant from Vienna itself. The number of the population and of the houses in the town of Schönbrunn is less than those of Versailles and of Potsdam near Berlin.

In front of the Emperor's palace there is a square. The carriage drove to the foot of a staircase within a corridor of the palace; and there, at the foot of the staircase the Emperor was awaiting us. Alighting, we gave our hand, went upstairs, and entered a room, where the princes of Austria and Germany, the Emperor's brother, and others, were assembled. We stayed there a certain time. The

Emperor offered excuses for the second son of the
Sovereign of Holland, who happened to be at Vienna,
and who had been invited to the dinner, but had not
arrived. For this reason we went late to the dinner
table. After a little, however, the son of the Sovereign of
Holland came, whose name is Alexander, and we went to
table. All were there. This saloon is all in white, with
a few plaster ornaments and gildings. The ceiling is
painted, as though with designs executed on the plaster.
All the rooms and halls are plain, and there are not a
great many objects of luxury, such as pictures, portraits,
and the like; though a few pictures were noticed of
events in the life of the present Emperor, of Maria-
Theresa, and others.

In front of this saloon there is a park, with beautiful beds
of flowers, lawns, and avenues. The whole of the leaves
of the trees on both sides of the avenue have been clipped
with shears, and the resemblance of walls of verdure has
been thus produced. At the further end of the garden was
a lofty green mound, and on the summit of this a small
building with many columns overlooking the garden. At
the foot of the mound, within the garden, there is a basin
of water with fountains that send their water to a great
height, but do not always play. When it is wished, their
sources are opened (and the fountains play).

At the conclusion of dinner we went to another room,
where the whole of the guests at dinner were assembled
and conversed with one another. Prince Hohenlohe, one
of the grandees of the Emperor's Court, Minister of the
Palace and first person there, a handsome young man,

was also present. I gave to the Heir-Apparent the decoration of my own Portrait set in diamonds.

We then went to the station, and by train returned home and retired to rest. During the night a violent wind with rain set in, which cooled the air and watered the ground.

Saturday, 7th (2nd August).—This day we have to go to the city of Vienna and visit the Exhibition.

When we rose in the morning, the air, through the rain of last night and the clouds, which were a real godsend from the secret providence of the Lord Most High, was very cool and pleasant. Had it been otherwise, it would have been an extremely irksome task to go to town through that excessive heat and with the dust and dirt of the roads.

We offered our thanks to God, dressed, mounted, and started, the whole of our suite being of the cortège. By rail, the distance to the city was one hour or less. The country was most charming, the air pleasant, the fields green, and flowers of various kinds were noticed. There were many hares among the crops.

We came near to the city. As the town of Vienna is situated in a hollow, no trace of it is visible until one comes close upon it. On one side of it is a mound and the hills of Schönbrunn, the city being at the foot of these in an extremely low spot. From this cause, its atmosphere during the summer season is hot and unhealthy. It has neither a citadel, nor fortifications, nor a ditch. By reason of the lowness of the central parts of the city, the streets are all downhill to one who enters from the outskirts. The river Danube skirts one side of the town, and a canal therefrom, dug by hand, enters the city; but this is very much smaller than the river Seine in Paris. Very small steamers ply thereon. The water of this river is not fit to drink. In bygone days the inhabitants of Vienna had no (good) water to drink, and through the filthy state of the Danube that flows by the city, they were much exposed to sicknesses from using it; but now the Emperor, at the expense of the inhabitants of the city, has dug a large canal for the snowy waters of the mountain streams and springs, which he is leading into the town. Great expense has been incurred, and the work is not yet complete. It was said that it would be finished in another year. The population of the city of Vienna is six hundred thousand souls.

Well; the Emperor, with all his officials, and others, were on the platform waiting. We alighted, gave our hand to the Emperor, and together mounted a carriage. We drove through every part of the city and along a boulevard newly constructed, by an ancient building called the Belvedere, where they now have made a collection of paintings, and near to the Arsenal—a place where arms are kept, which has a high wall and towers, crossed a bridge over a branch of the river Danube, and so arrived at a long avenue with large trees on either side, which led straight to the building of the Exhibition. On both sides of this avenue is a spacious park and meadow. They have erected some elegant coffee-shops of wood, with numerous chairs and gas-lamps, the whole way to the vicinity of the Exhibition. From the first place of our entry into the town until we reached this spot, everywhere crowds were collected; but, by reason of the notoriety of the cholera sickness and of the unwholesomeness of the air of the city, the whole of the notables thereof had gone away to their summer residences in hill-stations.

We arrived at the Emperor's private pavilion outside the Exhibition building, where a table was prepared for breakfast. We sat down to this and partook of the breakfast; after which, in company of the Emperor, we went to the Exhibition, a large enclosure like an Eastern bazaar. In the centre of this bazaar a very spacious and lofty dome of a globular form was erected—a very magnificent structure and full of interest. There are stairs and a way by which people go to the top thereof to enjoy the sight. The whole of this circular apartment, of the bazaars, and of the rest, are of iron, common glass, and plate-glass. The bazaars branch off from this large dome in every direction, the contour of the whole building being also circular. It has two passages for entry and exit, being closed elsewhere. Beneath the great dome they had arranged a very beautiful basin of water with a fountain from which water flowed. Great multitudes were within the Exhibition. They had apportioned special sections and places to each nation and State that had brought its effects and productions there. For instance, the French nation had one long bazaar, and two other bazaars by the two sides of that; in which the various productions of their own country were arranged, even to the stems of such and such forest trees of such and such a province of France, with the dried leaves of the same; and whatever may be the forms of the cattle, wild beasts, or birds of such a town or such a place in France, representations thereof were exhibited there. From these minor particulars an inference may be drawn as to the principal commodities of choice, such as tissues of wool and silk, mirrors, plate-glass, warlike implements, and others, all of which were sent there in the best taste.

Other nations also in like manner, *i.e.*, some great States like Russia, England, Germany, and even Austria itself, had much space, and vast exhibits. The Ottoman State, Egypt, Greece, Japan, China, and others, had sent a sufficiency of every kind of commodities.

In this way did we make the tour of the bazaars with the Emperor, until we reached the part where the commodities of the Persian State were set forth. Although it was but three months that an edict had been promulgated that merchants and others should collect commodities and send them—which was much too late, and the greater part had not yet arrived,—still we saw a fair quantity of precious stuffs and productions. We stayed there some little while; and then the Emperor expressed the wish, as the Empress was indisposed and had gone to a summer-residence, to go there; we bade adieu, and the Emperor left. We, on our part, went a second time round all the bazaars, and in one of them lighted upon the Grand-Duke Constantine, brother of the Emperor of Russia, and a very charming prince. We stopped and exchanged salutations with him, which resulted in a long conversation. He was somewhat unwell, and looked pale. On my asking his ailment, he told me that on his return from Nicholaieff to (St.) Peter(sburg), he had gone to Cronstadt, and there, in passing from one ship to another he had wished to visit, he had had a fall and severely injured his foot. It was evident that he had been much hurt.

Well; after leaving the Exhibition, we went to view the specimens that had been put up of the buildings of various countries. There was one very beautiful building, and a grandiose mosque with a tall minaret from Egypt; also, a mansion and a coffee-shop from the Ottoman State, and one very beautiful house built by the Persian Government. With the exception of these, I did not examine those of any other country. We went to the Persian mansion, to which were several steps to be mounted. Its builder was a certain architect of the name of Ismāʻīl, together with one carpenter. Although it was but three months that they had been commissioned to build this house, they had executed their task with great taste, and had so quickly constructed the edifice as to elicit wonder and applause. The carpenter and the builder were both present, the latter in these three months' space having learnt the German language well, which was a subject of still greater astonishment. We sat down there, the Archduke Regnier—President of the Exhibition—being in our presence.

Next we went to the Ottoman and Egyptian buildings, viewed them, and then drove off in our carriage to town, passing through its remaining districts, by its buildings, and into its markets, until we reached the palace inhabited by the Emperor, and from thence arrived at the station, took our seat in the train, and went home. Thanks be unto God that all has gone well.

The expense of this Exhibition is at the charge of the Government, which has incurred an outlay of seven crores (1,120,000*l*.). Three months hence, when it shall have been removed, there will have been realized, from the sale of materials and the money taken at the doors from visitors, a sum of three and a half crores (560,000*l*.), half of the outlay being so much loss to the Government. They say, however, that from the traffic (hereby occasioned) there will be large sums gained in other ways by the inhabitants and by the State.

This Emperor has reigned for more than three-and-twenty years. Ferdinand I., uncle of this Sovereign, was Emperor, but abdicated the Crown and is still living, being eighty years of age, and resides at Prague, one of the great cities of Austria. The Sovereignty then fell to his brother, the father of the present Emperor; he declined it, and gave it to his son. This father of the Emperor is also living still. He is in Vienna during the winter, but goes to Ischl in the summer as a hill-station, where he now is at the present time.

Sunday, 8th (3rd August).—This day we had no engagement. In the afternoon we drove in the park and had a long row on the lake. The Grand-Vazīr and Mīrzā Malkam Khān also came with us in the boat. At sunset we returned home.

The Sanī'u-'d-Dawla and the Muḥaqqiq have gone to

the town of Baden, which is at a distance of one league from this palace. There are hot and cold mineral springs at that place, which have great efficacy in certain maladies, especially in the affection of paralysis and the like. At the present season invalids repair thither to undergo treatment.

Monday, 9th (4th August).—The Emperor has invited us to a shooting party for this afternoon, and to dinner at Schönbrünn for the evening. Towards the afternoon, therefore, we took our seat in a train, went to the palace and town of Schönbrunn, alighted from the train, and got into a carriage. The Emperor had left for the hunting-ground. We therefore pushed on, drove past the suburbs of the city of Vienna, where are the summer-residences of the citizens, as follows: after Schönbrunn came Stetzendorff, next Hitzing, and then Laintz, where are the shooting-grounds of the Emperor. The road was long. There are many mansions and hotels in these villages.

We drove on until we had left behind us all traces of human habitations, and came to a long avenue with dense forest on either side, leading to a spot where they had surrounded (a part of) the forest with screens of strong canvas, white in colour, and high, but in the folds of which no wood was used, each cloth, instead of rope, having a wooden frame that leant against the screen. This is a very excellent arrangement, as against the wind.

Well; around the forest for the extent of about two leagues had they set up this fence, and so cut off the passage of animals. We arrived there, and saw the

Emperor waiting on foot with the sportsmen, and dressed in the costume of a huntsman, having a feather stuck in his cap. At intervals, lurking-places of planks, resembling square boxes, were placed, and around them fir branches with their leaves masked the boxes, which were raised from the ground and ascended by two steps. There were about a hundred of these huts so arranged, and in each were three or four breech-loading rifles for balls, with a supply of ball-cartridges, and also two or three of the magnates seated, who were to fire the shots.

I wished to descend from the carriage and get on my feet; but the Emperor opposed this, and so we proceeded further on in the carriage, the Emperor, with the others, walking on foot, until we reached a hut, higher and further forward than any of the rest, which had been allotted to us. Here we alighted, got up on to the planks, and there took our station, the Emperor going to another hut further down. We now took up the Emperor's rifles placed in our hut, loaded them, and made ready.

The Emperor's huntsman, a man of Bohemia, and named Count Virbin, a person seventy years old, and hard of hearing through age, besides being nearly blind, was present; and with him we held a little conversation about the chase in Persia and as carried out by the Emperor, which latter is as follows:

We have already explained that a large number of screens had been set up. These screens came along in like manner, so that there were screens in front, opposite to us, and screens behind us, at our backs. From the place where we were seated, to the screen in front, was about thirty feet. There was a door arranged a little above the spot where I was, for the entry and exit of the game; and there was no other passage by which they could come or go. Forty or fifty men drove the deer from the forest, and caused them to enter by that door in batches of twenty or thirty each. As one of these batches entered and came along, the deer passed before the riflemen at a distance of about ten feet, and they began to fire, uninterruptedly shooting at the deer with bullets. If they did not hit them from this hut, they did from a second, a third, or so on to the last, which was a long way off. The animals scampered along in quest of a place of escape; but no means of flight was there, and at length all were slain. When not one of these was left breathing, a fresh batch was driven within the screen, and these were likewise slaughtered as their predecessors. I also fired a few shots. These deer are of the species of the stag, and are not very wild. Two or three batches were thus admitted and killed. In short, it was capital sport, and passed off very pleasantly.

The Emperor now came, and together we mounted our carriage, driving by the road along which we had arrived there, back to the Château of Schönbrunn, in the park of which we had a walk. It has beautiful avenues, lofty trees, with marble statues along the avenues. There is a mound at the end of the park, with a building on its summit, and a winding path to go up. On arriving there, we noticed a zoological garden, which we surveyed in a cursory manner. There was an elephant, a rhinoceros, some beautiful parrots, and some other animals. This park and the zoological garden are open to the public, and people are always walking about in them.

Well; we returned to the palace, went to the dinner-table, and enjoyed a good repast. After that we returned to our own quarters by train.

In the forenoon to-day the Corps Diplomatique of Vienna were received in audience, the names of some of the members of which may be here mentioned: Novikoff, Envoy from Russia; the Viscount de Jonghe, Envoy from Belgium; Mr. Jay, Envoy from the United States; Count de Robilant, Envoy from Italy.

Tuesday, 10*th* (5*th August*).—To-day a photographer came and took several negatives of us. We strolled about a while in the park. An individual brought a pump and apparatus which in ten minutes time bored a hole in the earth to the depth of ten ells (35 feet), and brought up water from thence, pouring out of the pump. The apparatus is made of steel and iron, and however hard or stony the ground may be, it pierces it. Each set of apparatus was of the price of fifteen tūmāns (6*l*.). I ordered several sets to be purchased and to be brought to Persia.

In the afternoon we went by train to the city, all the princes, and the greater portion of our household officers accompanying us. At sunset we reached the city station and alighted. The Emperor had gone to the theatre, and thither we repaired also. It was the Grand Opera-house of Vienna, and perhaps better than those of all other places. We alighted at the door of the theatre, and the Emperor was awaiting us at the foot of the staircase. Giving our hand, we went up together. The Emperor presented several of the Lady-Princesses, as follows: The Archduchess Elisabeth, wife of Charles Ferdinand; Marie-Renière, Princess de Joinville, wife of the son of Louis-Philippe and daughter of the Sovereign of Brasil; Princess Coburg, daughter of Louis-Philippe and wife of the Prince of Coburg. We went into the box, and took our seat in the middle, these Lady-Princesses being to our right and left, the Grand-Vazīr behind us. The princes of Austria and Germany were all present. In justice, it is a very noble theatre. The present Emperor has displayed in this theatre much architectural talent. It has five tiers of seats, and a lofty, spacious, handsome ceiling, together with most beautiful branches for gaslights, chandeliers, and other adornments. The audience was numerous.

The curtain rosé. So beautiful a play did they perform, with dancing and music, that the like had been witnessed in no pláce before. The costumes of the players were at every moment of a different shape and colour, all of rich stuffs and delicate tints. This evening there was a ballet. Each time the scene changed and the dance varied, they brought out apparatus for conjuring, with demons, genii, and fairies, in a way that set one beside himself. The daughters of the Fairy of the Night were in a green and most charming forest, the moon was declining to its setting, so that its sheen was reflected in the water of a stream,—the moon, the ripples of the water, and the forest, being all exactly like real. A stout tree had been blown down and had fallen across the stream in guise of a bridge, and on this the fairies danced. Suddenly demons made their appearance, and the fairies vanished; the demons danced, and genii came forth. Then the demons disappeared and the fairies were seen again. Now suddenly this green forest and spring view was converted into a north-polar region with mountains of ice; snow fell; the waters of the sea brought forward pieces of ice like mountains, and again washed them away. White polar bears, crocodiles, walruses—sea-elephants came and went away again upon the ice. A prince was held prisoner in this wintry scene, and was about to die, when suddenly the daughters of the pole and the fairies of the regions of frost came forth with dresses and hair white and covered with snow. They brought forth fire from the earth, warmed the prince, and all danced together in pretty costumes, and keeping time to the music, in every air played, in a manner truly wonderful. The prince, with his Vazīr, had been made a captive in the house of a sorcerer. So many magical effects did they represent that it is not possible to describe them.

Ultimately, there was a scene that represented the bottom of the ocean. Fishes, various shells, coral flowers, seaweeds, marine flowers, the undulation of the water at the bottom of the sea, nymphs of ocean—each a saucy, coquettish child—lying beneath those weeds and flowers, were shown. At one time, from within the shells and flowers, one sea nymph would come forth, most lovely; at another, the angels of the clouds would come down and dance; sometimes they would sink into the earth, and at other times would mount into the air in a balloon or on the back of a griffin, and again come down. The correct description cannot be written. Although I had not dined, I did not desire it to finish.

At length all was concluded; we rose and came down. The Emperor accompanied us to the side of our carriage, thence departing. We came to the station, took our seat (in the train), reached home, dined, and retired to rest late.

Wednesday, 11th (6th August).—In the morning, the Grand-Duke Constantine, brother of the Emperor of Russia, came, and some conversation ensued. On account of the pain caused by his foot, he had a stick in his hand. To-day we have to go to Schönbrunn in the afternoon to see a review of troops. At that time we went to the station and alighted at Schönbrunn, there mounting a carriage to proceed to the review. We passed through streets and arrived on a grassy plain with short herbage that had become yellow. The Emperor, surrounded by his staff, was waiting on horseback. We, too, mounted a horse, the Grand-Vazīr, the Husāmu-'s-Saltana, and our Generals being also mounted. The I'tizādu-'s-Saltana, the Nusratu-'d-Dawla, and the rest were on foot, and stood in front of a small room that had been prepared for us, and furnished with a chair.

We and the Emperor, with the Austrian and Persian officers, and others, rode forward. The infantry battalions, the cavalry, and the artillery, were drawn up in five long lines, one behind the other, like a column. We passed with the Emperor on horseback in front of each

z

of these five lines, composed of very handsome soldiers in fine uniforms; especially the regiments of Hungarian hussars and dragoons. The horses of the cavalry and artillery were all strong and handsome; they are procured in Hungary, the horses of that country being good. The dress of the Austrian infantry has been of white cloth from of old, as it still is; but according to what people said, the Emperor wishes to exchange that colour for light blue.

Well; after a long stroll, we came and took up a position in front of that same wooden hut, and the troops, infantry, cavalry, and artillery, marched past in our presence. Altogether they amounted to fifteen thousand men. There were also numerous spectators. Some few individuals of distinction among the Arabs of the province of Algiers, a portion of France, had come to the Exhibition, and were all there (at the review) on horseback in those white Arab clothes and turbans. The Emperor went, saluted them, and returned. The names of those Arabs were as follows: 'Alīyyu-'sh-Sharīfu Farhān; Muhammadu-'l-Hanafī; 'Abdu-'d-Dīn Mu'askar; Hasanu-'bnu-Aqdi-'bni-Ahmada-'l-Jazā'irī; Muhammadu-'bnu-Muhammadi-'s-Sayfī. They all spoke French well.

At sunset, when the review was over, we returned home. The Emperor and all the principal officers wore green feathers in their hats.

Thursday, 12th (7th *August*).—This afternoon we have to go to Schönbrunn because, the Empress having come in from her summer-residence, there is a party there.

After breakfast, the Emperor's brother, who has also

come from his summer-residence, and whose name is Charles Louis, was received. We gave hands and mutually saluted. He was a very pleasant-looking, pleasant-spoken man. It was about fifteen days that he had had a wedding, that is, he had married two wives before, and both had died; he has now taken a fresh wife from among the Lady-Princesses of the realm of Portugal, but born and brought up in the land of Bavaria, in which land also the Emperor's brother held his wedding. After a long conversation he left.

At sunset we went by train to Schönbrunn, arrived there, and were met by the Emperor at the foot of the staircase. We took one another's hands. At the top of the stairs the Empress was waiting; we reached her, mutually saluted, and then, giving her my hand, we went into the first room, where there was a congregation of the Lady-Princesses and Princes of Austria and Germany, who had newly come in from their summer-residences. The Emperor presented the men, and the Empress the women. The Empress has a very pleasant face and a very graceful figure; she is kind and is a superior person. In health, she is rather delicate, and for this reason passes the most part of her time at all four seasons away from the capital. She is thirty-six years of age.

Well; taking the hand of the Empress, we went into a large hall, where the members of the Diplomatic Corps, with their wives, the Princes of Austria and Germany, and the brothers of the Emperor, all were collected. In the hall a number of small tables were laid out for supper. The Arabs from Algiers, also, were all here this evening. After a good deal of conversation, a certain number of individuals took their seats at each table for supper. Around our table were the Empress, the Grand-Vazīr, Qabūli Pasha—the Ottoman Ambassador, Count Andrassy—the Austrian Premier, and one other elderly woman of importance. I sat a long while, and had much conversation with the Empress. She expressed great regret at not having come several days earlier and at having come this evening only to say adieu. I, too, moved by her demonstrations of kindness, expressed my friendship at great length.

When supper was over, all rose, and the Emperor came. I also rose. In this assembly the Emperor had taken a seat with a few other individuals at a separate table, and had there supped. We now went out on to a long and narrow terrace in front of the palace and looking on to the garden, for the purpose of witnessing some fireworks. Many chairs were placed there, and we sat down with the Empress on our right hand and the wife of the Emperor's brother on our left. The other Lady-Princesses and women also took their places to the right and left. The Emperor remained on foot, the rest of the company being some on foot also, and some seated. About five hundred musicians were stationed in the park and performed airs. There was also an immense concourse of spectators. The fountains of the basins played. The building on the hill opposite to the palace where we were sitting was illuminated and fitted with fireworks. The air, too, was clear, and the moon was shining most splendidly. The fireworks were superb.

They had executed the Order of the Lion and the Sun in fireworks very successfully. This was followed up by another display. A fortress of fire appeared on the border of the sea, and the sea itself was represented by fire to the very life. Ships of war came and besieged this fortress, cannon being fired from the ships and from the fort; while an electric light was thrown from the roof of the palace of Schönbrunn on to the mound and the basins of water, which was extremely beautiful, and resembled sunshine or moonlight.

At the termination to this display of pyrotechny we rose, and arm-in-arm with the Empress, while the Emperor, giving his arm to the elderly woman of importance, followed us, we arrived at the staircase of the palace, said adieu to the Empress and Emperor, and returned home. Thanks be to God, all passed off well.

Friday, 13th (8th August).—To-day we must go to Saltzburg. Rising early in the morning, the Emperor arrived about half an hour afterwards, accompanied by the whole of the Austrian princes, ministers, and officials. In the first instance, the Emperor, with his brothers and the princes, came into the room. We advanced and gave our hand; we sat down on chairs and had a long conversation, I expressing the great pleasure I had enjoyed during my few days' stay at Laxenburg. Grenneville, in attendance on us, came to say the time had arrived for us to start. We arose. In another room Count Andrassy—the Premier, with the other ministers, was waiting. We exchanged salutations, but I did not say a last adieu to the princes, Andrassy, and the rest, being under the impression that they would all come to the platform at the station. We took our seat in a carriage with the Emperor, and drove off. When we reached the station and alighted, the princes and Andrassy had remained behind and did not come. We felt great regret at not having bid them good-bye; but, exchanging adieux again with the Emperor, we took our seat in the train. The Emperor remained on the platform to the last, so that even as the train glided away, we saluted each other.

The weather to-day in Vienna and the country was very sultry. Again at the town of Lintz the train stopped for an hour; and in the same place where they prepared breakfast on our arrival, to-day also was breakfast made ready. We alighted and breakfasted. One hour afterwards we again took our places and were on our way.

At the station of Lambach the train halted. The Sovereign of Hanover, with his wife, daughter, and servants of distinction, was waiting on the platform. We alighted, went, and shook hands with him. We had a lengthened conversation, and I expressed the utmost sympathy for the Sovereign. The wife of the Sovereign is a woman of great good sense, and is of middle age. His daughter is exceedingly pretty, graceful, and modest. The summer-residence of the Sovereign is near to this place, and having heard that we were to pass, he came (to meet us). But we were excessively grieved at sight of the Sovereign. He was a Sovereign, of political importance, possessed of treasures, of an army, of a diadem. The Emperor of Germany, through his wish to weld all Germany into one State, was under a necessity to take the country of this Sovereign out of his hands. Hence, he made war, and quickly routing the forces of this Sovereign, made of his dominions a portion of Prussia. The Sovereign, with his family and certain of his choicest jewels, fled to the land of the Austrian State, and up to this time passes his days in the territory of the Habsburg Emperor. Added to this misfortune, both eyes of the Sovereign are sightless. His wife takes him by the hand and leads him about. The Sovereign is still quite young-looking, very tall and robust; but alas, his eyes are blind. According to what was told us, he had one weak eye in his childhood; upon that, he was once playing with a purse of money, or some other thing, which struck him in the eye and injured his sound eye. His age is sixty-four (*read*, fifty-four); his name is George the Fifth, that of his wife is Queen Mary,—a Lady-Princess of Saxony, and of his daughter, Princess Frederica. Well; we exchanged adieux with the Sovereign, went to the train, and again proceeded, reaching the city of Saltzburg at sunset. Our quarters here were again in the same palace where we had put up on our arrival, and the same honours were shown to us as then.

Qabūli Pasha, the Ottoman Envoy (*read*, Ambassador) to Austria, is instructed by his Government to accompany us to Brindisi.

Saturday, 14th (9th August).—We have to go to the city of Innsbruck, which is eight hours distant by rail.

In the morning we joined the train and started. We traversed the territory of Bavaria, and ascended the Inn, a very large stream that flows into the river Danube, so arriving at the fortress of Kufstein, built on the frontier between Austria and Bavaria. With respect to the river that flows by this fortress, the left bank belongs to Bavaria, while the right bank is in the Tyrol, and part of the Austrian dominions. It is a strong little fort, in a valley, upon an enormous rock. There was a garrison and artillery in the fort. They fired a salute. A wheel of one of our carriages showed a defect, and we had to wait a quarter of an hour until the load of that carriage was removed elsewhere. A battalion of infantry, with a band and numbers of officers were in attendance. The Governor of Saltzburg here received his *congé*, and left.

Again we got in motion. On our journey hitherwards, we had passed this region by night, so that nothing of it had been seen. To-day when all is visible, it shows itself to be a wonderful place—a very spacious valley, in the middle of which flows a river, and all around high mountains full of forests of pine and yews. The hill-tops, the hill-sides, and the hill-skirts are all under crops without irrigation. The villages are all at the foot of the hills, very charming and pleasant.

And thus we journeyed to the city of Innsbruck, near to which the air became cloudy, with wind; and a violent storm, with heavy rain, broke over us, and cooled the temperature. We reached the city three hours before sunset. It is a small city, with a population of about ten thousand souls; a pretty and delightful hill-station for summer, situate in the midst of a valley, while all around are lofty, snow-clad mountains. In spite of the rain, the number of spectators was great, with many troops and bands, infantry and cavalry. A salute was fired.

We arrived at a palace of the Government, which, though plain, was elegant and very pretty, with nice tables and chairs, a very large and long hall, and the most part of the apartments white, being adorned with gilt woodwork. In some of the apartments rich silk stuffs were on the walls, with oil-paintings—portraits of the family of the Emperor of Austria, ancient and recent, hung in the rooms. Other paintings, too, were on the ceilings of the rooms and other parts.

To-day the train, near to the city, passed over a bridge that crosses the river, and joins on to another bridge (viaduct) that comes over the meadows and marshes to the station of the town—a very long bridge, certainly two thousand ells ($2333\frac{1}{3}$ yards) or more in extent. The difficulty and expense of constructing railroads arise from structures of this kind, which must be made of great strength.

Sunday, 15th (10th August).—We have to go to the city of Bologna in Italy. In the morning we strolled about a while in the great hall and viewed the pictures. The rain had continued to fall all through the night until morning. The weather was cloudy and misty, but little by little it cleared up. Immediately opposite to this palace is a small theatre, closed at the present season, but open during the winter.

The time to start having come, we mounted carriages, and left for the train. Nazar Aqā received his *congé*, and proceeded towards Pâris. We took our seats in the train, and commenced our journey. As the road was all upon an ascent, we proceeded very leisurely,—about two and a half leagues per hour. Lofty mountains, lovely valleys, springs, rivers, cascades, villages, pretty detached houses, flowers of all colours, meadows, green fields, on both sides of the road were in profusion; the weather also, from the rain which had fallen, was like paradise. On our first journey through this part of the country it had been night, and nothing had been seen from the station of Franzansvest onwards as far as the city of Innsbruck,—Franzansvest being one of the strong fortresses of Austria,—we have now, therefore, given the above details.

Well; the road continued everywhere to ascend, and the train passed through ten "holes in mountains,"—not very long ones,—and so we arrived at the principal peak and eminence which is named the Brenner, and is four thousand three hundred and seventy-three feet above the level of the sea. It is a very excellent place for a summer hill-station, and is very picturesque, having snow-clad mountains on every side. From Innsbruck to this point the forests were dense, the trees being larches in general. The train stopped. The waters which flow from this peak in the direction of Innsbruck, towards the north, fall into the river Danube, and pass thence on to the Black Sea; while those which flow southwards towards Italy fall into the Po and the Adige, and thence into the Adriatic.

On proceeding again, we advanced only a few leagues and reached the spot named Schelleberg, when the train stopped anew, as henceforward our road was to be all downhill. I noticed the Grand-Vazīr, with the rest, alighting from their carriages and commencing the descent. On enquiring the reason, I was informed that it was a very interesting sight to watch the downward progress of the train from this place; and therefore alighted also, following them down the hill. We walked a considerable distance and came to the village of Gossensasse. We passed through the place on foot without seeing a single soul. At length I noticed the 'Imādu-'d-Dawla and the I'tizādu-'s-Saltana, who were walking alone, and asked them what they were doing. They answered: "We went to see the village church. As it is Sunday, all the villagers were in the church, and the priest was addressing them from the pulpit. When his eye fell upon us, his speech failed him in the pulpit, and he was thoroughly bewildered in conjecturing who we might be, with these caps and costumes of ours, that had arrived in the church of a village in so remote a corner of Europe." We then walked on a good bit further, but we did not see the train coming; it had got down before we had, and had stopped for us. Thus those who had expected to see a sight were all disappointed, and had fatigued themselves as well.

We mounted and went on. The further we proceeded, the smaller were the mountains and less covered with forest; the atmosphere became more sultry; and steep, rocky mountains began to be seen. Continuing our journey, we came to Franzansvest, alighted there, and they breakfasted. This occupied an hour. At all the stations the troops, the bands, the officials, and others, were in waiting to render the usual honours. Breakfast over, we resumed our journey and reached Ala, the frontier between Italy and Austria. It was now night, and the train stopped. Grenneville, the official in waiting, together with his subordinates on that duty, were received in audience, took their leave, and departed. We showered upon them every sort of civilities, and expressed ourselves warmly as to the gratification afforded us by the Emperor's kindnesses. Qastīqar Khān, the engineer, also went away from this place to his own country, and will return thence to Tehrān.

Well; as far as the fortress of Verona, we had seen the country on our upward journey, since it had been performed by daylight; but from Verona onwards to the city of Bologna I had not seen. True it was now night, but there was a most beautiful moonlight, the mountains were left behind, and we were upon the plains. I dined in the train; and after dinner I would not lie down, as I pictured to myself that I would take some rest on arriving at the end of our day's journey. All my companions went to sleep, while I continued to explore the plains with my eyes. The train, too, was now going ten leagues an hour. I observed that the whole plain bore crops of Indian corn or rice, with mulberry trees for silk. I noticed a few eminences and small hills; also numerous habitations on both sides of our path,—the mansions reflecting back the whiteness of the moonlight, and producing a pleasing effect. We passed through one "hole,"—not very long, and across two great rivers with five bridges; and so, at four hours after midnight, when the dawn had thrown out its first streaks of light, we arrived at the station of Bologna.

I was extremely worn out from not having slept. The Governor of the town, and the officer in command of the troops of the place, whose name was Mezzacapo, were awaiting us, with the other local magnates. These people of the city were also, the whole of them, worn out and sleepless; so that neither could they pay proper attention to us, nor could we rightly consider their condition. I mounted a carriage; when a telegram arrived from the Sovereign of Italy, who was at a hunting-place in the Alpine chain, which expressed his great pleasure at our having again arrived in his dominions.

We drove a long way to arrive at our quarters,—a hotel that had been designated by Narīmān Khān. We went upstairs. My room fronted the public thoroughfare. The noise of carriages, carts, cries and talk, as well as bands, was such that to sleep for one instant was simply impossible. However, in the best way we could, we lay down for four or five hours, and even this I esteemed a great prize.

In Vienna and in Italy, &c., excellent water-melons are raised. The milky Indian corn is also found in great abundance. Other fruits are no great things.

This night we crossed two rivers; first, the river

Adige, which passes by the little town of Rovigo, and is the same stream that accompanied us everywhere from the valleys of the Tyrol in Austria, after the road began to descend at Schelleberg; secondly, the river Po, which flows by the city of Ferrara, and enters the Adriatic Sea.

Monday, 16th (11th August).—A halt was made in the city of Bologna. We breakfasted at the hotel. In the afternoon we took a seat in a carriage with Dr. Tholozan and the Governor of Bologna, named Count Bardessone, and set out for a drive. We came to two towers, erected six hundred years ago, very large in diameter, being like square obelisks. They have steps within them, so as to be ascended, though this is attended with great danger; for it is possible for one to be suffocated inside them from lack of air. The one is a hundred and three ells in height (360 feet), and is somewhat out of the perpendicular. The other, not far distant, was expressly constructed by its builder to lean over in like manner, and had at first a great elevation. But, as its deviation from the plumb-line was very great, fears were entertained as to its safety, and it was partly demolished; so that now the half only is standing.

Next we drove through sundry streets and wards, passing by the Bank, which has recently been erected, and is a very handsome building. The streets are all paved with stone, and kept clean. Including the suburbs, the city has a population of one hundred thousand souls. Carriages and carts are numerous. It produces excellent fruits,—especially peaches and water-melons.

We then went out beyond the city, drove round the

walls, which are of brick, of ancient construction, and have several gates, as well as a ditch of no great depth; also passed by the Armoury—another recent structure. From thence the road began to ascend in a southerly direction to some hills, on which people have built a number of handsome mansions. There was also one on the summit of an eminence, that in olden times had been a place of worship, and where the great Popes used to lodge when they came to this city. At present the Sovereign of Italy has taken possession of it, and it has become his private property.

As this city was, fifteen years ago, in the possession of the Pope, and its government in the hands of the priests, so now it is entirely the property of the State. We arrived at the door of the edifice, entered, and strolled about awhile. It is a very ancient structure. Coming out again, we walked about all round it, enjoying the delightful view it affords over the city and country. I observed that, as far as the eye could reach, the whole country was green and populous, with abundant crops, and here and there isolated mansions that cast back a white gleam from among the verdure. One hill there was, higher than this eminence; and on its summit was built a beautiful mansion, the summer-residence of one of the Khāns (noblemen) of Italy, whose name is Vicini.

Well; at sunset we descended from thence, entered the city by a different gate, and passed by a noble old building in which is the library of the place. According to what they said, it contains many volumes of ancient manuscripts and others. We also passed by the house of the Governor, around which in the olden time a strong wall has been erected, like that of a fortress. It is a large and ancient structure. The greater part of the buildings of this city are old and venerable, the most of them being of stone.

The name of the hotel in which we are lodged is the Hotel Brune. We reached our quarters, and in the evening went to the theatre, a handsome edifice and large, with five tiers of seats. As we had expressed a desire to see some performances on horseback, they had arranged the pit of the theatre like a circus; that is, they had enclosed it with a circular barrier of wood, and had sprinkled it over with earth. The exhibitions of horsemanship were similar to those seen in Paris. There were chandeliers and beautiful sconces on the walls, all lit with gas. The theatre is white, with gildings on wood, the ceiling and other parts being decorated with paintings. The audience was numerous. Two women performed on the horses; of whom one was very awkward and continually fell from her horse. The other, an American, performed well. There was also a pantomime of vulgar tricks. As we had not dined, we soon rose and returned home, had our dinner, and retired to rest." The city is lighted with gas-lamps. A graceful, prettily-dressed girl took a whip in her hand at the theatre, and exercised the horses, so that they ran, stopped, or stood upright, as she commanded, yielding obedience to her whip, and submission to the beauty and gracefulness of the girl.

Tuesday, 17th (12th *August*).—We have to go to

Brindisi, the remotest port in Italy, where some Ottoman government vessels are already awaiting to convey us to Constantinople. In the morning we rose early and breakfasted. Our travelling companions, from eagerness to return towards Persia, all went to the station; but our departure is put off. until three hours before sunset. We lingered at the hotel for a short time after breakfast, and then, to pass away the time, mounted a carriage, and went to see the library. There we found a collection of the grandees and officials of Italy. It is a long corridor; and there we saw some writings in the Egyptian character, written, two thousand years ago, on the surface of wood, which had been rendered clear and delicate, like paper. Also, one of the Pharaohs of Egypt had sent one of his great captains to a certain place on a mission to purchase horses, three thousand years ago; and he too had written in detail the incidents of his journey on that kind of paper-wood, in Egyptian and in Hebrew. They said they had deciphered it; but the translation was not forthcoming. A considerable part of the wood and writing had fallen to pieces by decay. The writing, as is the case in Persian and Ottoman Turkish, is written from right to left.

There were also some objects usually found in museums, of the sculptures of Egypt and other places; and furthermore, some things which have been recovered from the cemeteries of Bologna itself were also placed there. Anciently it had been a custom that when any one died, they should bury with that person enough provisions for several days, together with certain other articles; and these very articles are the things that, after an interval of two thousand years, have been recovered. So much so, that the shells of the eggs that were so deposited for the dead man to eat, have been collected and placed here. The bones of several dead persons, so cleaving to the earth, have been brought forth, and set up on foot. In the hand of one of these dead men there was a copper coin of the period, which, as I saw, had remained in his hand. This coin was given into his hand for the purpose that when he came to the bridge of Sirāt (that spans the abyss between this world and paradise), he should hand it over to the toll-keeper of the bridge, in order that he might allow him to pass in safety. Another of the dead, that had been a woman, has, as I saw, a necklace on her neck, together with a ring on the bone of her finger. In short, it is a very comprehensive library and museum. The building, which is very ancient, was formerly a college with many professors, who had come from all parts and gave lessons of philosophy and other things within its precincts. After seeing as much as was possible, we returned to our carriage and drove to the railway station.

The time for starting, however, had not yet come; and so we had to wait half an hour in a room at the station. The Governor of the town, the commanders of the troops, and others, were all there. When the time came, we went and took our seat in the train, which was no longer the same (that brought us), but had been changed. The present one was the property of the Italian Brindisi Railway Company, the cars of which do not communicate.

In the car that followed behind the one in which we were seated, there was a coffee-maker and the like; so that whenever we expressed a wish for a galayān (hubble-bubble), or other thing, they stretched forth their hands and reached it (to us).

We started. For the first half league there were at all points on our right hand hills backed up by lofty mountains; on our left, a green plain, with populations, trees, and crops. Behind those mountains one can go even unto Florence, one of the chief cities of Italy. In Rimini, a small town, the Adriatic Sea was first seen, looking very pretty. But as we advanced a little further, some hills interposed an obstacle, hiding the sea from our sight. The mountains on our right, too, came nearer. There were populations, mansions, villages, and pretty towns, upon the hills and in the plain. We passed by Pesaro, Fano, and other places, where the train stopped for a few minutes, and where great crowds were collected with the hope of seeing us; so much so, that they even fell under the wheels of our carriages in their eagerness. Extremely pretty women, and very handsome boys, whose features were half-way between those of Persians and Franks, were noticed.

We then came to Ancona, a seaport of importance; but it was now dark, and nothing of it was seen. Crowds flocked on to the railway; a band also was there playing. The Governor, military officers, and magistrates of the town were received in audience. The Sovereign of Italy had specially commissioned the Minister of Commerce and Agriculture to present his congratulations on our arrival. His name was Baron Finál. After starting thence we dined and lay down to rest.

Wednesday, 18th (13th August).—In the morning, on awaking, the air was very cool. While sleeping, we had passed by the town of Foggia. We now reached Barletta, Bari, and Monopoli, stopping at each a few minutes; and so arrived at the town of Brindisi. From Barletta to the neighbourhood of Brindisi, both sides of the road was everywhere a plantation of olive-trees; and some ancient olive-trees, five hundred years old, were noticed. The greater part of the olive-oil of Firangistān is exported from these localities. Cotton also was cultivated.

Brindisi is an ancient, old-looking city; but since the railway has been established, it has begun by degrees to be repopulated, and is now a seaport. The post and despatches from England for India go by this route; also those from India for England, through the Red Sea and Egypt. The people of these parts are extremely poor.

The train stopped. Crowds had collected. Eshref Pasha, who was formerly Envoy in Tehrān, had come with the Ottoman ships; and the Grand-Vazīr introduced him to an audience, with Qabūlī Pasha, Serkīs Efendi—the Minister Resident in Italy, and others who had come from Constantinople; and with them we conversed. Qabūlī Pasha returns hence to Vienna. After that, the Governors, civil and military, with other Italian magnates residing here, and the foreign Consuls, were also received. We then walked to the ship.

Two ships have come from His Most Exalted Majesty the Sultan; one named the "Sultāniyya," a yacht of the Sultan himself, which has been brought for our accommodation. I had not seen in Firangistān a yacht so beautiful and so decorated. She has a spacious hall and rooms full of rich furniture. The other ship was named the "Talī'a," also a beautiful vessel. In our ship, room was wanting. The Grand-Vazīr, our household officers, and Dr. Tholozan, remained; and all the rest went to the "Talī'a." Through the transport of our luggage, and the dispersal of the people, we remained five hours at the anchorage; but we shall get under way for Constantinople at two hours to sunset.

In Firangistān, thanks be to God, all has passed safely and happily; God willing, the end of our tour will be equally pleasant and auspicious.

Our journey to-day from Foggia to this place was not through a part so much improved by man; the greater portion being a wilderness, with clumps of heather and such like. It had been arranged that we should start in another five hours; but in consequence of a high wind springing up, we remained all night in harbour.

19th (*Thursday, 14th August*).—In the morning I arose. At one o'clock of the day (eleven before sunset) we started. The princes and others who had gone to the "Talī'a," all came back to our vessel, with the exception of Ibrāhīm Khān, M. Richard, Narīmān Khān, the brother of Mīrzā Malkam Khān, and our horses, saying she was a very nasty place, and complaining of the dirt and biting beasts. Several had even been bitten by cockroaches, and not one of them had been able to sleep.

Well; the dinner and breakfast served up by the Sultan's cook were very excellent. Thanks be to God, the weather was fine, though there was a little wind, and the frequent waves kept the ship in motion. We lay down for a space, and on rising we had reached the land's-end of Italy, the parts about Otranto; that is, in three hours after leaving Brindisi, we had arrived there; and as we were close in with the shore, the waves were much diminished. We now took our breakfast.

At half an hour to sundown we were abreast of Corfu, which we passed to our left. The mountains of the island were visible; but it was at a distance of ten leagues or more from us. It is the largest of the seven Ionian islands, formerly in the possession of England. Ten years ago, however, she voluntarily ceded them to the kingdom of Greece. The weather was very fine and cloudless, free from wind. The stars twinkled, and, as the moon was twenty nights old, she rose late; but, as she emerged from the sea, she offered a glorious spectacle. Another singular sight, too, I witnessed from the ship's windows. The waters of the sea, cleft by the paddles of the steam-wheel of the ship, were converted into foam, and assumed the appearance of a white stream, in which I remarked a very curious phenomenon. Incessantly, from amid the water, and within the foam, did fire shoot forth, like lightning. As when the shoe of a horse strikes against a stone, or when a flint strikes a light, or when the wheel of a diamond-cutter gives out the electric light, in like manner did this fire incessantly shine forth. It was more abundant in the midst of the foam, less so in the rest of the water.

20th (*Friday*, 15th *August*).—In the morning, at one o'clock of the day, we were opposite to the island of Cephalonia, one of the seven Ionian islands, and passed it on our left. To-day the sea was calm, and there was no wind at all; so we breakfasted. We passed by the island of Zante,—one of the seven Ionian islands, and also by Navarino, where the ships of the three Powers—Russia, England, and France, fought with those of Turkey and Egypt for the independence of Greece, and entirely finishing off the Turkish and Egyptian ships, set fire to them; and at that epoch, the maritime preparations of Turkey being entirely destroyed, the kingdom of Greece was separated from the Turkish dominions, and obtained a separate Sovereign. That battle took place forty years ago, in the days of Sultān Mahmūd Khān, father of the present Sultan. In those days steamers were not in general use; all ships were sailing vessels.

Well; the shores of Greece are little inhabited. It was evident that in those mountains there was a great lack of water. I examined them through a telescope; they were generally barren, with only a few shrubs on some of them. The mountains further inland were higher. The land of Greece has offered to notice Aristotle, Plato, Hippocrates, Socrates, Alexander the Great, and the ancient philosophers and poets.

At sunset we were abreast of Cape Matapan, on the

skirts of the mountains of which a good many habitations were observed, all of which belonged to the population of Matapan itself. The houses and buildings were white. Each family establishment had a kind of tower, of great strength; as though these parts enjoy no great degree of security, and therefore, by way of simple precaution, the houses are built strong. The mountains hereabouts are extremely barren and waterless, having no verdure, not even a bush. All are rocky.

In the night we entered the straits of (Cape) Malea, passing between (Cape) Malea (Cape St. Angelo) and the island of Cerigo; this island being on our right, and the cape on our left. Hence we turned our faces towards the quarter where the sun rises, in the direction of (Continental) Greece and Constantinople. Up to this time there had been no wind; but, on reaching this strait, a light breeze sprang up, and caused the ship to oscillate.

21st (Saturday, 16th August).—When I arose in the morning, the wind was blowing; but the weather was fine, and the waves not very rough. Half an hour after the morning twelve o'clock, according to the Persian method of computing time (by which sunset is always at twelve in the evening), we arrived off the Gulf of Athens. Athens is the capital of the kingdom of Greece.

We next passed through the straits of Zea, leaving that island on our right, and the cape of Athens (Cape Colonna; Cape Sunium) on our left; but the city of Athens was far off, behind the Cape, and therefore was not seen. The island of Zea is very famous and celebrated, through a book written by Fenelon about the adventures of Ulysses, who was king of the island, and was lost in the war of Troy, his son Telemachus going off in quest of him; but it is very small, and barren;—destitute of water, grass, and trees. The coast of the promontory of Athens, too, has many barren mountains. On our left hand, upon the shore of Greece, were the remains of an ancient building, which I surveyed through a telescope. They are upon a rock on the edge of the sea, and have many stone columns, like the ruins of Persepolis; as was said, they are of marble; but some are broken, and have fallen down. These remains were in ancient days a temple. In Greece, and especially in the neighbourhood of Athens, there are many such remains.

After three or four hours we passed through the channel between the islands of Negropont and Andros. Negropont, on our left, is a very large island, and is attached to Greece; Andros, on our right, is a small island.

At one hour and a half to sunset we were opposite the little islet of Psara, which belongs to the Ottoman; and behind it was Scio, a large island, called Saqiz (Mastic Island) by the Ottomans. On our left again was the island of Skyros, which belongs to Greece; but it was far off and not visible.

The distance from Brindisi to Constantinople is seven hundred and eighty miles, which is, in Persian reckoning, two hundred and sixty leagues. The weather, thanks be to God, was beautiful; but an adverse wind blew uninterruptedly. The ship stoutly held her own against the billows, and made good way; but one league, out of her speed of three leagues per hour, was cut off; so that she only went at a rate of two.

I went to rest. At half-past six o'clock (from sunset) the ship suddenly stopped; which alarmed us. I asked, and was told she had been purposely stopped, since the channel of the Dardanelles was near at hand, and they did not wish to enter it by night. In order to be quite sure and to know that the ship had no defect, I said they might go on for another half hour. They then went on again, and I resumed my couch. When the half hour expired, the ship was again stopped. The moon had now newly risen, and the weather was very temperate. Two hours later, we again made way towards the Dardanelles.

CHAPTER VII.

TURKEY; 11 DAYS.

22ND (*Sunday, 17th August*).—When I arose in the morning it was two o'clock of the day, and we passed by a small island on our right hand, named Tenedos, from the fortress of which a salvo of guns was fired. On our left hand, opposite to Tenedos, was the island of Lemnos, rather large.

After breakfast we arrived at the (entrance to the) channel of the Dardanelles, on both sides of which they have constructed strong forts. The first of these forts is that of Tenedos, on the right hand; the second, on the left hand, on the European shore, is Seddu-'l-Bahr (Barrier of the Sea); and on the right, opposite the Sedd, is Qūm-Qal'asi (Fort of the Sands); the third, on the left, in Europe, Shāhīn Qal'asi (Fort Falcon), which is in ruins, and on the summit of a hill; it was formerly a stronghold, and still has a garrison, with guns. After this comes the Qal'a-i-Sultāniyya (Fort Sultan), on the left, in Asia; there being also, to the left, and opposite this fort, several other forts, towers, and batteries. Fort Sultan (at the town of the Dardanelles) has many guns, and its walls are built of stone. It had a garrison of troops, and around it were numbers of buildings and mansions, with beautiful houses. To-day we have noticed many ships, merchantmen, yachts, and others. The ships of the Austrian (Lloyd's) Company frequently passed by. These castles and fortifications have always been in existence from days of old, and the Ottoman Sultans have repaired them; not that they have newly erected forts. On the left-hand side, opposite the town around Fort Sultan, there was (another) group of buildings on the shore of the channel, which is named Kilīdu-'l-Bahr (Key of the Sea). The whole of these erections are portions of the Dardanelles (Chanaq Qal'asi, Fort Crockery; so named from the great manufacture of coarse earthenware carried on in and around the town, which also bears this name, and represents the ancient Abydos, as the village at the Kilīd represents the ancient Sestos).

Well; at five o'clock of the day we arrived before the town of the Dardanelles, and a salvo was fired from each of the forts. There was also a large Ottoman ship of war at anchor there, which fired a salvo,—a fine ship with three masts and thirty guns. Muhammad Rushdī Pasha, known by the patronymic of Shīrwānī-Zāda (son of the man of Shīrwān—in Georgia), and actual Grand-Vazīr of the Ottoman State, had come to the Dardanelles to meet us on the part of the Sultan. Our ship also cast anchor, and came to a stop in front of Fort Sultan. As it is but ten hours' steaming from this place to Constantinople, if we should go on at once to-day, we should reach there by night; hence we remain here until the afternoon; and, please God, we shall proceed during the night, so as to arrive at Constantinople in the morning.

The Ottoman Grand-Vazīr, and Hājjī Muhsin Khān—the Persian Minister Plenipotentiary, came on board from the shore in a boat. Our Grand-Vazīr introduced the Ottoman Grand-Vazīr to an audience. Shīrwānī-Zāda is a sagacious man of great intelligence and understanding, of a pleasing disposition and well-spoken, and is corpulent, thickset, and short, with a round black beard, and speaks Persian. After a few minutes' conversation he went out, and presently returned again, with our Grand-Vazīr, and presented the following personages who were with him: Kan'ān Bey—Amedī of the State Council (Secretary for all incoming official communications); Nazīf Pasha, Governor-General of the islands in the Egæan Sea; Eyyūb Pasha, commanding in chief the forces stationed at the forts in the channel of the Dardanelles; Emīn Efendi, Custos Rotulorum of the province; Esh-Sherīf Rushdī Efendi, judge of the province, who wore a turban; Nesh'et Bey, chief of the office of investigations, who also wore a turban; Mustafà Bey, colonel of artillery; another Mustafà Bey, lieutenant-colonel, aide-de-camp of the Grand-Vazīr; Sāmi Bey, colonel of police of the province; Hāfiz Bey, colonel; Rushdī Bey.

At one hour and a half to sunset we weighed anchor and resumed our voyage towards Constantinople. Some very graceful Frankish women had mounted in boats, and came near to our ship. There are many foreign Consuls at the Dardanelles, who have built handsome houses. Our Grand-Vazīr mounted a boat and went ashore to return the visit of the Ottoman Grand-Vazīr. The Ottoman Grand-Vazīr's steam yacht is a very handsome vessel, and followed in our wake, the Talī'a bringing up the rear.

We went on. On both sides of the channel were fine forts with many guns. We passed three or four forts and batteries of earthworks, erected after the system of the Franks. Those which are after the new system of Firangistān have been raised within the last ten or fifteen years; the rest, which have stone walls, are from times of old. On either side of the channel there are hills; and behind them again, mountains; all full of forests and trees. Gallipoli and its fortifications are at the (upper) extremity of the channel of the Dardanelles, from whence one enters into the little Sea of Marmara. From the commencement of this channel to its extremity next the Sea of Marmara is (a distance of) forty miles, that is, twelve Persian leagues. We passed Gallipoli in the dark, so that it was not seen.

23rd (*Monday*, 18th *August*).—When I arose in the morning, the coasts on either hand were visible at a distance. The ship, too, had proceeded slowly. On nearing Constantinople a speed was kept up that would bring us to the entrance of the Bosphorus at the prefixed hour of five o'clock in the day (about noon at that season). I dressed. By slow degrees we neared the land on our left—the Rūm-Eyli or European side; and some buildings and habitations became visible, beautiful houses being there built. Some manufactories were also noticed, which they said were small-arms works and cloth-mills. The whole of the shore was hilly and rolling ground, with fir and cypress trees, and also forest trees. They generally plant the cypresses in and about the cemeteries; but there are also cypresses in the valleys and upon the mountains.

Passing on from these habitations, Islāmbūl (a word that has been coined, in times gone by, as a substitute for the common Istānbūl, vulgarly Stāmbūl, formed from εἰs τὴν πόλιν, to or at the city—the capital, *i.e.*, to or at Constantinople, as we say: to or in town, *i.e.*, to or in London) came in sight. Again we took a turn about, in order that the time might arrive. Then the ship "Sultāniyya" stopped, and we went in a boat to a ship of the Sultan's, named the "Pertev-i-Piyāla" (Ray of the Goblet) which is the name of the Sultan's mother, — that had been sent with the Grand-Vazīr to the Dardanelles in order that we might enter the Bosphorus in her,—and in which the Grand-Vazīr was embarked, following in our wake. The Ottoman Grand-Vazīr came to our vessel, and again accompanied us to the "Pertev." This ship is smaller than the "Sultāniyya," but is extremely elegant and pretty. Its cabin is fitted up with inlaid-work, and is richly furnished. I went on to the deck of the vessel. About three thousand Persian subjects, of whom there are great numbers in Constantinople, had embarked in five large steamers, and come out to meet us. They brought their ships near to mine; and just at that moment our Grand-Vazīr, with the princes and others in a boat, was coming from that other ship to this one, when one of the vessels with the Persian subjects on board, turned on her steam and made way, so as to come nearer to our ship; and little did it lack that she did not strike against the boat of the Grand-Vazīr and others, and drown them all. God showed mercy, and by some means they escaped, reached (our ship), and came up (on deck). The greater part of our household officers were even in their State costumes. The other household officers, and others, all remained in the first ship.

Well; we proceeded. On our right hand were a number of islands (Princes' Islands), with hills and trees; some even with a spring of water. They told me that mansions are being built for certain Franks and wealthy Ottomans, so that in summer they may go thither for strolls; but we saw no buildings. It may be that they are in valleys and behind the hills.

We arrived at the beginning of the habitations of the city of Islāmbūl. On the left hand is the land of Europe; on the right, the land of Asia. We proceeded in the vicinity of the land of Europe. Certain steam ships, in which the foreign ambassadors were embarked to come and meet us, were observed. The first of the habitations were some houses. Next, there commences an ancient stone wall, with towers. This is a fortress dating from the days of the Cæsars. As this kind of fortifications are no longer of any use, they do not repair it; but, since it is all of stone and very strong, the most part of it still remains standing. This wall surrounds the old city of Islāmbūl, the whole of which is on the summits of hills, on their slopes, or in their valleys. The habitations of the city extend the whole length of the Bosphorus; but these have not much width; and the great bulk and busy part of the inhabited quarters, the city and stronghold of Islāmbūl, is within this fortress, and from hence to the old palace (at Seraglio Point), to the palace of Beshik-Tash, to the Sultan's waterside residence of Chirāgān, within which are the great mosques, like those of Saint Sophia and other imperial cathedrals, the Government Offices (the Downing Street of Constantinople—the "Porte"—the "Sublime Porte," as it is called in Europe),—in which the Ministers and Councillors of State have their places of business, the Ministry of War, the Ministry of Mines and Commerce, barracks of great extent, hospitals, bazaars, caravanserais, and the like;—all are there. Beyond these, too, every part of the Bosphorus, the summits of the hills and of the mountains, are all inhabited and covered with fine houses, mosques, and the like, as far as Bīyuk-Dera (Buyoukdereh) and Tarāpiya (Therapia), which are the summer-stations of the foreign Representatives. These, however, are detached and isolated from each other. On the right hand, again, which is the Asiatic shore, and is also called Iskyudār (Scutari), there are magnificent buildings and beautiful mosques; especially, the barracks of Selimiyya—most splendidly built. This side also, like the other, is all hill and vale, with woods of cypress, pine, and oak. Every one, too, who has a mansion and garden, plants orchards of fruit-trees, kitchen-gardens, and flower-gardens, bringing water to those gardens and trees with the greatest taste. The forest-trees, however, require no water, being independent of irrigation. According to information received, on the other side of these hills there are extensive and dense forests that cannot be penetrated; but, as the hills themselves are near to habitations, the greater part of their trees have been cut down; only a certain number of pines, cypresses, and others have been preserved to ornament the houses and hills.

Well; after the wall and towers, there was a place made famous by the name of the Seven Towers, which was, as it were, the ark, the citadel of this city. It has walls of stone and several large towers. It acquired its celebrity from this circumstance, that, formerly, the Ottoman Sultans, with whatsoever State they declared war or took offence, immediately seized upon the person of the Representative of that State resident in Constantinople, together with his subjects and attachés, cast them into prison in the Seven Towers, and sometimes even put them to death.

After that place, we came abreast of the cathedral mosque of Sultan Ahmed, of that of St. Sophia, and of others; and then reached the old Seraglio, the former residence of the Ottoman Sultans, which is built upon the summit of a lofty eminence, with a strong wall all round it. The Ottoman Sultans no longer inhabit it. The "Sublime Porte," also, and other edifices, were noticed at a distance. The residence of the Persian Minister Plenipotentiary, built by this our present Grand-Vazīr, is also within that part of the city, and is a very handsome building.

Next we reached the offing of Galata and of Bey-Oghú, *i.e.*, Pera, the winter place of residence of the Foreign Representatives, and where the greater portion of the Franks have their quarters. Then we came upon the palace of Dōlma-Bāgcha, — called also the palace of Beshik-Tash,—where the Sultan dwells, with the Harem, the Sultana-Mother, and others of the imperial family, as also the princes of the blood. This is a very fine and imposing edifice; and was built by the Sultan 'Abdu-'l-Mejīd Khān, who was the reigning Sultan's brother. Passing thence we came abreast of the seaside palace of Chirāgān, — an exceedingly beautiful structure. It was originally founded by the Sultan Mahmūd Khān, father of the present Sovereign, who has recently renovated and completed it. At last we came in front of the palace known by the name of Beyler-Beyi, our own quarters, situated to the right, on the Anatolian side, and on the brink of the Bosphorus. It is so called from being built in the parish of that name, and is a very stately structure.

As the current of the waters of the Bosphorus sets from the Black Sea towards the Sea of Marmara, and is very rapid, like that of a river, in certain places, especially in front of this palace, where it attains its utmost velocity, our ship could not cast anchor immediately opposite to the palace; but, passing about a thousand feet further up the channel, stopped there.

A few moments later, His Most Exalted Majesty the Sultan, who was at the palace of Beyler-Beyi, mounting a boat which he had caused to be specially prepared for us, came on board. We took seats, and the two Grand-Vazīrs also seated themselves. After a little conversation we arose, descended from the ship, got into the boat with the Sultan; the two Grand-Vazīrs, and Husayn 'Avnī Pasha—the Minister of War, were also with us in the boat. We arrived at the stairs of the palace, and landed. A battalion of infantry, with a band, were in the court and garden of the palace, the band playing. The Sultan led us upstairs, and pointed out to us the apartments and rooms of our quarters; then, after the exchange of numerous civilities, he returned to his own residence. The Sultan's age is forty-four—the same as our own.

To-day, as we came up the Bosphorus, numerous salutes were fired from the forts, and from the war-ships of the Ottoman fleet. We noticed four large war steamers in the Bosphorus,—some of which were armour-clad,—and which are always anchored in front of the Sultan's palace.

Well; half an hour afterwards I mounted my boat, with the Grand-Vazīr, the Mu'tamadu-'l-Mulk, and the (Ottoman) Grand Master of Ceremonies—'Alī Bey; and went to return the visit of the Sultan at the palace of Dōlma-Bāgcha. This is a very magnificent edifice, the greater part of the staircases, the panels of the walls, the columns, and the like, being of marble. The Sultan met us at the foot of the stairs. In the very warmest manner we gave our hand, went upstairs, sat a while conversing, and then, rising, returned to our quarters and made ourselves at home.

The palace of Beyler-Beyi is a most beautiful structure. Its stairs, and the panels of the walls of the staircases are all of marble. It is partly in the European, partly in the Persian, and partly in the Ottoman styles; being by this means extremely pleasing to the eye. The whole of the furniture in the rooms, such as curtains, chairs, sofas, tables, looking-glasses, chandeliers, and candelabras, are very rich and elegant. The rooms are hung with rich European stuffs; the windows are all in single sheets of plate-glass, very wide, long, and heavy; but arranged in such a manner that a child can easily raise and lower them ten times in succession, opening them to any desired extent, and leaving them so without support, prop, or assistance of any kind. As left, so they remain; and one can, without danger, put one's head out of window under them. We had seen similar windows in London. They are a very excellent contrivance. The whole of the windows in all the Sultan's palaces are of plate-glass and on this plan.

The width of the Bosphorus is more than a thousand ells (nearly 1200 yards). One can distinguish, without the aid of a glass, every one who passes along on the other side, in whatever coloured dress he may happen to be. A musket-ball could easily traverse the interval between the two shores. The depth of the water is from ten to twenty ells (35 to 70 feet, 6 to 12 fathoms); some parts being as much as a hundred and ten ells (385 feet, 64 fathoms) deep. The largest ship of war can navigate every part of the Bosphorus.

The position and site of the city of Constantinople are without rivals in the world.* For instance: One can purchase in the New World the chandeliers, tables, chairs, and furniture of a whole palace, and, without the deposition of a spot of dust upon them, or their being again moved, can bring them to the foot of the palace on the Bosphorus, and there open them. Marbles, &c., anything one desires for his mansions can be brought from all countries with the greatest facility to this place. In like manner, merchandize of every description can be brought in ships easily from all parts of the world, and exported hence in like manner.

There is one very spacious, handsome, and highly decorated hall in this palace of Beyler-Beyi. The greater part of the ceilings are of wood and boards, but exquisitely painted. The mats which cover the floors are of the finest quality; and over these are extended narrow slips of European carpeting, upon which people walk. Beneath this hall is a place with a basin of water, of marble, and very handsome. Water flows into the basin from certain figures, the basin being of one block of marble. The temperature here is very agreeable, and exactly suited to the summer weather. It has columns of marble also.

Our suite are all lodged in this palace. Within it is a handsome hot-and-cold bath of marble, with small basins of marble around it, each provided with taps for hot and cold water. As it was some time since we had taken a bath, we made use of this opportunity, and then went for a stroll in the gardens, where we walked about a considerable time. The garden being on the skirts of a hill, is subdivided into terraces, one above the other;

each terrace having marble steps on either side for going up and down. Around each terrace also are small handrails of bronze; and upon these are single gas-lamps, here and there. The sustaining wall of each terrace is covered with ivy—the plant that climbs up plane-trees and is always green,—which clings to it and clothes it, as it were, in a most beautiful robe of emerald. There are also pear-trees, peach-trees, plum-trees, apple-trees, and the like; as also lovely flower-beds of elegant composition, in the European style. There are handsome statues and sculptures of marble, of maned-lions of Africa, and others, around basins of water; as well as statues of bronze, of horses and bisons. Five or six terraces are thus laid out in handsome gardens, and are provided with marble steps, balustrades, and the like; having charming views over the Bosphorus. On the upper terraces there are also some beautiful lodges and pavilions, all forming part of the establishment of this palace of Beyler-Beyi. We went through them all; they are most elegantly furnished. There was one building with a basin of water and a fountain, of marble, very handsome; against the walls on two sides of the room were ranged sculptured marbles also, in the form of large vases, carved out in three rows; on the top of each one of the upper vases was a tap, and when this was opened a small stream of beautifully clear water ran out of it into the first vase. As soon as the top row of vases became brimful and running over, the water flowed into those of the second, and thence again into the third row, the vases of which resembled, small basins, and had each a hole through which the water disappeared. This was very chaste and pleasing; also spreading around in the room a delightful coolness.

In these upper terraces and gardens the Sultan has dovecotes, with large numbers of pigeons—very spacious. The keepers were at their post, and they preserve the place in the highest degree of neatness. They said the Sultan often comes there to see the birds. Besides these, there were parrots of all colours, sporting dogs, and a stud of hunters, cocks and hens, and other animals. We strolled about there a good long while; and then descending, returned to our quarters.

Between the original city of Constantinople proper (on the one hand), and Galata, with Pera and the parish of Qāsim-Pasha (on the other), there is another inlet besides the great channel of the Bosphorus; and the further extremity of this inlet (the Golden Horn) extends as far as the hills and mountains. The width of this inlet is much less than that of the Bosphorus itself. There are two bridges across it, that afford a passage between Galata and Constantinople.

24th (Tuesday, 19th August).—This day we breakfasted at home; and after breakfast the Diplomatic Body resident at Constantinople, as also the Ottoman Ministers, came to audiences. Before them, however, Ferīd Pasha had come on the part of the Sultāna-Mother with a message of welcome, congratulations for our safe arrival, and kind enquiries as to our health. The Ottoman Ministry were next received, and then the Diplomatic Corps.

First, Ignatief, the Russian Ambassador, came; and we had some conversation in a small room. He is young, good-looking, and pleasant-spoken. He shaves his beard, but has a moustache.

He left, and Elliot (the Right Hon. Sir Henry George Elliot, G.C.B.), the English Ambassador, came in. He shaves his chin, but has a beard on his cheeks. With him, too, we had a long conversation.

When he went out, we came into the hall where all the other Representatives of Governments, together with their respective suites, were drawn up and standing. In the first place, the Russian Ambassador presented his suite, to the number of about twenty souls. Next the English Ambassador presented those of his mission. We then approached the other Representatives, and some words were exchanged with each. The following are the names of these Representatives, and of the Ottoman Ministers:

OTTOMAN MINISTERS.

Muhammed Rushdī Pasha, Shīrwāni-Zāda, Grand-Vazīr;
Midhat Pasha, President of the 'Adliyya Council;
Rizà Pasha, ex-Minister of Marine;
Husayn 'Avnī Pasha, Minister of War;
Rāshid Pasha, Minister of Foreign Affairs;
Ahmed Pasha, Minister of Marine;
Jevdet Pasha, Minister of Public Instruction;
Hamdī Pasha, Minister of Finance;
Kyāni Pasha, Minister of Public Works;

Maḥmūd Pasha, Minister of Commerce;
Sādiq Pasha, Minister of Taxes;
Kemāl Pasha, Minister of Estates in Mortmain;
Gālib Bey, Custos Rotulorum of the Privy Domain.

FOREIGN REPRESENTATIVES.

Ignatief, Ambassador of Russia;
Elliot, Ambassador of England;
Lesourd, Chargé d'Affaires of France;
Ludolf, Minister of Austria;
Euhmann, Minister of Germany;
Grimberghe, Minister of Belgium;
Covo, Chargé d'Affaires of Italy;
Booker, Minister of the New World;
&c.

At five hours to sunset we went in a boat to the ship "Pertev-i-Piyāla," took our seat on board, and started for a promenade on the water to the upper parts of the Bosphorus in the direction of Biyūk-Dera (Large Valley). From the palace of Beyler-Beyi to the uttermost limit of the Bosphorus, which is at Biyūk-Dera, is half an hour's voyage in a steamer. The following are the most beautiful of the palaces and seaside-residences which we noticed on the Bosphorus. On our right hand, the shore of Asia: 1. The palace of Gyūk-Sū (Azure Rivulet), one of the buildings of the Sultan 'Abdu-'l-Mejīd Khān, is a small pavilion of two stories, the steps and walls of which are all of marble, this marble being carved and sculptured in the most charming manner. The ornamental furniture thereof is also entirely from the days of the late Sultan 'Abdu-'l-Mejīd Khān, as is attested by his cypher being on them. There is also a small park and garden around this pavilion, which are very pleasant places. A small stream flows into the Bosphorus near to it, the name of which is Gyūk-Sū, *i.e.*, azure rivulet; and from it the pavilion takes its name.

The greater part of the marbles that are used in the (construction of the) palaces of Constantinople is brought from the quarries of Italy.

2. The palace of the Lady-Sultāna 'Ādila, sister of the Sultan, is a very splendid palace and garden.

3. The house of the Sharīf 'Abdu-'l-Muttalib, former Sharīf (Prince) of Makka the Magnified, who now constrainedly sojourns at Constantinople.

4. The house of the late Fu'ād Pasha, Minister of Foreign Affairs.

5. The house of Rāshid Pasha, present Minister of Foreign Affairs.

6. The house of Res'ūf Bey (son of Rif'at Pasha, a former Minister of Foreign Affairs, &c.). And others.

On the European shore, being at our left hand:

The different mansions of the Foreign Representatives, which are generally handsome buildings with beautiful gardens. Such are:

7. That of the Russian Ambassador;

8. The sea-side residence of the Khidīv of Egypt, very beautifully built.

9. The sea-side residence of the Lady-Sultāna Fātima,

daughter of the late 'Abdu-'l-Mejīd Khān. These two edifices are built in the quarter named Emirgyān.

10. The house of Rushdī Pasha, the Grand-Vazīr.

In short, we went on until we had passed Biyūk-Dera, where the waters of the Bosphorus have produced a valley, that has swerved somewhat to the left, and around which are palaces and mountains. They have named it Biyūk-Dera; which means: Big Valley. We then returned, and the ship was stopped opposite to the palace of Gyūk-Sū, where we went in a boat to the palace, and strolled all over it. It was a very sweet place. Again we mounted our ship, returned, and came home.

25th (*Wednesday, 20th August*).—To-day we are the guests of the Sultan to breakfast at the sea-side residence of Chirāgān. We went. At the landing-place, the Ottoman Grand-Vazīr, Midhat Pasha, the Minister of War, the Minister of Marine, the Minister of Foreign Affairs, and others, were waiting. To each was addressed an enquiry as to health. The Sultan was on the stairs; we gave hands and saluted; then went up stairs. In the first place we adjourned to a private room, and sat awhile with the Sultan; our Grand-Vazīr being also present. We then rose and went into another room, where a table was laid out in European fashion. We took our seats, and breakfast was dispatched. We talked much with the Sultan. The Sovereign of England had addressed a telegram to us from Scotland, with an enquiry after our health, and containing a similar enquiry after the health of the Sultan. This selfsame telegram we this day communicated to the Sultan, and gave him the salutation of the Sovereign of England. Breakfast over, we retired to another room, sat down, and took coffee; after which, rising, we went home.

In the afternoon we went out of the upper garden-gate (the back or land gate) of this palace, mounted our horse, and went for a ride, as I wished to go to the top of a high hill (Chamlija),[1] more lofty than any of the rest, and from thence enjoy a view of the city, the Bosphorus, and their environs. We pushed on through streets, by inhabited places, and handsome isolated houses; and observed a beautiful house and garden belonging to the Khidīv of Egypt; so arriving at the summit, I rode the horse of the Yamīnu-'d-Dawla. I alighted on the summit of the hill, where the air was very cool. The condition of the hill, of the plants, and of the atmosphere, was very similar to that of the hills and atmosphere of Kajur-Kalā, a village of Māzandarān. A tomb, with a room for a single keeper, were there, on the top of the hill, extremely small. The keeper was there himself also. He said that there a Pīr (saintly Elder) and Dervish (voluntarily poor man) had been buried. I entered. The tomb was long. The view was most magnificent. Behind the hills to the east there is a vast plain that goes through Anatolia as far as Tehrān; perhaps, it may extend as far as China. Mountains were visible; but of habitations, not many were observed. Towards the west, the Sea of Marmara, five inhabited islands, together with ships that were either stopping, coming, or going, were visible. On the north side, were Biyūk-Dera and the Bosphorus. In short, it was a beautiful place.

We then descended by a different path, and arrived at a street paved with stones, where the horse had a difficulty to keep his feet. We even walked a certain distance, and so returned to the palace.

26th (*Thursday, 21st August*).—We breakfasted at home; after which we went to the city of Islāmbūl to pay visits to the mosque of Saint Sophia and the residence of the Persian mission.

Before we started, Yūsuf 'Iz̤zu-'d-Dīn Efendi, eldest son of the Sultan, who is sixteen years of age, and a handsome prince, came to see us. We took our seats in a room, had a little conversation, and the " Most Sacred Order," with its broad ribbon, which is one of the " most noble Orders " of the Persian State, was conferred upon the prince. A few minutes after he had departed, we mounted our boat and went to the palace of Chirāgān to return the visit of Yūsuf 'Iz̤zu-'d-Dīn Efendi. Rising from thence, we again mounted our boat and proceeded to the landing-place of the city. Crowds of the people of Constantinople, of Persian subjects, and of Franks, had assembled in ships and on shore. The Beyler-Beyi (lord of lords) of the city, named Ismā'īl Pasha, called also the Shehr-Emīni (Prefect of the City) was present with the members of the administration, some regular cavalry, and numerous policemen, to keep the people in order. We took our seat in an open carriage. Although the streets go up hill and down dale, still a carriage can go about everywhere. We drove along, and arrived at the mosque of Ayā-Sofiyā (Saint Sophia, ἡ ἅγια σοφία,, the holy wisdom), alighted, and entered. The servants of the mosque were drawn up in rows, and enquiries were made of their health. Kemāl Pasha, the Minister of Estates in Mortmain, was also present. This is a very imposing and ancient mosque, the whole of it built of stone. The area of the mosque is very extensive, the central part under the dome exceedingly spacious and lofty. The height of the dome from the floor may be about seventy ells (245 feet). Its building dates from one thousand three hundred and ten years ago (having been erected by the Emperor Justinian I. who died in A.D. 565). It had been an idol-temple at first, then became a Christian church, and after the taking of Constantinople by Sultan Muhammad the Conqueror, was converted into a mosque, as it now is. From the reason that it was not originally a mosque, the praying-direction of its altar is slantwise. It has numerous pulpits, and in the days of Ramazān and the like, sermons and worship are conducted in several parts of it, (simultaneously). There is a place constructed especially for the Sultan in the first gallery, so that whenever he may come (here), he performs his devotions in that place and no one sees him. There are some sculptures and carvings in the stone capitals of the columns in the upper story; and in the ceiling there are some mosaics of stone also. But, through the lapse of time and the great duration of this mosque, it has fallen from its original splendour. One side of it is even somewhat cracked and sunk. It is like a venerable tree from which the freshness of youth has departed.

Well; we here performed our midday and afternoon

devotions (together); and then proceeded to the library, where there are about two thousand volumes of books, the whole in Arabic, on jurisprudence, theology, rhetoric of sense, rhetoric of expression, history, metaphysics, and the like, open to the use of every one who may come there, sit down, and study.

We next went up to the gallery, the middle story of the mosque, around which are columns, and which looks down over the (floor of the) mosque; whenever the congregation is very numerous, people sit here likewise. The way to it was long; but there were few stairs to mount, as the path was a wide flagged corridor on an incline and in zigzag. We went about here a little, and then descended again. In this story it is plainly visible that one side of the building has given way.

We now drove off to the residence of the Persian Minister, an edifice erected by our Grand-Vazīr himself (when Minister Plenipotentiary). We reached the gate, where a crowd of Persians, Ottomans, and Franks had assembled. We entered and went up stairs by a marble staircase. It is a very grand building, furnished with curtains, chairs, sofas, chandeliers, and the like. We remained there a while, partook of some fruit and tea, returning home afterwards.

For the evening there was an invitation to a state banquet at the palace of Beshik-Tash, to which I went in court costume. The whole of our princes and officers of state, all the Corps Diplomatique and Ottoman Ministers were present. We entered the palace; the Sultan came to the foot of the stairs; we gave hands, went up, and took seats at first in a private room, the Grand Vazīr being also present. After a short interval dinner was announced. We then went into a hall where all the members of the Diplomatic Corps were standing in a row. The Sultan, with the interpretership of Rāshid Pasha— the Minister of Foreign Affairs, addressed words of compliments and recognition first to the Russian Ambassador, next to the English Ambassador, and so on to each one of the others. After him I too, with the interpretership of the Grand-Vazīr, conversed likewise with the Representatives ; only that I was not so much in need of an interpreter, as I spoke French myself. This (ceremony of) conversing with the Diplomatic body occupied half an hour; after which we went down stairs to a large and very magnificent hall, where the dinner-table was spread. I and the Sultan were at the upper end of the table ; I to the right, the Sultan to the left. Considerably lower down, away from us, to the right was the Russian Ambassador, then the English, next the 'Izzu-'d-Dawla, the Husāmu's-Saltana, Midhat Pasha, the Mu'tamadu-'l-Mulk, &c., to the end ; while on the left, far away from the Sultan, was first the Persian Grand-Vazīr, then the Ottoman Grand-Vazīr, next the I'tizādu-'s-Saltana, the Nusratu-'d-Dawla, the (Ottoman) Minister of War, &c., to the end. There was a very large and beautiful chandelier suspended in the middle of the hall, lighted up with gas; and there were other gas-lights in candelabra and in sconces on the walls. This hall, together with its furniture, is one of the constructions of the late Sultan ('Abdu-'l-) Mejīd Khān. Around it is a gallery, in which was an orchestra playing airs; but when they struck up their music, one's ears were filled, and nobody could converse. An excellent dinner was served. When this was over, I and the Sultan, with the two Grand-Vazīrs, the Minister of War, the Russian and the English Ambassadors, again retired to a separate room, where coffee was handed round, and where much conversation took place. Then we rose and returned home. The night being dark, caution had to be used in conducting the boat across the Bosphorus.

27th (Friday, 22nd August).—Breakfasted at home to-day; after which the Spanish Chargé d'Affaires at Constantinople, and a deputation of Armenians, were received in audience. After them came two individuals, magnates of the Jews, dressed in Frankish costume, who read a prolix address in French. Next we dressed in state costume, and 'Abdu-'l-'lāh, the photographer, who takes good likenesses, and is by origin a Christian and a Frenchman, but who has assumed this name, took several negatives of us. After this we mounted our boat, went on board the (Ottoman) ship of war the "'Azīziyya," and inspected her above and below. This ship was built in London, and is a very fine vessel. The sailors and marines on board went through their exercise.

Leaving her, we went by boat to the "Pertev-i-Piyāla," and started for the (Princes') Islands. Salutes were fired from all the men-of-war. We reached the islands, which are five in number, two small, and three comparatively large. They have many forest trees of oak, and verdant hills, with various shrubs and herbaceous plants. European merchants and others have there built pretty houses, and there is a Naval College—a fine building, where pupils study for the sea service. Opposite to the college a ship of war was anchored, in which they are taught afloat certain practical parts of their profession. On each of the islands there are habitations and handsome houses. They have no soft water or fountains; but what they have is drawn from wells. Taking them all together, these islands contain about two thousand houses.

On our return, we coasted along the shores of Asia and Scutari. The following are the few villages and inhabited sites we observed on the seashore or on the hillsides: Yaqajiq, Qārtāl, Māl-Tepa, Fener-Bāgchasi, and then Qādi-Kyūyu, which joins on to Scutari, and is reckoned as one of the parishes thereof. In Yaqajiq and Qārtāl large quantities of grapes are produced, and these of excellent quality. We reached home by sunset.

28th (*Saturday, 23rd August*).—In the morning after rising and dressing, the Sultan came. We went downstairs, mounted on horseback together, went to the upper gate of the palace garden, and there, taking our seats in an open carriage, drove off, the sun being right in our faces, and scorchingly fierce. Our drive was to the vineyard of the Sultāna-Mother, there to take breakfast. It was a good distance off, at the termination of the inhabited parts and parishes. Alighting there, we ascended the stairs of the pavilion, which is a pretty, though plain building, with richly furnished apartments. After a little preliminary waiting, we went to breakfast, then returned to the first room, and had a long desultory conversation on all manner of topics. We then rose, remounted our carriage, and drove back to the lower entrance gate of the palace of Beyler-Beyi, dismounted at the foot of the staircase, the Sultan accompanying us upstairs and taking a seat, when we resumed our conversation, the two Grand-Vazīrs being also present. The Sultan evinced much kindness, then rose, and returned to his own palace, we escorting him to the foot of the staircase.

Every day several large steamers, making five or six trips each between the morning and the evening, convey passengers, and ply to and from Biyūk-Dera, and other quarters of the capital. These ships belong for the most part to companies of foreign nationalities; and by means of this conveyance of passengers to and from the different quarters, each ship earns about ten thousand tūmāns (4000*l*.) yearly. Each time a ship takes in passengers, she becomes crammed with people. In one place they stretch a partition for the women to have their seats, the rest of the ship being used by the men. These ships are a source of great danger in the Bosphorus to persons who go about in boats. If a boat should come near a steamer, the force of the paddle wheels, causing the sea to rise in waves, wrecks the boat; as was the case three days ago, when several women and men of quality were drowned in the Bosphorus, only one child and a few of the boatmen having been saved. It is, however, the custom of the boatmen of the Bosphorus that, whoever may be drowned, they tell no tales, and no one knows anything of what has happened. The cause of this is said to be their fear lest people should take alarm at going in boats, and their craft thus fall into desuetude. Every year numerous persons are drowned of nights or during rough weather on the Bosphorus. But as the accident mentioned above took place in broad daylight, it was witnessed and reported.

Last evening, as we were sitting at dinner, there came successively the reports of several guns being fired. I was astonished at this, and on looking out of the windows, saw that at various parts of the environs of the Bosphorus there were numerous flames of fire; showing that a conflagration had broken out. There is a very high tower and signal in the city, where watchmen are stationed every night; and whenever a fire happens in any quarter, it is an established rule that, in order to warn the public, seven guns shall be fired, so that they may go and help to extinguish it. In the morning we learnt that eight hundred houses had been burnt in the parish of Qāsim-Pasha. Since the houses at Constantinople are for the most part of timber, it is very frequent that the woodwork takes fire.

Well; in the afternoon I mounted my boat and went to the seaside palace of Chirāgān. There is a public street that separates the palace from its gardens; and over this street they have thrown a bridge. Whenever the Sultan, with his harem or others, wishes to go into the gardens, he passes by this bridge. We drove along the avenues in a carriage uphill. The garden is full of trees like a forest, running up the hill and down along a valley. Here and there, upon knolls and eminences, there are pretty detached structures, not yet completed, as workmen were busy on them. The Sultan's wild animals are kept in this garden. We saw many peacocks. There were several cages with handsome tigers, and one of these was extremely savage, the like of him not having been seen by us in any of the zoological collections of Firangistān. He roared continuously,'and came rushing at those who were looking at him. There was another curious tiger that I had not hitherto seen. He had many white spots upon his back and sides; *i.e.*, his body was the same as that of any other tiger, and with the very same black stripes; in which respect there was no difference. These white spots were in addition to them, and resembled the white spots on the young of the red deer. There were also some birds and parrots of beautifully-coloured plumage.

From thence we drove in the carriage to another place, where were the cages of birds (an aviary). It was one long cage divided into compartments, in each of which were trees and a basin of water, most neat. There were many kinds of birds, especially some golden pheasants from the lands of Australia. There were about fifty or sixty of these in all the cages. In (the country of) the Franks I had seen but few of them. There were also various other kinds of pheasants, from India, China, and Africa.

After a good stroll I came down the hill and went into the palace. Here, too, there were many dovecotes, as they have preserved the pigeons near to the garden of the Sultan's palace. Across the garden-bridge I went to the palace itself. The columns of this building, with the greater part of the walls, floors, and stairs are of marble—a kind of marble that is brought from quarries in the Sea of Marmara, whence this sea itself has received its name. The marble has two defects; one, in that it is much marked with dark streaks; the other, that, however much they work it, it never becomes smooth and glossy. In reality, it is a kind of stone. The columns are monoliths, and the flags of the pavement are very large. There is a marble bath-room within the palace. These baths are not like those of Persia, outdoor buildings far away from the houses; nor are they excavated. On the contrary, they are inside the house, and their floor is level with that of the other apartments; so that they are quickly heated. It has small and large basins, into which, taps being opened, hot and cold water flows. Beneath the bath-room is a vacant place, and the furnace is lighted and fed from outside. As soon as the flags of the floor become warm, and the hot-water taps are opened, the bath-room gets heated. The sources from whence these taps derive their water are also outside the bath, where they heat the water.

Although it was now late, and darkness was coming on, we went over the whole of the apartments of the Sultan, those of the Sultāna-Mother, of the female establishment and garden special to this. It is a very sumptuous palace, fitted with rich furniture. According to what was asserted, much money has gradually been expended upon the edifice. It was originally founded by the Sultan Mahmūd Khān; but the present sovereign pulled that down, and has rebuilt it. Serkīs Efendi, the Sultan's architect, a fine young man, who speaks French well, has built the whole of this palace, and was present with us.

At sunset we remounted our boat and went home. In the evening they brought us a conjurer, who made his preparations in the hall, where we went after dinner and took our seat in a chair. The whole of our suite were present. Four days ago the Muhaqqiq had left for Persia with our photographs and despatches.

Well; the conjurer was an ungainly-looking man, who spoke in French, and performed some wonderful tricks. A few of the more surprising of them are the following:

First of all he drew from his breast-pocket a thin stick without a hole in it, and held it in his hand. Out of this stick he produced a live canary bird, which he let go, and which went and perched at a distance. He then took a ruby ring from the finger of the I'tizādu-'s-Saltana, and placed it on a table. He now produced two large lemons, and laid them also on the table; asking that one of them might be chosen, and this was done. Upon that, he cut the other lemon in two, to show there was nothing in them. He next took the ring and caused it to disappear within his hand; after which he went and fetched back the canary-bird, a thing of the size of a sparrow; he caressed it with his hands, and it disappeared also. Now he took the selected lemon, cut it in two with a pocket-knife, and from within it drew forth the canary with the prince's ring firmly bound to its foot by a delicate red silk ribbon.

He took the pocket-handkerchief of the Grand-Vazīr and held it for the Sanī'u-'d-Dawla to cut through with a pocket-knife. He then made it into a roll, rammed it into a pistol, and fired this off. Next he produced a winebottle, free from any defect, and placed it on the table. He took another pocket-handkerchief, and this also the Sanī'u-'d-Dawla cut in twain and set fire to. The conjurer rubbed it up in his hand and caused it to disappear. Next he took four cigar-cases that some of our officials had about them, placed them on the table, and requested that one of them might be chosen. The Grand-Vazīr selected one and gave it into the hand of the Husāmu-'s-Saltana. He (the conjurer) took an axe in his hand; struck the bottle with this, and broke it; out of it came a live dove, with the Grand-Vazīr's pocket-handkerchief bound round his leg. It was the very same handkerchief; for the Grand-Vazīr had himself marked it with his own name. To conclude he now drew forth safe and sound, from the cigar-case held by the Husāmu-'s-Saltana, the other handkerchief that had been cut in two and burnt.

He took three finger-rings from our people and gave them into the hand of one of our own officials. He brought out a wine-glass, into which he broke an egg, white and yolk together, casting the three rings into this. He now took the hat of Dr. (Sir Joseph) Dickson, and poured into it from the wine-glass the liquid contents of the egg, together with the rings; after which, turning the hat upside down, the three rings fell out of it, each fastened to a nosegay; the inside of the hat being in no wise wet or soiled by the egg.

Again he took the ring of the prince I'tizādu-'s-Saltana and laid it on the table; produced two water-melons and asked for one of them to be chosen, which was done. He took the ring in his hand and made it vanish; then cut the melon in two and brought out an egg, sound and uncooked. This he broke and drew from it a walnut without a flaw, which he brought and placed on the floor in front of us. He gave a hammer to the Amīnu-'s-Saltana, who with one blow completely cracked the walnut, and from it dropped the ring of the prince.

Many other curious tricks did he also perform.

29*th* (*Sunday,* 24*th August.*)—Breakfasted at home to-day. Kyāmil Pasha, President of the Privy Council, a most charming and noble man, came to an audience. He had not come during the last several days, having been suffering from illness. He is a son-in-law of the celebrated Muhammad-'Ali Pasha of Egypt, and is an old man of very great wealth. When he left, Rāshid Pasha, the Minister of Foreign Affairs, came to return thanks for an Order we had conferred on him. With him, too we had some conversation.

At two hours to sunset we went by boat on board the "Pertev-i-Piyāla," and proceeded to the waterside residence of the Ottoman Grand-Vazīr, sat there awhile, and partook of coffee. He has a delightful house. It is a considerable distance from Beyler-Beyi to this residence of the Grand-Vazīr, which is on the left hand side (of the Bosphorus), on the European shore, in the village of Yeni-Kyūy (New Village,) from whence there is a road to Tarāpiya, and from thence to Biyūk-Dera. Returning from thence, we reached home, and landed there at sunset.

Monday, 1st of Rajab the Respected (25th August).— Our departure from Islāmbūl took place, for Poti, by way of the Black Sea. In the morning we arose and breakfasted at home. At four o'clock in the day (eight hours to sunset) we have to go to the Sultan's palace to say adieu, when, exactly as on the day of our arrival, will ceremonial honours be carried out.

We came down stairs and mounted our boat, our Grand-Vazīr, Mīrzā Malkam Khān, and 'Alī Bey, being with us. We pushed off and reached the palace of Dōlma-Bāgcha. The Ottoman Grand-Vazīr, with the whole of the Ministry were at the landing-place, and the Sultan had come to the foot of the staircase. We gave hands and went upstairs, took our seats in a stated room, the two Grand-Vazīrs being present, and a long conversation ensued. We rose and returned home, when the English Ambassador came to an audience, and with him, too, somewhat of a conversation ensued.

About an hour afterwards the Sultan came. I went to the foot of the staircase; we gave hands, came upstairs to a room, sat down a while, and again conversed; then we rose, went down to a special boat, in which the seats occupied by us, the Sultan, and others, were canopied over; here we took our places and pulled off to the "Sultāniyya," the ship in which we had come from Brindisi, and which, in justice, was an extraordinarily fine vessel. Our suite had come on board in the morning or yesterday, with the baggage, and were present. We now again took seats in chairs, with the Sultan and the two Grand-Vazīrs, for a few minutes; after which the Sultan rose, and I accompanied him to the ship's ladder. Salutes were fired from the other ships. We had to wait about half-an-hour while the anchor was being got up and other matters seen to. At length, at two hours and a half to sunset, we bid adieu to Islāmbūl, and commenced our voyage. The ship progressed slowly up the Bosphorus. Opposite to Biyūk-Dera and Tarāpiya, where are the summer-residences of the Diplomatic Corps, the ships in attendance on the Embassies, that had come to see us off, made their appearance. The ships of the English and Russian Ambassadors were very large and handsome vessels, each having a numerous crew, who went up on to the yards and shouted hurrahs. The ship of the French Representative and those of the others did the same. Our ship stopped; the Russian Ambassador came in a boat, mounted on deck, was received in audience, and much conversation followed; after which he left. Mīrzā Malkam Khān, our Minister resident in London, with Hājjī Muhsin Khān—our Minister resident in Constantinople, and Narīmān Khān—who is returning to Paris, left in company with the Russian Ambassador for the city. Tamsūn Sāhib (Mr. R. Thomson)—the English Chargé d'Affaires, who had been with us everywhere throughout this tour, remained behind in Constanṭinople to go to England, from whence he will return.

We now steamed on, and quitted the Bosphorus. At the extremity of the channel, both sides of which are mountainous, there are constructed on the brink of the sea some strong forts and batteries, all with guns. These fired salutes. The ship "Talī'a," that had accompanied us from Brindisi, not having given satisfaction, had been replaced by another named the "'Asīr" (Difficult—Impregnable), which was a ship of war. They said she was a comfortable vessel, and the greater part of our servants are in her, as follows : the Ilkhānī ; General Hasan-'Ali Khān ; the Minister of Public Works ; the Mukhbiru-'d-Dawla ; the Nasru-'l-Mulk ; the Shujā'u-'s-Saltana ; the Ihtishāmu-'d-Dawla ; M. Richard ; Sātūr Khān ; Lt. Ibrāhīm Khān ; and also our horses. But as she is a ship of war, she is not a speedy vessel, and by degrees lagged behind, so as ultimately to be lost to sight. As they said, she will, God willing, reach Poti the day after us.

During the night we slept tranquilly. We saw the new moon of the month of Rajab the Respected (as it were sinking) into the sea, as we contemplated some handwriting of the Commander of the Faithful, 'Alī son of Abū-Tālib, upon whom be the blessings and benedictions of God. This evening, Eshref Pasha, the Ottoman official in attendance upon us, fell down twenty steps of a ladder in this ship, poor fellow, and broke his head and arm. Dr. Tholozan and others treated him. To-day Tholozan brought Marco Pasha to an audience, who is the Sultan's Chief Physician ; and with him I had a good deal of conversation. He is a man forty-five years of age, thin, sallow, who shaves his beard and wears mustachios. He speaks French well; they say that, by origin, he is a Greek. For a long time he has been the Sultan's Physician.

Tuesday, 2nd Rajab (26th August).—When I arose in the morning from sleep, the weather, through the mercy of the Lord Most High, was like paradise, and the sea as smooth as a looking-glass. To our left all is water as far as Sebastopol, and to our right is the land of the Ottoman Anadōli (Asia Minor, ἡ ἀνατολή, the region of sunrise). Everywhere we went close along the shore, and high mountains were visible on all parts, the whole of them clothed in dense forests and larch trees. On the slopes of the hills every here and there cultivation and villages were noticed; and there are some very beautiful mountains with charming valleys.

In the afternoon we gradually increased our distance from the land, and at night, three hours after sunset, we were abreast of the harbour of Sinope, from whence onwards, until we reached Poti, the land was no more visible. Sinope has acquired a (terrible) celebrity since the time of the war of Sebastopol, when the Russians (there) set fire to the Ottoman squadron of ships. When we had reached the offing of Sinope, a breeze sprang up from the direction of the Crimea, striking the ship abeam. It was light and gentle, but caused the ship to roll violently. To-day, from morn until noon, while the sea was calm, large fishes (porpoises), of the size of horses, came up out of the sea, and sported about on the surface of the waters.

Wednesday, 3rd (27th August).—Last night, praise be

to God, the weather was very fine and the sea still. No shore in sight. In the morning we arose, performed our devotions, read the Scripture, and again lay down. Three hours later, on getting up, thank God, the sea was calm.

While at Constantinople a courier came in from Tehran, and brought dispatches from our Ministers, with detailed news from the province of Sīstān. Praise be to God, every part of Persia has been in the perfection of security and tranquillity.

This sea, which has received the name of Black Sea, really merits it; the name and the named fit each other. In one's eyes it is much blacker than other seas. Yesterday, from some not distant shore, a few small and pretty birds flew off to the ship, and there perched, remaining hungry and without food. The shore has become distant, and they cannot fly to it. At times they essay to do it; and although no land is visible, still, with the instinct given them by God, they fly off towards our right hand, where are the shores of Anadoli, and which is the nearest to land; but they come back again. One of them was caught and put in a cage. It drank some water, but died in a minute or two.

To-day, at an hour to sunset, we again approached the shore, so that the town and seaport of Trebizond became visible. I saw the town and its houses through a telescope. It is a pretty town on the skirts of a mountain, and in a valley. Again we left the shore at a distance. At night, about dinner-time, thunder and lightning began to be perceived towards the west, and the sky darkened over, though there was no wind. Through this western darkness, thunder, and lightning, which gave a bad presentiment respecting the weather, the sea became convulsed. We dined, went on deck, and walked up and down awhile. All around, the sky was cloudy and dark; and in every direction vivid lightnings played, while the mutters of thunder came rumbling on. The mid-heaven was clear, and only a breath of air was stirring; so I again lay down. Violent lightning and thunder continued until morning in a terrific manner, while gradually the clouds overspread all, and gave every appearance of rain being at hand.

[1] The hill of Chamlija (p. 381), so called from a few pine-trees (cham) that crown its summit, is erroneously called Mount Boulgourlou on the maps and by European strangers. Bulgurlu (Furmity or Frumenty Village) is the name of a village in the valley west of Chamlija ; and at its back, still further west and a little more inland southerly, is the real Bulgurlu-Dăgi (Mount Bulgurlu), entirely uninhabited and treeless ; whereas Chamlija teems with vineyards and summer residences almost to its summit, having the city of Iskyudăr, with its suburbs, on its skirts and at its foot, along the shore of the Bosphorus.—J. W. R.

CHAPTER VIII.

GEORGIA, RETURN; 11 DAYS.

THURSDAY, 4th (28th August).—To-day we are to reach the anchorage of the port of Poti. During the night, by reason of the commotion of the sea in all directions, sleep did not overcome me for more than an hour altogether. I rose early in the morning, performed my devotions, and read a portion of Scripture. The weather was very threatening, and heavy rain poured down. A thunderbolt struck the sea not more than fifty feet from the ship, with a roar equal to that of a thousand cannons, scattering the water on all sides. Had it struck the ship, it would have shivered it to fragments. The sky remained in the same tempestuous state. Again I lay down for an hour or two. From the motion of the ship it became evident that we were near shore; and I arose. Praise be to God that we had escaped from the high sea, and had reached the coast; the shores of Poti were visible, all forest and mountain. The temperature and nature of the country were very much like those of the Gīlāns.

As the ship in which we had travelled was very large, it could approach no nearer to the land, and therefore stopped. We saw a vessel in the distance coming towards us on our beam, and she was made out to be the "'Asīr," our consort, of which it had been said that, since she was not a fast ship, she would not arrive until about ten hours after us. It became evident that in consequence of the bad state of the weather they had taken our vessel further out to sea, to avoid the neighbourhood of land, thus steering a different course to that which would have led more directly to our destined anchorage at Poti; whereas that other vessel, having the wind astern, had made sail and had arrived at Poti considerably before us. Very thankful was I that she too had safely turned up, and not lagged behind.

A small steamer came out from Poti to convey us ashore. Prince Menschikoff and Colonel Bazāk, formerly in attendance upon us, and who had first come to Enzeli (to meet us), were on board of her. I was exceedingly pleased to see the Prince again. But, as the sea was still very rough, all their efforts to bring his vessel alongside the "Sultāniyya" were fruitless,—they could not effect it. Several times they brought her near; but the two ships were dashed together, and the bows and stem of the Prince's steamer were slightly injured. Again they tried to get her alongside, and now she damaged the "Sultāniyya's" ladder. At length they resolved to exercise a little patience, and the sea calmed down somewhat. Then they fastened the two ships together, and transferred a few of our private effects and some of our princes and officers to the Prince's vessel; and to her we went also. I then saw Eshref Pasha, the (Ottoman) official in attendance on us, with his head broken and his right arm in a sling bound up to his neck, his face being all black and blue, in a state of suffering. This caused me great sorrow. They had passed a narrow plank from one ship to the other, which was very dangerous, and over this we passed to the Prince's steamer. The Sanī'u-'d-Dawla, remained behind in the "Sultāniyya," to see after the rest of the baggage; and several others remained there also with him.

In half an hour we arrived at the mouth of the river of Poti, which flows into the sea, and is named the Rion. It is a large river, but vessels cannot go up it more than the distance of half a league. There are some few habitations on both banks of the stream—houses like those of the peasantry of Māzandarān and Gīlān. The soil is wet, and the climate bad, fever and agues abounding there. But by degrees they are beginning to improve the place. This seaport town of Poti has no good anchorage either. Large ships cannot by any means enter the river, neither can they approach the shore. They are therefore constrained to keep at a distance from the town, and to load and unload goods and passengers by means of small shore craft. We noticed one large English steamer, and two Ottoman sailing vessels in the roadstead. The plain is all forest, and extends as far as the mountains, which are also one dense forest.

Many flags were hoisted on both banks of the river, and a small room had been prepared to receive us when we should land from the vessel. The Grand-Duke Michael, brother of the Emperor, Viceroy and Governor-General of the Caucasian Provinces, was at the landing-place with his officials and generals, waiting to receive us. We disembarked and gave our hand to the Prince. We then went and inspected a battalion of infantry that was drawn up between the landing-place and the railway terminus. There was a multitude collected of various tribes and nationalities: Circassians, Lesghians, Armenians, Georgians, Dāgistānī Muslims, Open-Heads (Mingrelians; who go bare-headed like the Blue-Coat boys of London), Franks, and others. This region is part of the country of the Open-Heads (Mingrelia), *i.e.*, of the Bare-Heads, and in reality they are so. The whole of the inhabitants of the Open-Head country go bare-headed. Never do the women, men, or children adopt the practice of wearing hats or caps on their heads. The chief-town of the Open-Heads is Kùtāïs, situated between Tiflīs and Poti.

Well; we exchanged many salutations and conversed much with the Prince, who, in justice be it said, is a very agreeable prince. During the time of my visit to (St.) Petersburg, the Prince was not there, and I was therefore very glad to see him. Of all the Emperor's brothers he is the youngest. He wears his beard (whiskers) on either side of his cheeks, but shaves his chin. His eyes are blue, and betoken good-nature. He is tall of stature and strong of frame.

In half an hour's time we took our seats in the train and started, leaving behind us the Hakīmu-'l-Mamālik to bring on the luggage by railway. The interpreter of the Viceroy, Begliaroff, a son of Shāh-Mīr Khān the Persian, spoke French very well. The cars of the train all communicated with one another. This line of railroad has been recently constructed, and consists of a single line of rails all the way to Tiflīs, the whole of the traffic having to go over that one line. Much difficulty was experienced in its construction, the whole of the lands being forest, marsh, and inundation. To drain such a country and lay down a railway is a very onerous task. Once past the marshes all is mountain and valley, so that the line is very tortuous and on an assent, passing over a river and bridges, until it begins to descend again towards Tiflīs. From these causes the train could not travel with the rapidity usual in Firangistān; but went at about two and a half leagues per hour, not more.

Well; it wanted five hours and a half to sunset when we started, the sky being entirely overcast, and heavy rain falling without an interval; the road, too, was forest and mountain. By sunset we arrived at a station in the neighbourhood of Kutāïs, where they had prepared food (for us). The train stopped; we alighted and went into a room where the table was laid. A light dinner was partaken of. A company of infantry was also drawn out, of the Open-Head people of Georgia, who were dressed in a peculiar manner, after the fashion of the costume of the ancient troops (of the country), with open-breasted red coats, a red cloth round their heads by way of turban, a pistol and a large knife in their sashes. Their uniform thus resembled those of the Zouaves in France and of the tribes of Hindūstān; but their muskets were needle-guns made in the factory of Tula.

We again mounted and went on. I had a restless

night of broken sleep. We arrived very early in the morning (of Friday, 29th August) in the neighbourhood of Tiflīs, when I arose very much worn out, and dressed. The train stopped, and we alighted. The Viceroy was waiting with a large staff of officers and a battalion of infantry. We mounted an open carriage with the Viceroy. The air was very cold; and by reason of the rain which had fallen, a piercingly cold wind was blowing, which raised up the dust and earth. The lamps were still burning in the streets. We arrived at the gate of the Viceroy's palace, where a battalion of infantry and numbers of military officers and civilians were drawn up in attendance. To each of these we addressed a word of inquiry after his health. The Governor of the City of Tiflīs, together with the mayor and aldermen, came and brought the usual bread and salt. They had prepared a lengthy address, written out in Persian; and we stood while an individual, learned in Persian, read it out with perfect propriety of utterance.

We now went up-stairs, where, in one room, Prince Orbelianoff, a Georgian prince, and Baron Nicholas, the Administrator of Foreign Affairs in the Caucasian Provinces, were waiting; whom the Viceroy presented. I knew the Prince Orbelianoff seven years ago; as, on the occasion of our visiting the seaport of Farah-ābād in Māzandarān, he had come there on the part of the Emperor with several Russian ships of war.

Next, the Viceroy showed us our rooms and apartments, there leaving us. We breakfasted, and then lay down to rest.

The town of Tiflīs is in a valley and is surrounded by mountains, with some of its houses on the flanks and summit of a hill. The river Kur (the ancient Cyrus) flows through the town, but its water was not very abundant at that season. A bridge has been built across it. To the north of the stream is the new town and the Frank quarters, wherein also are the palaces of the Viceroy and of the Governor. On the south side is the old town of Tiflīs, and, on the summit of a hill, the ruins of the ancient fortress of the Sovereigns of Georgia. Fifty years ago, this town was very wretched and filthy; now, by degrees, private houses and public buildings, schools and colleges, broad streets paved with stone, are being constructed. The peak of Mount Qāf (Caucasus), which the Franks name Kazbek, is visible. This is a very lofty mountain, covered with snow. The Russians have made a road for carriages, so that now they cross the mountains to the other side in coaches, the town of Vladi-Kaukas being there, and the land route to Moscow and Hājjī-Tarkhān. Immediately around Tiflīs the mountains are bare, but further away from the town they are wooded. The air of the place is not healthy, being very hot and variable in the summer and autumn. When rain falls in the neighbourhood, or in the town, it becomes exceedingly chill, and then returns to a sultry heat again. Its climate is therefore a source of fevers and agues. The population of the town is fifty thousand; for the most part foreigners and strangers, a mixture of all nationalities—Persians, Georgians, Russians, Dāgistānīs, Circassians, Germans, Armenians. It has excellent fruits; such as water-melons, grapes, pears, cucumbers.

To-day we went to see the Viceroy, who lives in this same palace, where are our quarters. We passed through several rooms, and reached a hall built by Persian workmen, and adorned with embellishments in plaster and looking-glass work. This part of the palace was very beautiful, and the furniture of the rooms was all of Persian stuffs—large and small carpets, of Farāhān (Furrah *of the maps*), of Qā'īn (Ghayn *of the maps*), and of Kirmān; tables and couches, &c., of inlaid work of Shīrāz and Isfāhān; curtains of carpets to the rooms; while Rasht patchwork in flowers of broadcloth was used for the covers of the seats, backs, and cushions of the couches, chairs, &c., and as covers for the tables. This furniture and these works of Persian art were not placed there for the reason that we had come to the palace; but were there before. There was a large black bear, formerly killed in the chase by the Viceroy himself, set up like life in a corner of one of the rooms; so that should one see it suddenly unawares, he might take it for a living bear.

The Viceroy has also made a very varied collection, hung up on the walls of the rooms, of weapons, such as sabres, swords, muskets, and pistols; also of ancient arms and armour, such as shirts of mail, helmets, saddles, barbs, stirrups, horse-trappings, jewelled and gilt; besides many other objects of interest, even to an ancient tallow-burning lamp,—which formerly was in use in Persia, being found in a niche of one room. We took a survey of all the rooms; from the windows of one was an excellent outlook over the town of Tiflis and its streets.

We sat there a while, and then proceeded to the apartment of the Viceroy's wife, adjacent thereto; and there also tarried a small space. The Viceroy's wife is a sister of the Grand-Duke of Baden, and with her brother I had breakfasted in the city of Carlsruhe in Germany. She has five sons and one daughter by the Viceroy, her eldest son being fourteen years of age. Her children were away at a summer-residence. The name of the Viceroy's wife is Olga Feodorowna.

Rising, we returned from thence to our own room, and without any interval the Viceroy's wife, with the Viceroy, came to return the visit.

In the evening we went in a carriage with the Viceroy to the summer theatre, a very small building, all white, with one brass chandelier lighted with gas. The theatre was filled with Russian officers and others. At the utmost it will hold about two hundred persons. The music was good. The curtain was raised, and a few acts performed; the dialogue being in Russian. They sang nicely; they represented with much spirit some interesting plots, with dancing, that called forth much laughter. The women and young Russian men were good-looking and graceful. There was one French dancer, very graceful, who danced well, and had been at Tiflis two years. To conclude, they performed a Russian national dance, followed by a Georgian dance which was very pretty. A number of Georgians were drawn up on each side, who clapped hands, while one played the Persian tomtom, and two others blew the Persian horn, very melodiously. One girl and one boy danced, much after the manner of Persian dancing.

Between the acts, while the curtain was lowered, we went down into a small garden where an illumination had been got up. We sat awhile in a tent pitched on a raised platform, and there the Viceroy presented to us some Georgian women and others. We returned home and dined.

Meanwhile, our private secretary, the Hakīmu-'l-Mamālik, and the Sanī'u-'d-Dawla, who had remained behind (at Poti), had come up to Tiflīs, bringing the luggage. But they gave a tremendous account of the sea storm. The secretary and the Sanī', who had remained on board the "Sultāniyya" after we left her, said that immediately after we had got out of that ship and gone to Poti, the sea had become convulsed in such a manner that, however much endeavour had been used to put the little Russian steamer alongside the "Sultāniyya," it had been impossible, through the violence of the waves. At length, the two ships came into collision, breaking the paddle-wheel of each of them. At length, after a thousand toils, they had managed to get the two ships close together; and, whenever the waves lifted the little one up, they tossed a bale of luggage from the other into her, or else one person threw himself on board of her; and so, with a thousand perils to life, they had got the luggage and men on shore. The secretary further added that, although the shore was near, the waves so tossed them up in the air, and then precipitated them down again, that it was like one's falling down from a mountain peak. Praise be to God that this commotion did not happen a few hours earlier, while we were on the sea.

It had been at first arranged that we should go by way of the mountain Qāf and (the village of) Kāzbek to the seaport of Petrowski, en route for Enzeli; and orders had been sent to this effect along that road, where carts and carriages, &c., had all been got ready. But, as it would be all the more advantageous, by how-muchsoever we should shorten the sea voyage, I formed the desire to embark on board ship at Bād-Kūba (Baku). It was therefore settled that we should go to Bād-Kūba with ten of our people, and all the others to Petrowski, there to embark, come round to Bād-Kūba, take us on board, and then all go on together to Enzeli. We commissioned the Sanī'u-'d-Dawla to remain at Tiflīs and bring on to Enzeli all the baggage that could not be sent by courier, and all the rest of our party. We thus spent Friday at Tiflīs in the way described.

Saturday, 6th (30th August). — This day Bahman Mīrzā (a fugitive uncle of the Shāh), who had come over from Qara-Bāg, was received in audience. He has six or seven grown-up sons also, who were all admitted to the audience.

In the afternoon we took a seat in a carriage with the Viceroy, and drove a little about the city. The weather was sultry, and there was much dust. We went to the outskirts of the town, to a park called Bāgi-Mujtahid, laid out by Aqā Mīr Fattāh. The greater part of the inhabitants of Tiflīs are in the regular army or in the enrolled Cossacks.

In the evening we were the guest of the Viceroy to dinner. We first went to a hall where a great number of officials, military and civil, with others, were standing. The Viceroy presented them all. Bahman Mīrzā was also present. We then proceeded to another hall and sat down to table. The Viceroy sat on our left, his wife on our right; the others taking each the place assigned to him according to his rank.

Dinner over, we rose and went to a balcony of the room, like a terrace, and looking on to the palace garden. There was a very nice illumination arranged in the garden, together with a magnificent display of fireworks on the hill fronting the palace. In the garden there was a great multitude assembled of the notables and common people, of women and beautiful girls, Georgians and Franks. After the fireworks and a Cossack dance, which was performed with great spirit, and during which they fired off their pistols, we went down into the garden and walked about, having the Viceroy's wife on our arm. We walked through the whole of the avenues. Everywhere they had made (transparencies of) the device of the Lion and Sun, illuminated from behind. A telegram had come from the Emperor, and the Viceroy handed it to us. We read it. It was an enquiry after our health. We now returned upstairs, sat a while, and then retired to our own apartment.

This day a priest came from the Great Vice-Patriarch

of Uch-Kilīsa (Etchmiazin), near Irwān (Erivān), bringing a memorial. A telegram also came from Tehrān to the effect that Hājjī Sayyid Asadu-'l-'lāh, of Isfāhān, the authoritative legist, who had gone on a pilgrimage to the holy shrines (in Babylonia), had died at Kirind. This caused me great grief.

Sunday, 7th (31st August).—Having to leave Tiflīs for Bād-Kūba, we rose early in the morning and breakfasted. The Muʻtamadu-'l-Mulk, with the princes, also started this day for Petrowski. At six hours to sunset we began our journey, the Viceroy and all the officials of the Caucasus being present. Five carriages had been made ready, each harnessed with many horses. We mounted and drove through the old town of Tiflīs, where crowds were assembled. We quitted the town and broke into a courier's pace. All along, the river Kur was on our left; but by degrees we increased our distance from it. The banks of the stream are lined with willows and a few forest trees, creating a little verdure. The weather was very sultry, with dust beyond conception. Once outside of Tiflīs, there was not a single trace of the works of man on either side of our road; as far as the eye could penetrate, all was a melancholy plain or brown mountains; only that at each interval of two leagues a post-house has been erected, where they change horses. For about six leagues from Tiflis they have made a road, and sprinkled gravel, so that the dust was not so bad. But, where this (made) road came to an end, the dust was very great.

We stopped and changed horses at several of the

posthouses. At each of these stations there were some Cossack and Muslim cavalry, who relieved our escort also. At the station of Al-Git,—which, being Turkī, means : Take it and depart,—they had prepared breakfast. It wanted then but one hour to sunset. Afterwards, we again mounted our carriages and drove on, as it was moonlight. Before reaching the posthouse of Al-Git we passed a river (Monteith's Algeth), which had a bridge over it, and which joins the Kur. Three hours after sunset we arrived at the river Agistafa (Akistafa, Monteith), which is a large stream, but at this season has not much water. The posthouse, here, too, is named after the river; and there was on the far side of the stream another station where we were to rest for the night, and which had two or three rooms. We dined. It was sultry. They informed us that Hājjī Mīrzā 'Alī, the Mishkātu-'l-Mulk (the Lighted Wick of the Kingdom), had arrived. I marvelled exceedingly. The Hājjī had come from Tabrīz by way of Irwān, and had arrived here two days before. We had a little conversation as to news from Tehrān, and the like; after which he left, and was to start early for Tiflīs.

Monday, 8th (1st September).—We have to reach the town of Ganja (the Russian Elisabetpol; the birthplace of the Persian poet Nizāmī). We rose early and commenced our journey through a disagreeable, sultry, dusty wilderness. These regions are the abode of the Tatar Cossacks, who are all Muslims, and number about four or five thousand families; but of their habitations no traces were seen hereabouts. To our right and not far off, there was a chain of hills, on the other side of which is the way to the lake Gokcha of Irwān. To our left was another chain of hills, dust-coloured and bare, visible in the distance. We arrived at the posthouse of Hasan-Sū. On the other side of this place are the territories and lands of the tribe of Shamsuddīnlu, also of five or six thousand families. Hasan-Sū (Hasan River) is a stream, but had very little water indeed. A little further we came to the posthouse of Tāwūs-Chāy (Peacock River), the stream of which had also but little water. Thence reached the posthouse of Zakam, where we breakfasted. At each of these posthouses there was a large congregation of horsemen and pedestrians, inhabitants of those parts, who all, even to the little children, carry arms. They are all Muslims.

After breakfast we pushed on to the posthouse of Shamkūr, where the tribe of Shamsuddīnlu ends, and the jurisdiction of Ganja commences. On the summit of a little hill we noticed the remains of an old brick fort of great strength. A stream passes at its foot, but it had little water, though there were the ruins of a brick bridge across it, one half alone being still erect. These plains are, in the same manner as before mentioned, parched and little inhabited. We now reached the post-station of Qarā-Barāz; and pushing on from thence we reached the town of Ganja at two hours to sunset. The Governor of the districts of Ganja had come to Zakam with some horsemen; and the Governor of the town also, with some other horsemen and notables, came out half a league from the place (to meet us).

Gardens surround the town of Ganja; but within it the houses are poor and miserable. The old castle of Ganja, which was a strong brick fort, is now in ruins, and only a part remains. It had a good ditch and glacis, and is now used as a prison. A stream runs through the town, but it was nearly dry; a bridge has recently been built over it. The farther side of the stream is the quarter of the Franks and Armenians, while on this side live the Muslims. The Governor's house is in the Frank quarter, and in it we had our apartments. It is a very wretched tenement on the top of a hill, at the foot of which it had a small garden. According to what we could judge, the population cannot be above seven to eight thousand.

Tuesday, 9th (2nd September).—We have to go to Turyān-Chāy, a place in (the district of) Shaki. In the morning we mounted (our carriage), passed through the town and (surrounding) gardens of Ganja, into the open country. The same line of hills as yesterday was seen again to-day on our right for the first three leagues; after which, it gradually became more distant. At about half a league from the town, or rather more, is the tomb of Shaykh Nizāmī (the poet) by the side of the road—a very wretched brick building; and beyond that we reached Kūrak-Chāy (Shovel-River); which is the name of a stream. On our left also runs at a distance that same range of brown bare waterless mountains, which stretches away to Shaki.

Well; the weather was excessively sultry, the soil parched and disagreeable; and so we arrived at the post-house of Qarqali-Chāy (River of many crows or rooks, Rooky River), passing on from thence to the station of Mangi-Chāwūr (Advanced-Outwork) on the bank of the river Kur, where they had erected a felt tent for us, closed on all sides, and hot as a bathroom. For the Grand-Vazīr and the others they had built a hut of the branches of trees, nice and airy, but many people were there.

The princes and others had remained a long way behind with the baggage-cart containing our jewels, which had broken down; and before they could get another to use in its stead, they were left far in the rear. Previously to their arrival, we took our breakfast off a very large fish caught in the river with a net. The lessee of this river was a young Armenian, who was there present. The farm of the fishery at this place is a branch of that of the fisheries of Sālyān.

Here the river Kur is of great width, but with a sluggish stream, and a depth of not more than an ell (42 inches). They had lashed two barges together, had made a platform upon them floored with planks, and had stretched a stout rope across (the stream) from bank to bank. Within the vessels were a few articles of gearing bound upon a large mast. They pulled at the rope, and the craft moved, carrying goods and passengers over to the other side. In the first place they so transported our carriages, then I went across, and lastly the Grand-

E E

Vazīr and others came over with the luggage: after which we again resumed our journey.

As far as this station of Mangi-Chāwūr the jurisdiction of Ganja extends, while this side the river belongs to the district of Shaki. The range of hills to our left continued still of the same aspect, but we were now approaching nearer to them. Behind those brown hills are the mountains of Dāgistān; and the town of Shaki (Nukhi *of the* Monteith map) is at the foot of the hills. On the summit of the mountains of Shaki there was much snow. From where we now were to the town of Shaki, to which the Russians have given the name of Nūkhā, is a distance of about five or six leagues. In some parts of the plain are woods, in some parts thorny bushes, and in others tamarisk shrubs, while some parts are bare. As we were going along at post speed, I fired my gun from within the carriage, and shot several birds, flying in the air, of the kind called in Persian Sabza-qabā (Green-Coats).

We now arrived at the post-station of Chomaqlu (Tchemakly *of* Monteith—Club-Village), in the district of Shaki, where I performed my devotions and partook of an afternoon meal. Again pushing on, we reached the posthouse of 'Arab, still in the district of Shaki, and, at two hours after sunset, arrived at Tūryān-Chāy (Turganchaisk of Monteith—*probably*, Tūrgān-Chāy—Stagnant-River), a large and beautiful river that comes down from the mountains of Dāgistān and Shaki. In these plains cultivation is carried on. From Tiflīs, until reaching this spot, we had seen no other trace of human habitations than the posthouses; the names of all other places being merely official, and neither house nor village is visible. The posthouse here was very hot and full of musquitoes; so that I was forced to have a felt tent pitched, and to sleep out of doors. Some of the Beg-zādas (sons of Begs—sons of chieftains, lords, lairds, or gentlemen, of Turkī tribes) and grandees of Shaki had come (here to greet us and pay their respects).

Wednesday, 10th (3rd September).—We rose early in the morning. The magnates of Ganja and Shaki received their *congé*, and departed. We then resumed our journey, having a plain on our right hand, within which are the territories of Aq-Dash (White-Rock), called also Arish, which is under the jurisdiction of Shaki. Numerous villages and gardens were in sight, the latter being irrigated from the Tūryān Chāy. Before we had proceeded far, the territory of Aq-Dash came to an end, and we reached the posthouse of Gok-Chāy (Azure-River). Here the Governor of the whole country of Bād-Kūba and the Shīrwāns was awaiting us, as this place was the first station within his jurisdiction. He was an extremely courteous young man of pleasing appearance, Stracelski by name. We stopped and changed horses. A large concourse of the people of Shīrwān and of the Doctors (of Law and Divinity) of Islam had come to meet us, and with them we had a little conversation. Again we drove on, and again to our right was a vast plain, forming part of the Shīrwāns, and irrigated from the river Gok-Chāy. Many villages were in sight. This is a fertile plain, but is very sultry. To our left the same range of mountains

E E 2

accompanied us all day, and so we came to the posthouse of Qura-Yazi (Black-Flat), where we changed horses. We observed the villages of Qara-Muryān, Yaka-Khāna, and Gard-Kand, in which they have planted colonies of Russian peasants also; but they are not places of any importance. We next came to the posthouse of Gululu (Smiling Village), where we breakfasted, and where we received Wīkhman, who was formerly Governor of Shamākhi, and who, at the epoch of our journey to Rasht, had come there with Qūlībakan the Governor of Bād-Kūba. He was as fat as ever. Some Russian families are settled there.

After breakfast we resumed our travel and passed the stream of Kardama (*perhaps the* Kurdamir *of* Monteith), which had but little water. The villages of Pādār and Galagāylu (of him who comes) were noticed, which are portions of the Shīrwāns. The streams which I have mentioned all come down from the mountains of Dāgistān, which are beyond the chain of hills on our left; and wherever the mountains form valleys and give an exit, these waters, flowing along the valleys, pass forth into the level lands of Shaki and Shīrwān.

We then came to the post house of Aq-Sū (White River; New Shamaka), a village of considerable size and importance, having numerous gardens of pomegranates, figs, and the like. It much resembles the village of Kand near Tehrān; but the gardens of Kand are more numerous and extensive than these. The river of Aq-Sū runs through the midst of the gardens, and the larger portion of the village is on the eastern bank of the stream. To the west of the stream are the quarters of the Hawáwiz, and on its east the camping-ground of the troops; all parts of (the jurisdiction of) Shamákhi.

The village has numerous fruiterers' shops, and others. We alighted, partook of some fruit, performed our devotions, and again set out. From hence the road went winding and twisting towards the north, and up into that very chain of hills that had been on our left hand. We therefore ascended the valley of the stream of Aq-Sū, and first of all a small, but very lofty hill came in sight. The carriage road here has been beautifully constructed, so that our horses and vehicles travelled along comfortably, and by degrees we reached the summit of the ridge. The other side of the hills was a forest of oak, abounding with pheasants. From this summit, proceeding towards that other side, the whole country is mountainous as far as Bād-Kūba. We now took a downward course, the sun set, and we arrived at the post house of Sharādīl, stopped there a short time, and again pushed on, so that we got to the town of Shamakhi (Monteith's Shamaka) at two hours after sunset.

Great crowds had assembled, and all parts were illuminated, the people making demonstrations of the greatest joy. We alighted. Two sons of Wīkhman, one five, the other seven years old, and in Circassian costume, were standing before the door with Wīkhman's wife. The Doctors of Islām were drawn up in line; and saluting each one of them, we arrived at the palace, which is the property of Lālāyaf, an Armenian of Shīrwān, a man of importance, and wealthy. It was formerly the residence of the Governor of Shamākhī, but has now been bought by Lālāyaf, and overlooks the whole town.

The Armenian and Frank quarters of this place are on the upper parts of a hill; the quarter of the Muslims being in a valley, and lower down. Two years before, a severe earthquake had occurred and devastated the town, which, up to that period, had been very flourishing, and even now has a population of three or four thousand families, or from ten to fifteen thousand souls. Earthquakes are very frequent. All round the town are hills and peaks; but these are so dry that not a vestige of vegetation, trees, or water, exists. A small stream flows from the mountains at a lower level than where the town stands, and by its means they manage to cultivate a few gardens. There is a mosque in the town, dating from the days of Shāh-'Abbās, in which divine service is still performed; and a certain Hājjī Muhammad Rizà has also built a mosque and a convent of dervishes, of very imposing appearance. The far greater portion of the inhabitants of the town and of the country districts are Muslims, the Armenians being only a small minority. The tombs of Mustafà Khān, of Shīrwān, and those of his children, are on the summit of an eminence at the far side of the town. The palace of Lālāyaf commands a very beautiful and extensive view. It is built of timber.

Thursday, 11th (4th September).—We have to go to Bād-Kūba. We rose early, dressed, and mounted our carriage. Great crowds had collected to witness the spectacle. We drove off, and reached the top of an uphill-downdale road, in the dry valleys of which we noticed the homes of a few families of nomade tribes. They said they were tribes of Arabs (by descent). The first posthouse reached was that of Aji-Chāy, a stream the water of which is bitter; then that of Marzi (Marusy), a large village occupied by Russians; then Naqi-Kirpi (Nahi-Kopru); and next, Jangi, where we breakfasted; then Haltamā; and Arbāt, which has a stream of the same name; next Sarāyī, and then the town of Bād-Kūba (Baku).

The whole road to Bād-Kūba was dry and bad. In fact, a plain and mountains so dry and so wretched we had neither seen nor heard of. Our journey to-day was over a part of the country called the Burying-Ground— a fit name for such a region.

The Governor of Bād-Kūba was waiting for us at Sarāyī, with a party of horsemen; we dined there, and reached the town two hours after sunset. As there are naphtha pits here, they had this night lighted up the whole country and town with lamps of naphtha. Through its being night, we did not see the place well; but, being moonlight, we made out that pretty houses are being newly built along the seashore in the European style. The Governor's house, too, looked on to the sea; and there we arrived amidst the blessings of a concourse of people of various nationalities, and a band playing. I first saw Colonel Bazāk, and concluded that the steamers had arrived with my party from Petrowsky. The Governor presented his officers, and after dining we proceeded on board the "Constantine." It is a wonderful harbour, as large ships can lie alongside the shore. We offered our most sincere thanks for having once more reached our ship in safety. The Governor and others took leave. Our suite were in a vessel named the "Shāh-Suwār" (king of horsemen—chevaleresque king); and the Grand-Vazīr, our personal attendants, Colonel Bazāk, Prince Menschikoff, and Bigleroff were with me, as also the same admiral as before. In another half hour we started with a calm sea and fair wind, so that I slept all night.

The regions of Shaki, Shīrwān, and the rest, produce excellent camels. Buffaloes are used to draw the carts and waggons, as well as other animals; but the wheels of these vehicles are of wood alone, having no iron about them.

Friday, 12th (5th September).—The anniversary festival of the birthday of the Prince of Believers 'Alī son of Abū-Tālib, on whom be the peace and blessings of God, is close at hand; we must therefore get to Enzeli. When I arose early in the morning the sea was most pleasant. With the utmost joy we went on until within two or three leagues of Enzeli, when we all dressed in our state uniforms, and prepared to reach our destined port. But now black clouds were seen to arise from the west and south, while the sea began to be disturbed. Still we despaired not, but continued our course until we reached the roadstead. A Russian man-of-war named the "Bukhārā" had come over from 'Ashūr-Ada to do honour to our arrival. Through a telescope we could see that she was being sadly rocked by the waves, and this alarmed us; for when a large war-ship was thus suffering, how could we hope that our vessel would be quiet. A sailing merchantman, anchored further in, was tossing about in the same way.

Well; we reached the anchorage, and the man-of-war with great difficulty fired a few guns. The tower of Enzeli and the people on the beach were all visible; but, as large ships cannot go closer in, and enter into Enzeli itself, it was a matter of necessity for lighters and our own small steam-yacht to come out and carry us in. With this storm, that was not practicable; and we therefore despondingly left the deck of the steamer, where we could no longer stand upright, went into our cabin, took off our state clothes, and resigning ourselves to God's decree, sat down. The others, who had put on all their orders, in like manner threw off their finery in the midst of heavings and vomitings, casting themselves down in the first corner, from whence they had no power to move.

It was now two hours to sunset, and heavy rain began to pour. The waves rose so that one could not bear to look at them, and the ship rolled to that degree that the yard-arms touched the water each way. The sea broke over the vessel, and she heeled over so fearfully that we thought she would capsize and shoot us all overboard. At each roll, the chairs, tables, and other furniture of the cabin were upset with frightful clatter; and the hull of the ship, with straining, groaned again. Little did it want for her to go to pieces. Thus with fierce rain from above, and a raging sea below, the ship became full of water; and it was impossible to walk about, by reason of her violent movements, and also because the planks were so wet that one's feet slipped, and could not retain their hold. "Such is the end of our tour in Europe! To be so near home—for our tower of Enzeli to be within sight, at a distance to be measured by feet, and for one to be in this condition! Should this go on for three days, we shall surely drag our anchor, and then there is no port except at Langarān! All these servants and others who have come to Enzeli, what will they do?" Such were our thoughts; and so much bitterness did they engender that I cannot describe it. I also felt indisposed; I perspired from agitation and the heat; the wind struck to my chest, and I coughed. Neither was there a chance of sleeping, by night or by day, by reason of the storm. The rain was unceasing.

Saturday, 13*th* (6*th September*).—In the morning the storm and motion of the ship were as before, or even worse. The other ship with the princes on board had also come in after us and anchored. So things went on the whole day—clouds, rain, storm. I slept about two hours. Suddenly a cry was raised that a boat had come alongside. I rose and saw her with twelve men who had undertaken to come out and obtain tidings of us. The sea also was a little less agitated, and we were somewhat calmed. The Mu'tamad wrote an answer to the missive that had been addressed to him. In another hour—it being now dawn of the 14th (7th September), a second boat came alongside, into which Mahdi-quli Khān and

Mírzá 'Abdu-'l-'láh cast themselves and went away. Morning broke, and other lighters came. Some more of our people got away in them. The weather was inclining to become fair, and the water of the lagoon had begun to flow into the sea.

At length our steam-yacht came in sight, paddling out of the lagoon. She came near; but it was still difficult to get from one vessel to the other, as they kept her somewhat at a distance. They then brought our barge alongside, and somehow or other I got into her, pulled to the yacht, and there I was hauled on board by hand. Once on deck, I felt safe; and immediately offering up my thanks to the Creator, whose name be glorified, arrived at Enzeli. Those who had come from Tehrán were admitted to an audience; after which we went to our tower, mounted to our apartments, and there again poured out our heart in thanks to God. At night there was a general illumination, and we slept in peace. Praise be unto God Most High!

D   Naser al-Din Shah
919   The diary of H. M.
N26

PLEASE DO NOT REMOVE
CARDS OR SLIPS FROM THIS POCKET

UNIVERSITY OF TORONTO LIBRARY